THE LITERACY OF
THE LAITY IN
THE MIDDLE AGES

THE LITERACY OF
THE LAITY IN
THE MIDDLE AGES

By

JAMES WESTFALL THOMPSON

BURT FRANKLIN RESEARCH & SOURCE WORKS SERIES # 2

BURT FRANKLIN
New York 25, N. Y.

1960

The first edition of this work was published as

UNIVERSITY OF CALIFORNIA PUBLICATIONS IN EDUCATION
Volume 9
UNIVERSITY OF CALIFORNIA PRESS

Published by

BURT FRANKLIN
514 West 113th Street
New York 25, N. Y.

Printed in the United States of America by
NOBLE OFFSET PRINTERS, INC.

CONTENTS

PREFATORY NOTE

LITERACY *during the Middle Ages may be measured almost wholly by the extent of the knowledge and use of the Latin language.*

Among many problems in the history of medieval culture one of the most obscure is the question of how extensively and how deeply a knowledge of Latin obtained among the laity. By the laity, of course, is here meant the upper class of medieval society, or the noblesse; for the illiteracy of the common people is not open to question. The interrogation is in itself a challenge to the old and widely accepted opinion which since the Italian Renaissance has held that illiteracy was almost universal, so far as the laity is concerned, throughout the medieval period, that is, before the thirteenth century.

It would be beside the mark to append a list of the standard works on the history of medieval education, for the good reason that none of them has given any attention to this subject.* Even historians of medieval culture have ignored this theme. Apart from a few rare articles, information upon the education and literary ability of the noble class in the Middle Ages must be searched for in the sources of the period. Unless I am greatly mistaken, this monograph fills a gap in the history of medieval education.

                                                            J. W. T.

---

* For a bibliography of the history of medieval education see L. J. Paetow, *A Guide to the Study of Medieval History* (2d ed.; New York, 1931), nos. 58–59, 117–118, 836–849, 1012.

BIBLIOGRAPHICAL ABBREVIATIONS USED

AA. SS.—Acta Sanctorum

AA. SS. ord. S. Bened.—Acta Sanctorum: Annales ordinis Sancti Benedicti

DGQ—Deutschlands Geschichtsquellen im Mittelalter bis zur Mitte des dreizehnten Jahrhundert (Wattenbach)

HF—Recueil des historiens des Gaules et de la France (Bouquet)

HZ—Historische Zeitschrift

MGH. AA.—Monumenta Germaniae Historica: Auctores antiquissimi

MGH. Epist.—Monumenta Germaniae Historica: Epistolae

MGH. LL.—Monumenta Germaniae Historica: Leges

MGH. Poet. Lat.—Monumenta Germaniae Historica: Poetae Latinae medii aevi

MGH. SS.—Monumenta Germaniae Historica: Scriptores

MGH. SS. rer. Langob.—Monumenta Germaniae Historica: Scriptores rerum Langobardicarum et Italicarum

MGH. SS. rer. Merov.—Monumenta Germaniae Historica: Scriptores rerum Merovingicarum

PL—Patrologiae cursus completus: Patres Latini (Migne)

Chapter I

THE EARLY MIDDLE AGES

THE COMMON and widely accepted belief that in the Middle Ages no one not a cleric was able to read or to write Latin, is a gross exaggeration.[1] A greater amount of evidence pertinent to this subject is to be found in medieval sources than is generally believed. Notwithstanding that "the tendency of the Church's teaching was undoubtedly to depreciate secular, and especially literary, education,"[2] we know that the Roman secular schools continued to exist in Gaul until the early seventh century, and that those in Italy persisted throughout the Middle Ages. Besides the evidences of lay learning afforded by the history of medieval education, a sizable body of data on the subject is to be found in chronicles, charters, and private documents such as letters and wills. From the very depths of the feudal age we have the testaments of several nobles who bequeathed the contents of their libraries, enumerating the books by title. Furthermore, allusions can be found to the favorite reading of certain cultured nobles, and even of a few noblewomen, who lived in the days when "letters" still signified Latin literature alone. That there had been a serious decline in education is of course true, and it will be pertinent to our study to give here a brief account of the decline of Roman education in the late imperial period. By the fourth century the decay of interest in learning and culture even among the élite of Roman society attracted the attention of the government. Abortive and clumsy endeavors were made to stimulate learning by establishing the Athenaeum at Rome, and chairs of rhetoric and law in the important schools of the provinces, such as Beirut in Syria, Athens, Milan, Carthage, Seville, Lyons, Bordeaux, and others. In all, there were ten such "universities" under government supervision.[3] These governmental measures soon proved ineffective in checking the tendency of the times.

The decline of education is also seen in the history of private charters, which, owing both to the increase in illiteracy and the growing practice of forgery, were now required by law to be registered in provincial or municipal archives.[4] The fate of the libraries, either neglected, or destroyed by decay and dispersion, is another

---

[1] Superior figures refer to notes on pp. 17–26.

symptom of the intellectual decline.[5] Already in the fourth century Ammianus Marcellinus (A. D. 378) had mournfully written:
"bibliothecis sepulcrorum ritu in perpetuum clausis"—the libraries were shut forever like tombs.[6]

The increasing poverty of creative imagination is reflected alike
in the decay of literature and the loss of vigor in education. Education slowly ceased to be a discipline and became a rhetorical
art. Grammarians degenerated into mere antiquarians; thought
became repetitious and added nothing to the ancient store of
knowledge. The splendid endeavor of cultivated pagan nobles, like
Symmachus in the Theodosian epoch, who gathered together kin-
dred spirits in Rome and strove to keep the candle of vision alight,
failed to relieve the growing intellectual darkness. Finally, the
triumph of Christianity had divorced almost all men from fellow-
ship with the classical tradition.

Fortunately for culture and humanism, the Church, while it was
able to revolutionize the religion of the ancient world, and even
its morals, did not create a new educational system. The method
of teaching, and even the textbooks, remained in large part pagan
in character.[7] The last public schools of the Roman Empire, however, except those in Italy, expired in the seventh century, at a
time when Benedictinism was still in its infancy and its great
school system yet to be developed. Education was not an original
function of monasteries; that office was, so to speak, thrust upon
them by later circumstances.[8] Thus in the seventh and eighth centuries education in Western Europe reached its nadir; its future
belonged to the Church.

Nevertheless, although the monastery and cathedral schools became almost the sole centers of learning and literature, and were
to remain so for centuries to come except in Italy, the sweeping
statement often made,—that a knowledge of letters in the Middle
Ages was limited strictly to the clergy, and that the laity, including kings and emperors, were totally ignorant of Latin and could
neither read nor write,—must be rejected as untrue.

It is the purpose of this study to examine in detail the evidence
on this question, and to determine how large a part of the laity in
the Middle Ages was able to understand Latin, both to read it and
to write it. We shall find that the lay class was not so completely
ignorant of Latin as is generally supposed; that in every century

of this period a number of lettered men and women were to be found outside of the ecclesiastical confines. There is evidence to show that even some of the barbarians acquired a fair knowledge of Latin.

As early as the fifth century, Latin was the official language at the Burgundian and Visigothic courts. The Burgundian king, Gundobald, must certainly have understood Latin, for he had spent many years at Rome under Ricimer.[9] His niece, Clotilda, the future wife of Clovis, may also have had some knowledge of Latin.[10]

Concerning the knowledge of Latin by the barbarians, Mr. Dalton has said that "probably most of the principal barbarians could speak it, at any rate among the Visigoths."[11] There is no doubt about Theodoric II, the Visigothic king (452–466). Sidonius Apollinaris represents him as thanking Avitus, the poet's father-in-law, for having inculcated in him an appreciation of the cultural value of Vergil.[12] There seems to be some question about the ability of Euric, Theodoric's successor, to use Latin. According to Ennodius, Euric had need of an interpreter;[13] but Sidonius, in a letter to Euric's Latin secretary, urges him to "lay aside awhile the universally applauded speeches composed for the royal lips, those famed deliverances with which the glorious monarch from his exalted place strikes terror into the hearts of the tribes beyond the sea."[14] It may be that Euric was sufficiently familiar with Latin to be able to deliver a prepared address although he was unable to use the language independently. The letters of Sidonius are sufficient proof of the persistence of Latin culture among the native Roman aristocracy in Visigothic Gaul,[15] although there is intimation of a decline in culture even among this class.[16] Among the lower classes a knowledge of Latin was doubtless confined to the native Roman population.[17] The sermon of Sidonius at Bourges in 472 which Dill[18] adduces as evidence of a knowledge of Latin among the common peoples of fifth-century Gaul, seems to be valid only for the Roman part of the populace. The Goths were Arians and would hardly have been present at the address of the orthodox bishop. Among the Goths the language of the common people was undoubtedly Gothic, and while most of the aristocracy understood Latin, their use of the language was not such as to arouse the admiration of the cultured Romans.[19]

Latin culture seems to have flourished appreciably in the Visigothic kingdom of Spain. "Education may have held a higher place [there] than in other Teutonic countries."[20] Kirn has pointed out[21] that the validity of private documents among the Visigoths depended on the personal signature of the witnesses. The genuineness of a document brought in question was established by identifying the signatures in the subscription. Under King Athanagild (554–567) the Visigothic court at Toledo was probably more cultured than that of any of his Merovingian contemporaries.[22] In the period following, "amongst the writers and cultured men of the time there were a few laymen, such as the kings Recared, Sisebut, Chindaswinth, and Receswinth, duke Claudius, the counts Bulgaranus and Laurentius."[23]

Perhaps the most remarkable of these learned laymen was King Sisebut (612–620), who composed a *Chronicle of the Kings of the Goths,* now lost, and probably also a metrical piece entitled *De eclipsibus solis et lunae,* which in old MSS was commonly appended to Isidore's *De astronomia* and often erroneously ascribed to him.[24]

In a recent article, M. Henri Pirenne[25] has directed attention to a significant and little known fact concerning the relative merits of the Merovingian and Carolingian periods with respect to literary activity. What the latter period gained in quality, it lost in quantity. At the same time that learning became more refined and deeper in the Carolingian age, it became in large part the monopoly of the Church, and the more superficial but extensive literacy of the Merovingian period gradually disappeared. M. Pirenne supports his belief in the widespread and lay character of instruction in the Merovingian period by ample evidence, and interprets its existence in terms of his favorite thesis, as a survival of the civilization of the Roman Empire in the West until the expansion of Islam into the western Mediterranean put an end to the more complex social and economic system of antiquity and marked the beginning of a purely agrarian and illiterate society.

The Franks, it would seem, took up Latin more readily in Neustria, where the mass of the population remained Gallo-Roman, than in Austrasia.[26] Since Latin was the language used in all public documents, in the Church, and in the courts of the provincial towns, the Franks naturally "would be compelled by the necessities of business and social life to adopt the language of a population which immensely outnumbered them."[27] Latin early became the language of the Merovingian court. Though the tongue of Caesar must, to the end of his days, have sounded strange to the ears of Clovis, his queen, Clotilda, may have acquired a smattering of Latin.[28] Notwithstanding their coarseness and brutality the Merovingian kings were culturally above the level of the early Carolingians. Sickel, it has been pointed out,[29] has proved[30] that whereas most of the Merovingian kings, and very likely all of them, were able to write, Pepin the Short was unable to do so, and Charlemagne did not learn to write until late in life. At least, the Merovingian kings were all capable of signing their own documents,[31] and the firmness of their signatures may indicate that they were not strangers to the pen.[32] When the king was prevented for any reason from signing the royal diplomas, the queen (or the queen-mother, for a minor king) corroborated the official acts which emanated from the royal chancellery. Thus in an extant charter, Childeric II, then a mere child, is made to say,—unless the charter be a forgery, which is probable,—"propter imbecillam aetatem minime potui subscribere: manu nostra subtersignavi [i.e., he has affixed the royal seal] et regina subterscripsit."[33] Gregory of Tours tells us that the royal children were instructed in letters.[34]

Among the Merovingian kings of the second generation after Clovis, there was at least one who considered himself a master of Latin, and that in more than one sense. Of Chilperic I (king of Soissons, 561–584) we are told that he even added certain letters to the alphabet, and composed "books in verse, in which he tried to imitate Sedulius."[35] Although Fortunatus' verses in praise of Charibert I (king of Paris, 561–567) are transparent panegyric, nevertheless they indicate the king's acquaintance with Latin.[36] The literary interests of certain Merovingian queens are also well known. Radegunde, the saintly wife of Clothar I (king of all the Franks, 558–561), who retired to the convent of Poitiers and befriended the poet Fortunatus, evidently possessed an excellent knowledge of Latin, although she was by birth a Thuringian, the daughter of King Berthar.[37] The famous Brunhild was doubtless able to understand even the *Epithalamion* which Fortunatus composed for the occasion of her wedding to Sigibert.[38]

A knowledge and appreciation of Latin letters was not limited to the royal families, however, but was widespread among the lay aristocracy of Merovingian society, especially among the descendants of those ancient Roman senatorial families, particularly numerous south of the Loire, which had successfully survived the period of invasions, and whose culture remained wholly Roman.[39] Just as the letters of Sidonius Apollinaris reflect the culture of Visigothic Gaul in the fifth century, so the poetry of Venantius Fortunatus casts light upon the intellectual life of Merovingian Gaul in the sixth century. The names of the persons to whom the poet addressed his verses supply us with examples of the educated aristocracy. Among these are Gogo, mayor of the palace in Austrasia under Sigibert;[40] Duke Bodegisilius;[41] and his wife Palatina, whose sweet speech so enchants the poet that at the sound of her voice he despises the lyre.[42] There are also Duke Lupus;[43] and Flavus, whose learning as described by Fortunatus[44] has caused Mr. Rand to dub him "a walking library."[45] Asteriolus and Secundinus, favorites at the court of Theudebert I and apparently wealthy Gallo-Roman nobles, are described by Gregory as "well-educated men and versed in rhetoric."[46] Parthenius, a high official under the same king, even went to Rome to complete his literary education.[47] Sulpicius, of ancient Roman senatorial stock, on whom King Guntram conferred the bishopric of Bourges, was "learned in rhetoric, and second to none in poetic skill."[48] We read also the illuminating story of Domnolus, bishop of Le Mans, who begged King Clothar I not to appoint him bishop of Avignon, where, because of his simple nature, he would be "teased by sophisticated senatorials or philosophizing counts."[49] That the women of the Frankish aristocracy also enjoyed some education is proved by the fact that some of Hermenfreda's letters to her son, Saint Desiderius, are contained in his biography.[50]

As to Frankish laymen, the too-sweeping statement has been made that they were almost universally illiterate. "Many high-born Franks, unless in their youth they had been trained at court ... were probably unable to write their names, relying wholly upon signets."[51] The *History of the Franks* by Gregory of Tours, however, in some measure modifies if it does not refute this judgment. The glory of the Frankish lady of Paris, Vilithuta, according to Fortunatus, lay in her having become by training and study a cultured Roman, despite her barbarian origin.[52]

M. Pirenne explains this preservation of a certain degree of literary culture among the laity of Merovingian Gaul, not only by the fidelity of the old Roman families to the ancient tradition, but also by the character of the state, whose administrative organization, a direct survival of the imperial machinery, demanded the existence of a corps of trained and educated officials.[53] There is sufficient evidence to prove that the training and instruction necessary to the official class was still dispensed as late as the first half of the seventh century by public lay schools of grammar and rhetoric, "the pale but authentic survivals of the schools of the Empire,"[54] although it is still generally but erroneously believed that these schools disappeared in Gaul at the time of the barbarian invasions in the fifth century. It is apparent from our sources that the curriculum of these schools included not only grammar and rhetoric, but also legal studies, in particular the explanation of the Theodosian Code. The *Life of Saint Bonitus,* for example, an anonymous but contemporary and trustworthy source,[55] tells us that Bonitus, a precocious young man, received his education at the hands of "sophists," or teachers, from whom he learned grammar and the Theodosian Code, before being sent to the court of Sigebert (634–656).[56] Though he ended his life as bishop of Clermont, his education and early career were distinctly lay in character; like many others of his class, he received a bishopric as a reward for his services to the state.[57] A similar education and career were had by Desiderius, future bishop of Cahors, who was instructed in "Gallic eloquence" and "Roman law" before he assumed the office of royal treasurer at the court of Clothar II (613–620).[58] Another Desiderius, future bishop of Vienne (d. 608), was put to the study of grammar when he had reached "the age of learning"; this statement undoubtedly means that he was sent to a school of grammar, according to Pirenne.[59] Evidence from the lives of Leobardus and of Saint Hermeland (d. 720), as well as Gregory of Tours's statement concerning a school at Marseilles where grammar, "calculation," and Roman law were taught, are also adduced by Pirenne as proof of the continued existence of public lay schools in Merovingian society.[60]

Another scholar, Franz Anton Specht, basing his contention in large part upon hagiographic literature, has agreed that it was well-nigh a general custom among the nobility in Frankish Gaul to send their children to school.[61] Hagiographic sources, however, must be used with extreme care, if we are to extract the reliable bits of information from the mass of legend. Of the passages from the *Vitae Sanctorum* cited by Specht[62] only one may be regarded as fairly contemporary and reliable. Of the remaining two examples, one, the *Vita S. Walarici,* seems to have been written about the middle of the eleventh century,[63] and cannot therefore be considered trustworthy evidence concerning conditions in the seventh.[64] The other, the *Vita S. Pauli Virodunensis,* though more applicable in view of the phraseology of the pertinent passage,[65] was also written at too late a date to make it acceptable.[66] But a passage in the *Vita S. Chlodulfi* (bishop of Metz, died *ca.* 694), written probably about fifty years after the saint's death,[67] is worth noting. It runs thus : "The venerable Chlodulfus, therefore, when he was a boy, was sent to school, and was given over for instruction in the liberal arts, as was suitable, and as was customary among the children of the nobility."[68] This, unless we regard it simply as empty verbiage, would seem to strengthen belief in the continued existence as late as the seventh century of lay schools in which at least the noble class acquired a knowledge of Latin letters.

There are also indications of the persistence among the Frankish aristocracy of the Roman custom of having servants whose function it was to read aloud to their masters and assist them in their literary activities. The most striking example of this custom is revealed by implication in the life of Saint Desiderius, cited above. While he was at the court of King Clothar II, his mother, Hermenfreda, frequently wrote letters to him.[69] That these letters were usually written by a scribe at the noble lady's dictation, although she was perfectly capable of writing them herself, seems to be implicit in the following subscription to one of the letters : "With my own hand : may the Lord see fit to keep you safe and to make you an heir of his kingdom."[70] Hermenfreda's *lector* was possibly one of the last of his race,—who, however, were probably not uncommon figures at the courts of Gallo-Roman and Frankish noblemen in Gaul in the preceding period.[71] The bishops, too, employed scribes or notaries. Gregory of Tours, for example, mentions his own notaries, and also the secretary of Aegidius, archbishop of Rheims.[72] Although these men were professional scribes, they were apparently servants and laymen.

Up to this point, we have been concerned almost entirely with the extent and character of the knowledge of Latin and Latin literature among the upper classes of Merovingian society. There is reason to believe, however, that some of the less favored groups of society were also literate. Pirenne has pointed out that both the juridical and economic conditions of the time, as well as the administrative functioning of the state, made constant recourse to writing absolutely necessary.[73] Since the greater part of the population in Gaul, as well as in Italy, Africa, and Spain, continued to live under Roman law, there must have been clerks who could read the law[74] as well as numerous scribes to answer the need for drawing up and copying legal documents. Only a few such records remain, written, as they were, on the perishable papyrus of the time. Similarly, the economic life of the period, still characterized by extensive Mediterranean commerce, demanded a knowledge of writing on the part of the merchant class or their "mercenarii litterati," clerks who were charged with the correspondence and accounts of their masters. Although no such documents survive, Pirenne believes they can be taken for granted because there existed a class of professional merchants living on long-distance commerce, and because a great abundance of papyrus was imported into Gaul from Egypt up until the beginning of the eighth century.[75] Exactly what proportion of the merchant class was literate is, of course, indeterminable, but it seems unreasonable to deny that at least some merchants were able to read and write. We cannot argue, as some scholars have done, that the merchant class had little or no education, merely from the statement of Caesar of Arles (d. 542) that he knew "some merchants who, since they were ignorant of letters, were forced to hire clerks; and who, although they themselves knew no letters, nevertheless engaged in big business transactions by the aid of others who kept their accounts for them."[76] It should be noted that Caesar seems to have regarded these unlettered merchants as exceptional; he says quite definitely "some merchants," not merchants as a class.[77]

Among the non-noble elements of society, not only the merchant class but the freemen also apparently received some education. Gregory of Tours supplies us with two examples of children of freemen who were sent to school. The story of the early training of Saint Patroclus (496–576) is especially interesting in this re-

gard. His father, Aetherius, a native of Bourges and a man of free
but not noble blood, had two sons, Patroclus, who at the age of ten
years was sent out to become a shepherd, and Anthony, who was
put to the study of letters. One day when the brothers came home
to dinner, each from his task, Anthony put on airs and made sport
of his brother because of Patroclus' rustic occupation. Patroclus,
seeing in this taunt the hand of God, straightway abandoned his
sheep, and set out to school, where he advanced so rapidly that he
soon surpassed his brother both in knowledge and in mental acumen.[78] Later in his life, after Patroclus had entered the Church,
he himself instructed boys in the study of letters.[79] The early education of the hermit Leobardus, a native of Auvergne, seems to
have been similar to that of the sons of Aetherius. He was sent
together with other boys to school, where, it is noted, he committed
to memory certain psalms, and, not knowing that he was to be a
cleric, prepared himself for the service of the king.[80]

This reference to a part at least of what the boy learned at school
raises an important and difficult problem. Were all the schools for
the education of the laity still under lay control; that is, did they
exist outside the framework of the Church? Pirenne[81] makes a distinction between what he calls special schools for the aristocracy,
which preserved a knowledge of Latin literature and classical literary Latin, and the greater number, which taught some letters
and some practical subjects, such as were required by administration and commerce, and used the "low," living tongue. He believes,
however, that the lower as well as the higher type of school existed
outside the Church and was distinctly lay in character, though
probably the masters were in great part clerics, that some simple
religious instruction was given,—similar to that given to Leobardus
(cited above),—and that some of the pupils may have been intended for Church careers.[82] It is difficult for me to accept without
reservation, however, Pirenne's insistence on the completely lay
character of such a school as that run by the dissolute cleric of
Lisieux. This adventurer, in a fit of gratitude for receiving pardon
for certain offenses, promised Aetherius, the bishop, "to perfect in
grammar any boys who might be entrusted to his charge." Thereupon the bishop assembled the boys of the city and handed them
over to the priest to be instructed.[83] It is likewise difficult to be
certain of the character of the school which John, archdeacon of

Nîmes, conducted in the deanery for the instruction of the little ones.[84] As time went on, the education of the lower classes undoubtedly fell more and more into the hands of the Church.

By far the greater number of the people in Merovingian Gaul must have been illiterate. The condition of the swineherd Brachis, as described by Gregory of Tours, is probably typical. Brachis, later an abbot, is said to have poured forth prayers unto the Lord, evidently in a sort of religious ecstasy, but without knowing for what he prayed, "because he was ignorant of letters" (*quia litteras ignorabat*).[85] Even in cities like Marseilles, where the cultural influences of Roman civilization may be supposed to have long persisted, the mass of the population seems to have been unable to read Latin.[86] Illiteracy was prevalent even among the lower clergy of the period. One of the canons passed at the Council of Orléans in 533 stated that "a priest or deacon who is unlettered and does not know the baptismal service ought in no wise to be ordained."[87]

It is worthy of note in passing, however, that notwithstanding the prevalence of illiteracy and its increase as time went on, there was apparently no lack of reading material or scarcity of books. Caesar of Arles, in the sermon cited above, scoffs at the idea that the Scriptures are not accessible to his listeners and exhorts them to find time in which to read them.[88] Vergilius Maro, the grammarian, who lived in the late sixth or early seventh century, and who was certainly a layman, since he was once described as a teacher of rhetoric of Toulouse, records the custom of having two separate libraries, one of Christian, the other of pagan literature, as still obtaining in his time. He also reveals the intense activity of the grammarians, one of whom, his old master, wrote a work on the twelve kinds of Latin while others wrangled for a fortnight over the vocative of *ego* or inchoative verbs.[89]

The evidence for the spread of the knowledge of Latin among the barbarian invaders who established themselves in Italy during the fifth and sixth centuries is scarcer and less satisfactory than that given above concerning the Merovingians. It is, of course, common knowledge that the Ostrogoths, like the other German peoples, regarded Roman institutions and culture with profound respect, and that Roman cultural influences upon the Ostrogoths were far greater than Gothic influences upon the Romans. Although a few Romans undoubtedly learned Gothic,[90] the more common course

was for the Goths to learn Latin. Since the administrative person-
nel was made up almost exclusively of Romans, and the official
language of the government was Latin, a knowledge of this tongue
must have been imperative, at least among the Gothic magnates.[91]
All the Ostrogothic kings, from Theodoric the Great on down, could
at least understand and speak Latin.[92]

The question of the degree of Theodoric's literacy or illiteracy
is a complex one. His speech to the people on his visit to Rome in
500 A. D. may not have been delivered faultlessly, but, as Hodgkin
has pointed out: "It is possible that historians somewhat under-
rate the degree of Theodoric's acquaintance with Latin as a spoken
language. There was a great deal of Latin used in the Pannonian
and Moesian regions, in which his childhood and youth were
passed; and some, though certainly not so much, at Constantinople,
where he spent his boyhood."[93] It is impossible, however, to take the
word of Cassiodorus without great caution. For he makes Theodoric both cite and interpret Homer, Terence, and Vergil, and
even quote Tacitus.[94] Whether or not Theodoric could read or write
Latin, is another problem. The *Anonymus Valesii*[95] says of Theodoric that he was illiterate, and that he had a sort of stencil made
by means of which he was able to trace out on his documents the
four letters of the word *legi* ("I have read"), which was the official
subscription indicating the king's approval of a document.[96] If we
accept this story as valid evidence, and limit the interpretation of
legi to personal reading, excluding the possibility that the word
here means that the document was read aloud to the king, then this
passage would indicate that Theodoric was able to read Latin, if
not to write it.[97] There are reasons, however, for believing that this
anecdote must be rejected. Hodgkin comments thus on the validity
of the story: "I strongly suspect that this paragraph was originally
written concerning the Emperor Justin (of whom precisely the
same story is told)[98] and has been transferred to Theodoric by mistake. The paragraph immediately preceding refers to Byzantine
affairs."[99] The historian of the barbarian invasions might have gone
farther in his proof. He translates the passage "ut in decem annos
regni sui quattuor litteras subscriptionis edicti sui discere nullatenus potuisset" to mean "that after ten years of reigning he was
still utterly unable to learn the four letters of his own signature to
one of his edicts." A more correct translation, however, would be

"that during the ten years of his reign he had in no wise been able to learn the four letters of the subscription to one of his edicts." This translation of the passage would seem to prove that it is simply a tale originally told of the Emperor Justin (who reigned from 518 to 527) and later clumsily imposed, by mistake or more likely by design, upon Theodoric. It is hardly possible that the anonymous author deliberately borrowed the story because it was applicable in all its details, and that he meant to say that Theodoric did not learn to write until after the first ten years of his reign.[100] In another place the *Anonymus Valesii* again says that "although he [Theodoric] was unlettered, he was of such great wisdom that some of the things which he said are still popularly regarded as proverbial."[101] It is evident that the *Anonymus* believed that Theodoric was and remained unlettered. He knew the story of Justin's stencil and apparently thought it a good anecdote with which to adorn his account of Theodoric, but he neglected to make the necessary change in the number of years of the reign! Just what does the author mean by *inlitteratus?* It seems probable that he meant in particular that Theodoric was unable to write. One other bit of evidence should be considered at this point. Several of the letters which Theodoric addressed to the bishops assembled in Rome in the year 501 for the trial of Symmachus conclude with the words "Orate pro nobis, domini ac venerabiles patres,"[102] which were written in a hand other than that of the scribe. According to Hodgkin, "Notwithstanding the depreciatory remarks of the *Anonymus Valesii* as to Theodoric's penmanship, one cannot repress the conjecture that this subscription was in the original added by the king's own hand."[103] Such a conjecture, however, belongs to the sphere of pure hypothesis.

The general intellectual interests of Theodoric are attested in a letter sent by Athalaric to Cassiodorus in 533. Here the king describes his grandfather as "a royal philosopher" who "when he was free from the cares of state was wont to seek the maxims of wise men" from the stories (*fabulis*) of Cassiodorus.[104] In summary; the evidence concerning Theodoric's knowledge of Latin seems to establish that he could understand and speak the language, that possibly he may have been able to read it, but that probably he could not write it.

Although the statements of Cassiodorus in praise of the intel-

lectual accomplishments of Amalaswintha and her consort, Theodohad, are doubtless colored by exaggeration, nevertheless they
are worth recording. Amalaswintha is said to have possessed an
excellent knowledge of both Greek and Latin, as well as of Gothic,[105]
and both she[106] and Theodohad[107] are credited with a laudable
knowledge of letters. These statements seem to indicate a rather
rapid spread of the knowledge of Latin among the élite of Ostrogothic society. It should be remembered, however, that there was
also a "national party" among the Ostrogoths, the partisans of
which violently resented the pro-Roman attitude of Amalaswintha
and her following. The Gothic (and Arian) priests in particular
opposed all Roman (and Catholic) influences; they probably encouraged the use of Gothic even for literary and business purposes,
but apparently with slight success.[108] The hostility of many of
the Ostrogothic leaders to Roman life and culture is brought out
clearly in Procopius' account of the education of Athalaric:

> Now Amalasuntha wished to make her son resemble the Roman prince in his
> manner of life, and was already compelling him to attend the school of a
> teacher of letters.... But the Goths were by no means pleased with this....
> And all the notable men among them gathered together, and coming before
> Amalasuntha made the charge that their king was not being educated cor-
> rectly from their point of view nor to his own advantage. For letters, they said,
> are far removed from manliness, and the teaching of old men results for the
> most part in a cowardly and submissive spirit.... They added that even Theod-
> oric would never allow any of the Goths to send their children to school; for
> he used to say to them all that, if the fear of the strap once came over them,
> they would never have the resolution to despise sword or spear.[109]

In the business world of Italy in the sixth century, a knowledge
of Latin was undoubtedly indispensable. The documents of the
period show that every businessman had to be able to read Latin
or at least understand it when read to him; he had also to be able
to write,—at least, sign his own name. A document could be drawn
up either by the contracting party or by a professional scribe
(*tabellio*), but in the latter event the document had to contain the
personal signature of the man who had authorized the scribe to
write it.[110] Many of the documents state that the party or parties
concerned, and the witnesses to the transaction as well, were present when the document was drawn up, and that they either read
it themselves or had it read to them. Such statements are found
in documents drawn up even as late as the Lombard period.[111] The

conditions revealed by these facts, however, are in no way startling, since it is probable that throughout the sixth century there were still abundant opportunities for lay education. Theodoric the Great and Justinian after him maintained chairs of grammar and rhetoric at Ravenna; and Justinian even reopened the university at Rome.[112]

The seventh century was undoubtedly a darker period, but, according to Specht, there are known to have been a few "schools which were still in a flourishing condition under the Lombard kings."[113] By the eighth century, however, Italy was again famous for her learning; illustrious grammarians were to be found in Benevento, Rome, Milan, and especially at Pavia.[114] But educated laymen among the Lombards were few in number. Hodgkin[115] claims for Theudelinda, daughter of the Bavarian Garibald, and wife first of Authari (584–590) and then of Agilulf (590–615), that she was able to sign her own name. He cites as evidence the autograph of Theudelinda in an early codex of the Four Gospels in the museum at Cividale. This claim, however, cannot be substantiated. C. L. Bethmann, whose article Hodgkin quotes as authority for his statement, points out that Theudelinda's signature, like all the signatures as of Lombard princes in this MS, is a sixteenth-century forgery, that most of the names which appear in the book were evidently written in by scribes, and that none of them is older than the late eighth century.[116] It is highly probable, nevertheless, that Theudelinda possessed some knowledge of Latin. She was a Catholic and a friend of Saint Columban and of Gregory the Great, who wrote several letters to her.[117] These facts, although they afford no definite proof, seem to indicate that Theudelinda was not wholly ignorant of Latin letters. She may have been able to write, and she could probably speak and read Latin.[118] If we can attach any significance to the Gospel lectionary which Gregory sent to Adaloald, the young son of Theudelinda and Agilulf, it is possible that the queen provided her children with some sort of training in Latin letters.[119]

We hear of no other Lombard prince or princess who is credited with a knowledge of Latin letters, until the second half of the eighth century. Both Adalperga, daughter of the last Lombard king, Desiderius (756–774), and her husband, Arichis, duke of Benevento, were cultured and educated persons, well versed in

Latin letters. Paul the Deacon says of Adalperga that "in imitation of her husband she diligently and sagaciously explored the sacred mysteries of wise men, so that the golden eloquence of the philosophers and the jeweled wisdom of the poets were at her command."[120] From the same source we learn that Paul had sent her Eutropius' *Roman History,* which she had read and found too short, as well as barren of all references to Christianity. Paul therefore wrote for her his own *Roman History,* continuing Eutropius and adding the desired material on Christianity.[121] Concerning Arichis' wisdom and learning Paul speaks in equally glowing terms.[122] Romuald, the son of this noble and enlightened pair, seems to have been a worthy successor.[123]

Notes to Chapter I

¹ A typical example of this misconception is the statement of Hallam: "When Latin had thus ceased to be a living language, the whole treasury of knowledge was locked up from the eyes of the people. The few who might have imbibed a taste for literature, if books had been accessible to them, were reduced to abandon pursuits that could only be cultivated through a kind of education not easily within their reach. Schools, confined to cathedrals and monasteries, and exclusively designed for the purposes of religion, afforded no encouragement or opportunities to the laity.... The very use of letters, as well as of books, was forgotten. For many centuries, to sum up the account of ignorance in a word, it was rare for a layman, of whatever rank, to know how to sign his name.... Still more extraordinary it was to find one who had any tincture of learning.... Whatever mention, therefore, we find of learning and the learned during these dark ages, must be understood to relate only to such as were within the pale of clergy...."—H. Hallam, *View of the State of Europe during the Middle Ages*, chap. 9, pt. 1.

As recently as December 30, 1935, Professor Charles Seignobos, of the Sorbonne, repeated the fable. "Du Vᵉ au XIIᵉ siècle, quand les clercs seuls écrivaient...." See his lecture published in *Revue des cours et des conférences*, XXXVII, no. ii (December 30, 1935).

² H. Rashdall, *The Universities of Europe in the Middle Ages* (Oxford, 1895), I, 27.

³ "Under the later pagan emperors, and under Constantine and his successors, the private schools of grammar and rhetoric had tended to decline. There were fewer pupils with inclination and ability to pay. So the emperors established municipal schools in the towns of Italy and the provinces. The towns tried to shirk the burden, and the teachers, whose pay came tardily, had to look to private pupils for support."—H. O. Taylor, *The Medieval Mind* (3d ed.; New York, 1919), I, 249–250.

⁴ O. Redlich, *Urkundenlehre: Die Privaturkunden des Mittelalters* (Munich and Berlin, 1911). Cf. *English Historical Review*, XXIX (1914), 118–121; this is a review of Redlich's book by H. W. C. Davis.

⁵ Bernhardy, *Grundriss der römischen Litteratur* (5th ed.; Brunswick, 1872), 88.

⁶ *Historia*, XIV, vi, 18.

⁷ "We must keep in mind that we are approaching mediaeval thought from the side of the innate human need of intellectual expression—the impulse to know and the need to formulate one's conceptions and express them consistently.... The Latin language contained the sum of knowledge transmitted to the Middle Ages. And it had to be learned.... Men would not at first distinguish sharply between the mediating value of the learned tongue and the learning which it held.... Any one really seeking learning, studied and worked and thought in the medium of Latin.... Because of the crudeness of the vernacular tongues, the Latin classics were even more untranslatable in the tenth or eleventh century than now. One may add, that it was fortunate for the prog-

ress of mediaeval learning that Latin was the *one* language used by all scholars in all countries. This facilitated the diffusion of knowledge."—Taylor, *op. cit.*, II, 360–361, and 361, n. 1.

⁸ Mabillon, *Tractatus de studiis monasticis* (Venice, 1729), pt. 1, p. 3. "Falsa procul dubio fuit quorundam imaginatio, qui praecedenti saeculo scripsere, monachorum coenobia non aliter ab initio instituta fuisse, nisi ut inservirent tanquam lycea, aut publicae academiae, in quibus scientiae humanae traderentur."

⁹ S. Dill, *Roman Society in Gaul in the Merovingian Age* (London, 1926), 277.

¹⁰ Gregory of Tours, *History of the Franks*, trans. by O. M. Dalton (Oxford, Clarendon Press, 1927), Intro., I, 413. See below, note 28.

¹¹ O. M. Dalton, *The Letters of Sidonius* (Oxford, 1915), Intro., I, p. cxxvi, n. 3.

¹² Sidonius Apollinaris, *Carm.*, VII, 495–498 (*MGH. AA.*, VIII, 215):

> "mihi Romula dudum
> per te iura placent, parvumque ediscere iussit
> ad tua verba pater, docili quo prisca Maronis
> carmine molliret Scythicos mihi pagina mores."

Cf. T. Hodgkin, *Italy and Her Invaders* (Oxford), II (1880), 380, n. 1; Dalton, *Letters of Sidonius*, Intro., I, p. xvi, n. 3; and Dill, *op. cit.*, 277.

¹³ Ennodius, *Vita B. Epiphani (Corpus script. eccles.*, VI, 353), where Euric's reaction to the speech of Epiphanius, bishop of Pavia and envoy of Nepos, is described thus: "At Euricus, gentile nescio quod murmur infringens, mollitum se adhortationibus eius uultus sui serenitate significat." Euric's reply is then introduced with "taliter tamen fertur ad interpretem rex locutus."

¹⁴ *Epist.*, VIII, iii: Dalton, *Letters of Sidonius*, II, 141.

¹⁵ See, e.g., *Epist.*, II, ii, v; IV, xii, xvii; and V, xv: Dalton, *Letters of Sidonius*, I, 36, 45; II, 24, 30, 68.

¹⁶ *Epist.*, IX, x.

¹⁷ Cf. *Epist.*, VII, ix: Dalton, *Letters of Sidonius*, II, 115.

¹⁸ *Op. cit.*, 278.

¹⁹ See the letters of Sidonius (*Epist.*, II, i: Dalton trans., I, 34, 35) to his brother-in-law, Ecdicius, in which Sidonius says of Seronatus, the "Catiline" of his day, "To the universal amusement he will rant of war in civilian company, and of literature among the Goths."

²⁰ Dalton, tr., *History of the Franks*, Intro., I, 413.

²¹ *Archiv für Urkundenforschung*, X (1928), 130.

²² Cf. Dalton, tr., *History of the Franks*, Intro., I, 69 and 413, and below, note 38, on Brunhild, the daughter of Athanagild.

²³ R. Altamira, "Spain under the Visigoths," *Cambridge Medieval History*, II, 192.

²⁴ A Leyden MS, Voss quarto 33, definitely attributes the piece to Sisebut by name. See E. Bishop, *Liturgica Historica* (Oxford, 1918), 173, n. 3.

²⁵ "De l'état de l'instruction des laïques à l'époque mérovingienne," *Revue bénédictine*, XLVI (1934), 165–177.

²⁶ Cf. Dalton, tr., *History of the Franks*, Intro., I, 165, 168–169.

²⁷ Dill, *op. cit.*, 278.

[28] So Dalton, tr., *History of the Franks*, Intro., I, 413, conjectures, on the basis of Clotilda's being seemingly well acquainted with classical mythology.

[29] P. Beckmann, *Revue des questions historiques*, IV (1868), 293–294.

[30] In *Acta regum et imperatorum Karolinorum digesta et enarrata*, Intro., pt. 1, *Die Urkunden der Karolinger* (Vienna, 1867).

[31] A. Giry, *Manuel de diplomatique* (Paris, 1894), 708: "The royal subscription was ordinarily an autograph, and was worded, 'N. Rex subscripsi.' "

[32] Pirenne, *op. cit.*, 167.

[33] L. Levillain, *Examen critique des chartes mérovingiennes et carolingiennes de l'Abbaye de Corbie* (Paris, 1902), 328–329.

[34] *History of the Franks*, Bk. VI, 16: Dalton, II, 254.

[35] *History of the Franks*, Bk. V, 32: Dalton, II, 218. At another place (VI, 33: Dalton, II, 279) Gregory says of Chilperic, "but as, in his ignorance, he put short syllables for long and long for short, his feeble lines had no feet to stand on."

[36] Fortunatus, *Carm.*, VI, ii (*MGH. AA.*, IV, pt. 1, 133):

> "cum sis progenitus clara de gente Sigamber,
> floret in eloquio lingua Latina tuo.
> qualis es in propria docto sermone loquella
> qui nos Romanos vincis in eloquio?"

[37] Cf. Ch. Jourdain, "Mémoire sur l'éducation des femmes au moyen âge," *Mémoires de l'Institut National de France: Académie des inscriptions et belles-lettres*, XXVIII, pt. 1 (1874), 83–84, and E. K. Rand, "The Brighter Aspects of the Merovingian Age," *Proceedings of the Classical Association*, XVIII (1921), 172.

[38] Cf. Dalton, tr., *History of the Franks*, Intro., I, 69 and 413, who suggests that at this time the Visigothic court at Toledo—Brunhild's home before her marriage—was probably more cultured than any court of the Merovingian kings.

[39] Pirenne, *op. cit.*, 166 f.

[40] Fortunatus, *Carm.*, VII, i, and esp. ii (*MGH. AA.*, IV, pt. 1, 154), where Gogo is praised thus: "tu refluus Cicero, tu noster Apicius extas."

[41] *Ibid.*, VII, v.

[42] *Ibid.*, VII, vi, 158:

> "blandior alloquio, placidis suavissima verbis:
> despiciamque lyram, si tua lingua sonat."

[43] *Ibid.*, VII, viii, 162.

[44] *Ibid.*, VII, xviii, 172.

[45] *Proc. Class. Assoc.*, XVIII (1921), 176. The exact social status of this Flavus seems indeterminable. Fortunatus himself gives no indication; and R. Koebner, *Venantius Fortunatus* (Leipzig and Berlin, B. G. Teubner, 1915), p. 67 and n. 1, says only that he seems to have been from southern Gaul. But he was undoubtedly a layman, since the poet, as was his custom, would surely have added Flavus' ecclesiastical title if he had had one. The only difficulty is that Fortunatus usually indicates the rank of laymen, too. Probably, as the name would seem to suggest, Flavus was simply a country gentleman of noble Gallo-Roman stock.

[46] *History of the Franks*, Bk. III, 33: Dalton, II, 109. See also Pirenne, *op. cit.*, 168.

[47] *History of the Franks*, Bk. III, 36: Dalton, II, 111.

[48] *History of the Franks*, Bk. VI, 25: Dalton, II, 271.

[49] *History of the Franks*, Bk. VI, 9: Dalton, II, 244; cf. also Dalton's note, II, 554.

[50] *La vie de Saint Didier*, ed. by R. Poupardin (Paris, 1900), 10–12. The *Vita* as we have it today was probably written either at the end of the eighth or at the beginning of the ninth century, but the author, probably a monk of Saint-Géry at Cahors, "if he was not a contemporary of Saint Desiderius, at least wrote his work on the basis of authentic documents and reliable information."—Poupardin, p. viii.

[51] Dalton, *History of the Franks*, I, 411. Cf. M. Prou, *La Gaule mérovingienne*, 46.

[52] Fortunatus, *Carm.*, IV, xxvi, 95:

"sanguine nobilium generata Parisius urbe
Romana studio, barbara prole fuit.
ingenium mitem torva de gente trahebat:
vincere naturam gloria maior erat."

[53] *Op. cit.*, 169.

[54] *Ibid.*, 172–173. See also Pirenne, "Le commerce du papyrus dans la Gaule mérovingienne," *Académie des inscriptions et belles-lettres, Comptes rendus des séances*, 1928, 178, n. 3.

[55] Cf. A. Molinier, *Les sources de l'histoire de France* (Paris, 1901–1906), I, 142, no. 454.

[56] *Vita Bonita*, chap. 2 (*MGH. SS. rer. Merov.*, VI, 120): "... grammaticorum inbutus iniciis necnon Theodosii edoctus decretis, ceterosque coetaneos excellens, a sophistis probus atque prelatus est." As the editor, B. Krusch, remarks in a note to this passage, "sophistae sunt oratores, qui una cum grammaticis eloquentiae doctrinam profitentur." Cf. also Du Cange.

[57] Pirenne, *Revue bénédictine*, XLVI, 169.

[58] *La vie de Saint Didier*, ed. Poupardin, p. 2: "Desiderius vero summa parentum cura enutritus, litterarum studiis ad plenum eruditus est, quarum diligentia hauctus est. Ubi post insignia litterarum studia Gallicanamque eloquentiam quae vel florentissima sunt vel eximia, contubernii regalis adulcisce indidit dignitatibus, ac deinde legum romanarum indagationi studium dedit, ut ubertatem eloquii gallici nitoremque sermonis gravitas romana temperaret."

[59] *Revue bénédictine*, XLVI, 173.

[60] *Ibid.*, and n. 3.

[61] *Geschichte des Unterrichtswesens in Deutschland von den ältesten Zeiten bis zur Mitte des dreizehnten Jahrhunderts* (Stuttgart, 1885), 2.

[62] *Op. cit.*, 2, n. 3.

[63] Molinier, *op. cit.*, I, 151, no. 511.

[64] Especially not in view of the wording of the passage in question (Mabillon, *AA. SS. ord. S. Bened.*, II, 71): "audivit in locis vicinorum propinquis qualiter nobilium parvulorum mos est, doctoribus instruere scholas."

[65] Mabillon, *AA. SS. ord. S. Bened.*, II, 258: "liberalium studiis litterarum (sicut olim moris erat nobilibus) traditur imbuendus."

[66] Tenth or even eleventh century; see Molinier, *op. cit.*, I, 135, no. 417.

[67] *Ibid.*, I, 141, no. 447.

[68] Mabillon, *AA. SS. ord. S. Bened.*, II, 999: "Igitur Chlodulfus venerabilis indolis puer, ut par erat, et ut nobilium filiis fieri solet, scholis traditur, et liberalibus litteris docendus exhibetur."

[69] *La vie de Saint Didier*, 9: "Haec autem crebras ad eum epistolas dirigens pio studio filium choortabatur ut coepta perficeret,..." That the letters are genuine is shown by the statement following: "Quarum exemplar apud nos habito testamento memoriae gratia pagellae hujus inserendum credidi, ut ex his advertatur qualis fuerit mater, qualemque propositum tenere filium vellet."

[70] *Ibid.*, 11: "MANU PROPRIA: Incolumes vos Dominus custodire et haeredes regni sui preparare dignetur."

[71] The *lector* of Sidonius Apollinaris is mentioned by him in one of his letters (*Epist.*, IV, xii: Dalton, *Letters of Sidonius*, II, 24). We hear also of the servant of the senatorial Felix, who, "occupied with his master in the study of letters, acquired an excellent education," and "was fully versed in the works of Vergil, the books of the Theodosian code, and in arithmetical studies."— Gregory of Tours, *History of the Franks*, Bk. IV, 32: Dalton's trans., II, 154–155; cf. also Dalton's note, *ibid.*, II, 531.

[72] *De virtutibus S. Martini*, IV, 10 (*MGH. SS. rer. Merov.*, I, 652): "Bodilo unus de notariis nostris cum stomachi lassitudine animo turbatus erat, ita ut nec scribere iuxta consuetudinem nec excipere, et quae ei dictabantur vix poterat recensere." *History of the Franks*, Bk. X, 19: Dalton, II, 456: "But a confidential servant of his [puer eius familiaris] was called who had preserved shorthand copies of the letters in the volumes of the bishop's documents, etc."

[73] *Revue bénédictine*, XLVI, 170.

[74] A law of Dagobert (630) required that every count should have a *librum legis* in his court. This does not necessarily imply, however, that every count in Merovingian times was expected to be able to read. Probably more often the court clerk read the actual law. See Baluze, *Capitularia regum francorum*, I, 105, xv, 2: "Comes vero secum habeat Judicem, qui ibi constitutus est judicare, et librum legis, ut semper rectum judicium judicet de omni causa quae componenda est."

[75] See also H. Pirenne, "L'instruction des marchands au moyen âge," *Annales d'histoire économique et sociale*, I (1929), 13 ff., and "Le commerce du papyrus...," *Acad. des inscr. et belles-lettres, Comptes rendus*, 1928, 178 ff.

[76] J. P. Migne, *PL* (= *Patrologiae cursus completus. Patres Latini;* Paris, 1850–1853), 39, 2325: "Novimus enim aliquos negotiatores qui cum litteras non noverint, requirunt sibi mercenarios litteratos; et cum ipsi litteras nesciant, aliis scribentibus rationes suas ingentia lucra conquirunt."

[77] On the authority of this evidence, A. Marignan, *Etudes sur la civilisation française:* I, *La société mérovingienne* (Paris, 1899), 145, n. 1, believes that "the merchants in general had but little education" at this time, although Caesar of Arles's statement, "Les marchands étaient en général assez incultes,"

hardly seems to warrant such a sweeping conclusion. C. E. Arnold, *Caesarius von Arelate und die Gallische Kirche seiner Zeit* (Leipzig, 1894), 20, interprets the passage to mean that the merchants were unable to read as well as unable to write Latin. It is true that in other parts of the same sermon Caesar of Arles uses "nesciens litteras" or a similar phrase to mean inability to read Latin, but in the passage concerning merchants quoted above it is clear that the clerks were hired specifically to perform the work of writing.

The first three paragraphs of this sermon are full of tantalizing remarks on the general subject of illiteracy (Migne, *PL*, 39, 2325): "Nec dicat aliquis vestrum: Non novi litteras; ideo mihi non imputabitur quidquid minus de Dei praeceptis implevero. Inanis est et inutilis excusatio ista, fratres charissimi. Primum est, quod lectionem divinam, etiamsi aliquis nesciens litteras non potest legere, potest tamen legentem libenter audire." And again, after the reference to the unlettered merchants, the bishop suggests that, following the example of these businessmen, those of his hearers who are unable to read ought to be willing to pay to have the Scriptures read to them: "Et si illi qui litteras nesciunt, conducunt sibi mercenarios litteratos, ut acquirant terrenam pecuniam; tu, quicumque es qui litteras non nosti quare etiam non cum pretio et mercede rogas, qui tibi debeat Scripturas divinas relegere, ut ex illis possis praemia aeterna conquirere?" Since even peasants in the country round about knew by heart profane Latin verses, they should also be able, in Caesar's opinion, to memorize and repeat psalms, the Creed, and the Lord's Prayer: "Sed dicit aliquis: Ego homo rusticus sum, et terrenis operibus jugiter occupatus sum, lectionem divinam nec legere possum nec audire. Quam multi rustici et quam multae mulieres rusticanae cantica diabolica, amatoria et turpia memoriter et ore decantant? . . . Quanto celerius et melius quicumque rusticus vel quaecumque mulier rusticana, quanto utilius poterat et Symbolum discere, et orationem Dominicam et aliquas antiphonas et psalmos quinquagesimum vel nonagesimum et parare et tenere et frequentius dicere, unde animam suam et Deo conjugere, et a diabolo liberare possent?"

[78] Gregory of Tours, *Vitae Patrum (MGH. SS. rer. Merov.*, I, 702): "Igitur beatissimus Patroclus, Biturigi territorii incola, Aetherio patre progenitus, cum decim esset annorum [*ca.* 506], pastor ovium destinatur, fratre Antonio traditum ad studia litterarum. Erant enim non quidem nobilitate sublimes, ingenui tamen; cumque quodam meridie hic ab scolis, iste a grege commisso ad capiendum cibum paterno in hospitio convenissent, dixit Antonius fratri suo: 'Discede longius, o rustice. Tuum est enim opus oves pascere, meum vero litteris exerceri; qua de re nobiliorem me ipsius officii cura facit, cum te huius custodiae servitus vilem reddit.' Quod ille audiens et hanc increpationem quasi a Deo sibi transmissam putans, reliquit oves in campi planitiae et scolas puerorum nisu animi agile atque cursu velocissimo expetivit, traditisque elementis ac deinceps quae studio puerili necessaria erant, ita celeriter, memoria opitulante, inbutus est, ut fratrem vel in scientia praecederet vel alacritate sensus, adnuente divini Numinis auxilio, anteiret."

[79] *Ibid.*, 703: "venit ad vicum Nereensim [Néris], ibique aedificato oratorio ac sancti Martini reliquiis consecrato, pueros erudire coepit in studiis litterarum."

[80] *Ibid.*, 741: "Leobardus Arverni territorii indigena fuit, genere quidem non senatorio, ingenuo tamen. . . . Qui tempore debito cum reliquis pueris ad scolam missus, quaepiam de psalmis memoriae conmendavit, et nesciens se clericum esse futurum, iam ad dominicum parabatur innocens ministerium." Cf. Pirenne, *Revue bénédictine*, XLVI, 173.

[81] *Revue bénédictine*, XLVI, 174 ff.

[82] The existence, even in the Merovingian age, of ecclesiastical schools for the purpose of training clerics is affirmed by Pirenne (*Revue bénédictine*, XLVI, 176, n. 1).

[83] Gregory of Tours, *History of the Franks*, Bk. VI, 36: Dalton's trans., II, 267.

[84] Gregory of Tours, *Liber in gloria martyrum*, chap. 77 (*MGH. SS. rer. Merov.*, I, 540): "in archidiaconatu suo studium docendi parvulos habens."

[85] Gregory of Tours, *Vitae patrum* (*MGH. SS. rer. Merov.*, I, 713).

[86] See the letter of Gregory the Great to Serenus, bishop of Marseilles, in which the pope reproves the bishop for his iconoclastic activities and then goes on to explain to him why it is fitting and proper to have pictures in the churches (*Epist.*, IX, 208: *MGH. Epist.*, II, 195, 21): "Idcirco enim pictura in ecclesiis adhibetur, ut hi qui litteras nesciunt saltem in parietibus videndo legant, quae legere in codicibus non valent." In another letter to Serenus (*Epist.*, XI, 10: *ibid.*, II, 270, 14), Gregory makes a similar pronouncement: "Nam quod legentibus scriptura, hoc idiotis praestat pictura cernentibus, quia in ipsa ignorantes vident, quod sequi debeant, in ipsa legunt qui litteras nesciunt; unde praecipue gentibus prolectione pictura est." Gregory's use of *idiotae* and *gentes,* here, makes it appear that he had in mind the lower classes and especially the foreign (i.e., the German) element in the population.

[87] J. Mansi, *Concilia* (= *Sacrorum conciliorum nova et amplissima collectio;* Venice, 1765–1773), VIII, 837, canon xvi.

[88] Migne, *PL*, 39, 2325: "Qui vero litteras novit, numquid potest fieri quod non inveniat libros, quibus possit Scripturam divinam legere? Tollamus a nobis fabulas vanas, mordaces jocos; sermones otiosos ac luxuriosos, quantum possumus, respuamus: et videamus si nobis non remaneat tempus, in quo lectioni divinae vacare possimus."

[89] J. E. Sandys, *A History of Classical Scholarship* (Cambridge, 1903–1908), I, 437.

[90] See the letter of King Athalaric to Cyprian, the Patrician (in Cassiodorus' *Variae*, VII, xxi: *MGH. AA.*, XII, 253, 4), in which he says of Cyprian's sons, "Pueri stirpis Romanae nostra lingua loquuntur." F. Wrede, *Ueber die Sprache der Ostgothen in Italien* (Strassburg, 1891), 14, regards this as exceptional; but A. Th. Heerklotz, *Die Variae des Cassiodorus Senator als kulturgeschichtliche Quelle* (Heidelberg diss., 1926), p. 83, n. 20, says that a knowledge of Gothic among Romans was not so rare as Wrede would have us believe, and cites H. v. Schubert, *Gesch. der christlichen Kirche im Frühmittelalter* (Tübingen, 1921), 24, in support of his position; the reference given by Schubert, however, to Migne, *PL*, 33, 1161, which is supposed to indicate a passage of Saint Augustine stating that Romans pronounced the *Domine miserere* along with the Vandals in the barbarian tongue, is evidently incorrect. I suspect that

the passage under consideration may be open to another interpretation, namely, that the Vandals prayed in German, while the Romans prayed at the same time in Latin. It is difficult to believe that many of the Romans ever learned any of the Germanic tongues.

[91] Cf. Heerklotz, *op. cit.*, 36.

[92] Cf. Wrede, *op. cit.*, 14.

[93] *Theodoric the Great* (New York and London, 1909), 233, note.

[94] Cf. B. H. Skahill, *The Syntax of the Variae of Cassiodorus* (Washington, D. C., 1934), p. xxi.

[95] Briefly, it may be stated that according to Bethmann, Pertz, and Waitz (*Nachrichten der Göttinger Gesellschaft der Wissε ιschaften*, 1865, 112), and Holder-Egger (*MGH. SS. rer. Langob.*, 273), the *Anonymus Valesii* or *Valesianus* is a fragment of the lost chronicle of Maximian, bishop of Ravenna (546–556). According to Mommsen, it was written after the death of Theodoric, but before the end of the Ostrogothic dominion. See Potthast, *Bibliotheca historica* (2d ed.; Berlin, 1896), I, 110, and Wattenbach, *DGQ* (= *Deutschlands Geschichtsquellen im Mittelalter bis zur Mitte des dreizehnten Jahrhundert*) (6th ed.; Berlin, 1893–1894), I, 56, n. 3.

[96] *MGH. AA.*, IX, 326, 16: "Igitur rex Theodericus inlitteratus erat et sic obruto [Hodgkin, *Italy and Her Invaders* (2d ed.; Oxford, 1896), III, 268, n. 1, suggests the reading of "obtuso"] sensu, ut in decem annos regni sui quattuor litteras subscriptionis edicti sui discere nullatenus potuisset. de qua re laminam auream iussit interrasilem fieri quattuor litteras 'legi' habentem; unde si subscribere voluisset, posita lamina super chartam per eam pennam ducebat, ut subscriptio eius tantum videretur." Hodgkin (cf. *Italy and Her Invaders*, II [1880], 487) seems to have used the original edition of H. Valesius, published as an Appendix to *Ammiani Marcellini Opera* (Paris, 1636). Mommsen's text in the *Monumenta*, as given above, makes one wonder why Hodgkin so carefully explained that the four letters which Theodoric should have signed were *Thiud* if in Gothic, and *Theo* if in Latin. Hodgkin's translation of the passage describes the stencil as "having the four letters of *the royal name* pierced through it"; but the text says simply that the stencil spelled out the word *legi: I have read.*

[97] The passage would then also supply a definite example in which the word *inlitteratus* refers only to inability *to write.*

[98] Gibbon, *The Decline and Fall of the Roman Empire* (ed. by Bury), IV, 206.

[99] *Italy and Her Invaders*, III (1885), 297, n. 1.

[100] D. Coste, in *Geschichtschreiber der deutschen Vorzeit, Sechstes Jahrhundert* (Leipzig, 1885), III, 381, translates: "In den *ersten* 10 Jahren seiner Regierung." But the text says only "in decem annos regni sui."

[101] *MGH. AA.*, IX, 322, 20: "Dum inlitteratus esset, tantae sapientiae fuit, ut aliqua quae locutus est, in vulgo usque nunc pro sententia habeantur."

[102] *MGH. AA.*, XII, 420, 12, and 422, 12.

[103] *Italy and Her Invaders*, III (1896), 451, n. 2.

[104] *MGH. AA.*, XII, 290, 19: "nam cum esset publica cura vacuatus, sententias prudentium a tuis fabulis exigebat, ut factis propriis se aequaret antiquis. stellarum cursus, maris sinus, fontium miracula rimator acutissimus

inquirebat, ut rerum naturis diligentius perscrutatis quidam purpuratus videretur esse philosophus." Cf. Heerklotz, *op. cit.*, 37, and 82, n. 3.

[105] *Variae*, XI, i (*MGH. AA.*, XII, 328, 18): "Atticae facundiae claritate diserta est: Romani eloquii pompa resplendet: nativi sermonis ubertate gloriatur."

[106] *MGH. AA.*, XII, 328, 27: "iungitur his rebus quasi diadema eximium inpretiabilis notitia litterarum, per quam, dum veterum prudentia discitur, regalis dignitas semper augetur."

[107] *Variae*, X, iii (*MGH. AA.*, XII, 299, 5): "Accessit his bonis desiderabilis eruditio litterarum, quae naturam laudabilem eximie reddit ornatam. . . . etiam ecclesiasticis est litteris eruditus."

[108] F. Wrede, *op. cit.*, 15, believes that the two extant business documents written in Gothic were drawn up by Arian priests who refused to adopt the more advanced literary language of the Romans on patriotic-religious grounds. The fact, however, that there are only two such documents extant proves that Gothic made little headway; all other Ostrogothic documents are written in Latin.

[109] *History of the Wars*, V, 2 (*The Gothic War*, I, 2), edition and translation of H. B. Dewing ("The Loeb Classical Library"; London and New York, 1914–1928), III, 16–19.

[110] Redlich, *op. cit.*, 6.

[111] *Ibid.*, 25.

[112] Cf. F. H. Dudden, *Gregory the Great* (London, 1905), I, 71, 81, and 410, n. 4.

[113] *Op. cit.*, 2. Specht cites as his authority W. Giesebrecht, *De litterarum studiis apud Italos primis medii aevi saeculis* (Berlin, 1845).

[114] Cf. Gregorovius, *History of the City of Rome in the Middle Ages*, trans. from the 4th German ed. by Annie Hamilton (London, 1894–1902), II, 409 ff.

[115] *Italy and Her Invaders*, VI (1895), 40.

[116] "Die Evangelienhandschrift zu Cividale," *Neues Archiv*, II (1877), 115–116. Bethmann's conclusions are based on paleographical considerations; his arguments are quite convincing. Hodgkin evidently misunderstood the German scholar. We shall have occasion later to come back to this Gospel MS of Cividale.

[117] *Epist.*, IV, 4, 33; IX, 67; XIV, 12 (ed. P. Ewald and M. L. Hartmann, in *MGH. Epist.*, I, 236, 268; II, 87, 431).

[118] See, e. g., the passage in *Epist.*, IV, 4 (*ibid.*, I, 236, 22): "Decet ergo gloriam vestram ad reverentissimum fratrem et coepiscopum meum Constantinum [Mediolanensem], cuius et fides et vita olim mihi bene est adprobata, sub omni celeritate transmittere, eique *directis epistolis* indicare, ordinationem eius quam benigne suscepistis, et quia ab eius ecclesiae communione in nullo separamini," and a similar passage in IV, 33 (*ibid.*, I, 269, 12), as well as XIV, 12 (*ibid.*, II, 431, 1): "Scripta quae ad nos dudum a Genuensibus partibus transmisistis gaudii vestri nos fecere participem . . . [and a few lines further on] . . . Illud autem, quod excellentia vestra scripsit, ut dilectissimo nostro Secundo," etc. These words can hardly be taken to mean that Theude-

linda wrote the letters referred to with her own hand; she probably employed a scribe to whom she dictated her letters.

[119] *Epist.*, XIV, 12 (*ibid.*, II, 431, 26): "Excellentissimo autem filio nostro Adulouualdo regi transmittere filacta curavimus, id est crucem cum ligno sanctae crucis Domini et lectionem sancti evangelii theca Persica inclausum."

[120] See the letter of Paul to Adalperga (written between 765 and 774) published by W. Hartel in his article, "Eutropius und Paulus Diaconus," *Akademie der Wissenschaften, Wien*, Sitzungsberichte, phil.-hist. Klasse, LXXI (1872), 294: "Cum ad imitationem excellentissimi comparis, qui nostra aetate solus principum sapientiae palmam tenet, ipsa quoque subtili ingenio sagacissimo studio prudentum arcana rimeris, ita ut philosophorum aurata eloquia poetarumque gemmea tibi dicta in promptu sint. . . ."

[121] *Ibid.*, 294–295. Cf. also W. D. Foulke's trans. of the *History of the Langobards by Paul the Deacon* (Philadelphia, 1907), Intro., p. xvii; and Gregorovius, *op. cit.*, II, 410.

[122] See the words cited in the note above, "qui nostra aetate solus principum sapientiae palmam tenet," and Paul's epitaph on Arichis (*MGH. Poet. Lat.*, I, 67, 10; also *SS.*, III, 482, 18):

> "Facundus, sapiens, luxque decorque fuit.
> Quod logos et phisis, moderansque quod ethica pangit,
> Omnia condiderat mentis in arce suae,
> Strenuus eloquii, divini cultor et iudex."

[123] Romuald died at the age of 25. The epitaph on his tombstone (in the *Chronicon Salernitanum, MGH. SS.*, III, 483) describes him as "grammati pollens, mundana lege togatus, divina instructus nec minus ille fuit." Cf. A. Ebert, *Allgemeine Geschichte der Literatur des Mittelalters im Abendlande* (Leipzig, 1874–1887), II, 52.

Chapter II

THE CAROLINGIAN RENAISSANCE

THE PURPOSE in this chapter is not to enter upon a broad discussion of the Carolingian Renaissance, but rather to adhere closely to our problems: to what degree there was knowledge of Latin among the laity, and to what extent secular learning was diffused. There is, on the whole, general agreement on these matters among scholars, but several important considerations are frequently overlooked.

No one will deny that under the magnetic influence of Charlemagne and the galaxy of scholars and teachers whom he gathered round him, there was a marked advance in the knowledge of Latin among the laymen of the royal court. Einhard's words (*Vita Karoli,* chap. 19) on the education of Charlemagne's sons and daughters are too well known to require more than allusion. Furthermore, it would be possible to name a number of personages in the emperor's immediate entourage of whom we could say with certainty that they must have been able to read and understand Latin. It would be a mistake, however, to take for granted a widespread knowledge of Latin among the lesser Frankish nobility who lived away from the influence of the court circle. This influence probably did not penetrate very widely or deeply; certainly the lower classes were for the most part unaffected by the cultural developments which we call the Carolingian Renaissance. The masses still understood and spoke only the Vulgar Latin or "Roman," or else the Teutonic vernacular, German.[1] To write either language, however, was for them impossible.

The Carolingian Renaissance is usually represented as a period when Europe, temporarily at least, escaped from an abyss of cultural darkness and oblivion. The historical accuracy of this picture, however, is open to question, for the cultural achievements of the Carolingian age have been magnified at the expense of both the preceding and the succeeding periods. An illuminating instance of it occurs in a passage of the *Vita S. Urbani* (fifth-century bishop of Langres), written by a monk of Saint-Bénigne at Dijon in the eleventh century.[2] The author explains why the life of Saint

---

Urban remained so long unwritten : it was because until the time of Charlemagne there was hardly anyone to be found in Gaul who was adequately educated for such a task!³ Bollandus pertinently remarks in a note to this passage that, "although Charlemagne did much to encourage letters, this statement is greatly exaggerated, and false. There were learned men in Gaul before his time."⁴

I have referred above⁵ to M. Pirenne's arguments concerning the relative merits of the Merovingian and Carolingian ages with respect to instruction and learning among the laity. M. Pirenne believes that the so-called Carolingian Renaissance should properly be considered a cultural advance of the clergy only.

As remarkable as this Renaissance was [he says], as superior as the clergy of the ninth century appears in comparison with that of the seventh or eighth, it must nevertheless be clearly recognized that the progress of education in the Church had for its counterpart the definite disappearance of that secular education which the survival of the Roman schools had at any rate enabled to subsist into Merovingian times. Undoubtedly the Latin written after the time of Charlemagne was better than that written before, but the number of those writing was much smaller, since no one wrote except the clergy.⁶

M. Pirenne believes, moreover, that from the ninth to the twelfth century, not only education in the broad sense, but even the simple, practices of reading and writing were rarely to be found except among the clergy.⁷ Although we may accept this statement as being generally true, nevertheless we hope to show that there are perhaps more exceptions to the rule than M. Pirenne has indicated. Ordinarily, all we can prove by the exceptions is that these persons were able to understand and to *read* Latin; it is extremely difficult, indeed, to find satisfactory evidence that there were laymen who could also *write* Latin.

As further proof of the gradual restriction of instruction to the ranks of the clergy, M. Pirenne points out the significant change in the style of writing from the Merovingian to the Carolingian age. The change from the cursive to the minuscule is indicative of a changed order of society : from one in which writing is indispensable to the collective life, to one in which the art of writing is confined to a select, professional group—this time, as it happens, the clergy.⁸ In the dissimilar characteristics of these two styles of handwriting "is expressed the contrast between a time in which the practice of writing is still widely spread among the laity and a time in which it has become a monopoly in the hands of the clergy."[9]

The early Carolingian mayors of the palace and kings, since they could not write, had to be satisfied to make a dot or a line in the cross or monogram prepared by the chancellery.[10] Both Pepin the Short and Carloman signed their documents with a cross.[11] Charlemagne substituted for the cross a monogram composed of the letters of his name.[12] The monogram was drawn by a clerk of the chancellery, and probably all that was added by the hand of the sovereign was the bar of the letter *A*.[13] If Charlemagne learned to write at all, it was not until late in life. Some scholars hold that the meaning of Einhard's well-known statement (*Vita Karoli,* chap. 25), "Temptabat et scribere, etc.," is "not that Charlemagne could not write at all, but that he could not write the book-hand used in the MSS."[14] But is it not possible that Einhard's words are simply a kindly and discreet way of indicating that Charlemagne failed in the attempt to learn to write? The evidence from the documents certainly suggests that Charlemagne was unable to sign his name. The documents of Louis the Pious, as well as those of Lothar I, would seem to point to a similar conclusion for the later Carolingian kings.[15] It would be unwise, however, to assume with certainty that none of the Carolingian princes could write. The evidence of the documents is not wholly conclusive;[16] and it is difficult to believe that the young men and women who attended the school at the royal court did not learn the rudiments of writing. Generally speaking, however, it is doubtless true that the ability to write was much less widespread among the laity in Carolingian times than in the preceding age. But Einhard also makes mention (chap. 25) of Charlemagne's ability to speak Latin as well as he could speak his native tongue, and, though less fluently, Greek.

There can be no doubt that Louis the Pious was able at least to read and speak Latin. His learning receives glowing praise from the pen of Freyculf, who asks "what emperor was nobler, or wiser in either divine or secular lore than Louis, the unconquered Caesar?"[17] More specific information is given by Louis' biographer, Theganus, who says that the pious emperor knew both Latin and Greek, and that although he could understand Greek better than he could speak it, he spoke Latin as easily as his native tongue.[18]

It is probable that Louis was the author of a short Latin poem addressed to Waldo, abbot of Saint-Denis, written when he was king of Aquitaine.[19] In his youth he had learned to know the pagan classics, but later in life he turned away from them and devoted himself to the Scriptures.[20] The same change of interest from profane to sacred studies is seen in the life of Benedict of Aniane, the close friend and adviser of Louis. The monk is worthy of our attention here because he had acquired his learning in profane studies *before* becoming a monk, and while still a layman.[21]

It is highly probable that the empress Judith also had a fair knowledge of Latin. The evidence, though indirect, is sufficient to make this assumption reasonable. The *Annales Mettenses* say that she was "well instructed in all the flowers of wisdom."[22] Her praises are sung by Walafrid Strabo,[23] and by Ermoldus Nigellus.[24] Rhabanus Maurus dedicated to her his commentaries on the books of Judith and Esther;[25] and Freyculf dedicated to her the second part of his *Chronicle* that she might use it for the instruction of her son, Charles the Bald.[26] In the Bibliothèque d'Avranches there is still preserved (MS no. 2428) a *Universal History* extending from the creation to the end of the fourth century, written probably by Florus, the antagonist of John the Scot, which is dedicated to the empress Judith.[27]

The next generation of Carolingian princes also had some knowledge of Latin. As Specht has said, "Although lay culture declined rapidly after the time of Louis the Pious, nevertheless the royal princes—especially those designated as heirs apparent—were still instructed in the disciplines of the school, at least enough to enable them to read and to understand Latin."[28] With the exception of Pepin, who seems to have been something of a rake, more interested in strong drink than in study,[29] all the sons of Louis the Pious displayed marked cultural interests. "We know that both Lothar and Ludwig knew Latin and enjoyed reading theological tracts, especially commentaries on the Bible";[30] and Charles the Bald "had perhaps received even a better education than that of his brothers."[31]

There is satisfactory evidence concerning Lothar I's ability to understand Latin. Sound pedagogical principles were followed by his teacher, the Irishman Clemens, whose aim was to give the young prince a solid foundation and thus enable him later to pursue his studies independently.[32] Apparently the Irishman succeeded in his purpose. Rhabanus Maurus wrote for Lothar later in life a number of theological treatises the dedications of which offer sufficient testimony of the emperor's knowledge of Latin.[33] We possess also an illuminating letter of Lupus of Ferrières addressed to Lothar.[34] Lothar has been justly praised for his famous capitulary concerning schools and education in Italy.[35] This capitulary, however, testifies only to Lothar's concern for ecclesiastical education. Giesebrecht[36] has pointed out that there is not a word in it which refers to liberal studies; its sole purpose was to raise the intellectual status of the clergy.

Ludwig the German could certainly understand and very probably also read Latin. Here again the dedicatory letters of several works of Rhabanus Maurus afford valuable evidence. Rhabanus sent to Ludwig, his "most wise king, well instructed in all things," the *Commentaria in cantica,* that the king might read it.[37] He sent to him also his encyclopedic work, *De universo,* that Ludwig "might have it read in his presence," adding that, "if anything in it were found to be in need of emendation, he [the king] and his learned readers should take care to correct it, according to the dictates of reason."[38] Similar statements are found also in the letter in which Rhabanus dedicated to Ludwig his commentary on Daniel.[39] Walafrid Strabo wrote to Ludwig the German in Latin verse;[40] and Ermenrich, a learned monk of Ellwangen, expressed an intention of dedicating to Ludwig a book on the seven liberal arts.[41] As the Monk of Saint-Gall observed, Ludwig's "wisdom was quite out of the common, and he added to it by constantly applying his singularly acute intellect to the study of the Scriptures."[42] In 865 Ludwig asked Hincmar of Rheims for an explanation of a difficult passage in the Scriptures, and the prelate sent him a lengthy answer in reply.[43] As Wattenbach has pointed out,[44] Ludwig's lively interest in the learned theological discussions of the day could hardly have been possible without a sound education. Ludwig was also apparently interested in the vernacular literature. The German *Paraphrase of the Gospels* (ca. 865) by the monk Otfrid of Weissenburg was dedicated to him.[45] Moreover, a MS (Cod. S. Galli, 98) of a sermon by Saint Augustine against the Jews, which was given to Ludwig by Adalram, archbishop of Salzburg, contains the German alliterative poem on the end of the world known as the *Muspilli*

(*The Last Conflagration*). It has been conjectured[46] that this poem was inserted in the MS by the hand of Ludwig himself; a conjecture which Wackernagel believes is supported by the fact that the poem is written in the Bavarian tongue, and further, by the fact that it contains numerous violations of the proper forms.[47] That the poem was added to the MS by the hand of a layman seems certain, but whether the layman was Ludwig remains, after all, no more than conjecture.[48]

We have already noted that the empress Judith concerned herself with the education of her son, Charles the Bald. Charles certainly learned to read and to write Latin. Freyculf tells us that he was a precocious lad who gave promise of being another Charlemagne;[49] and, according to Heiric of Auxerre, he not only equaled but surpassed his illustrious grandfather in his zeal for learning.[50] Like his brothers, Lothar and Ludwig, Charles was interested in theology, but he was a learned "philosopher"[51] as well as a "theologian."[52] His interest in learning is, moreover, attested by the possession of a library. In the Kiersy capitulary of 877, he provided that at his death his books should be divided among Saint-Denis, Sainte-Marie-de-Compiègne, and his son, Louis the Stammerer.[53] In spite of his weaknesses as a ruler, Charles deserves to be remembered as a patron of scholars and of learning.[54]

Charles seems to have had a special fondness for history,[55] and for military affairs.[56] Although we cannot accept without reservation the praises sung in honor of Charles's learning, nevertheless the evidence seems to indicate that he had a much wider knowledge of Latin letters than most of his contemporaries. It is probable that he was also able to write. We know of four documents of his,[57] from the years 860–877, which contain the subscription "X legimus X" written in large characters in red ink; quite probably the *legimus* in at least three of these documents was written by Charles, *manu propria*.[58]

Irmintrude, the wife of Charles the Bald, was apparently not without education; John Scotus Erigena portrays her as "often reading books."[59]

Pepin of Aquitaine may have been intemperate and immoderate in character, but he was not wholly illiterate. He had undoubtedly received some instruction in Latin letters in his youth, and in later life could understand Latin and even read it after a fashion.[60] Ermoldus Nigellus, the Carolingian poet, occupied an important place at Pepin's court, first perhaps as tutor and later as chancellor of the king.[61]

It should not be imagined, however, that a knowledge of Latin among the laymen of the second and third generations after Charlemagne was confined exclusively to members of the royal family. There are also some evidences of learning among the lay aristocracy of the period.[62]

The most striking example of a cultured noble in the ninth century is Nithard, the son of Angilbert, lay abbot of Saint-Riquier, and Bertha, Charlemagne's daughter, who wrote the *Historiarum libri quatuor,* our leading source on the history of the civil wars of the ninth century.[63] Contemporary with this work is the *Liber manualis,* a sort of *vade mecum* written by Dhuoda, wife of Bernhard, duke of Septimania, for her son William, who was stationed at the court of Charles the Bald.[64] Dhuoda's book is valuable to us because it reveals the extent of her knowledge of Latin and of Latin literature. It is apparent that the noble lady had a reasonably good command of the language. The book is written in popular Latin and contains even some examples of popular Latin verse.[65] Manitius thinks it probable that someone, perhaps the court chaplain, helped Dhuoda write the treatise, but admits that the style may possibly indicate completely independent authorship. Whether or not Dhuoda could write *manu propria* cannot be determined; it seems that she did not write the *Liber manualis* with her own hand, but dictated it to a scribe.[66] She was evidently very well read, especially in the Christian authors;[67] her acquaintance with the classical Latin writers seems much more limited.[68] The fact that Dhuoda composed such a treatise for her son William would lead us to believe that he, too, could read Latin, even without the presence in the treatise of numerous passages supporting this conclusion. The fond mother hopes that he will read her little work frequently although he already has many other books.[69] She admonishes him, moreover, not to fail to acquire the works of the great Church fathers, and to study them with care.[70]

Another work of edification was composed by Jonas, bishop of Orléans (d. 843). This treatise, entitled *De institutione laicali,* is of importance to us because of the layman at whose request it was written and to whom it was dedicated, Count Matfrid of Orléans.

From the dedicatory letter we can determine not only that Matfrid himself could read and understand Latin, but also that there were others who would read and derive profit from the work—or so at least the author hoped. Jonas' remarks seem to indicate that a knowledge of Latin, at least the ability to understand the language when read, was not exceptionally uncommon among the lay aristocracy of the day.[71]

This conclusion receives interesting confirmation in the will of the Burgundian nobleman, Count Heccard (Ekkard, Ekkehard), which was drawn up about 875.[72] This document shows that Heccard was the owner of a collection of books which must be considered remarkable for that day. Especially worthy of mention are the books of secular character, Gregory of Tours's *History of the Franks,* Paul Warnefrid's *History of the Lombards,* copies of the Salic and Burgundian codes of law and of the code of Papinian, a book on agriculture, one on the military art (Vegetius, perhaps?), two books on prognostics, and a book on medicine. The library also included several theological works, some books on canon law, some hagiographical literature, a *libellum Isidori,*[73] and a German Gospel (perhaps Otfrid's paraphrase)[74] which seems to indicate that German was still understood and read in the western part of the Carolingian empire.[75] We can be sure that Heccard not only owned books but was also able to understand them, because he even went to the trouble of borrowing books.[76] He must have read them himself or had them read to him. The facts, moreover, that his cousin Bernhard also owned a number of books,[77] and that Heccard bequeathed several of his books to laymen,[78] afford additional support to the belief that the ability to understand Latin was not so unusual among the noble laymen of this time as is often believed.

Another contemporary layman of cultural interests was Eberhard, margrave of Friuli.[79] His relations with Rhabanus Maurus, Hincmar of Rheims, and many other learned men are one indication of his propensities in this direction. Sedulius Scottus addressed no less than five poems to him.[80] A letter of Rhabanus to Eberhard proves that the margrave certainly could understand Latin, though its evidence is not conclusive concerning his ability to read the language.[81] His library was even larger than that of his Burgundian contemporary, Heccard. At his death (864) he left his books to the members of his family;[82] from this fact we may perhaps assume that they, too, must have had some knowledge of Latin, especially his wife, Gisela (d. 867), the daughter of Louis the Pious.[83] The literacy of Eberhard's two youngest sons can be taken for granted, since they entered the Church. It is difficult to be sure about the two eldest sons, Unroch, who died in early manhood, and the more famous Berengar, who became king of Italy in 888 and emperor in 916. The gift of a number of books to each of them makes it seem probable that they could at least understand Latin.[84] The same can be said of the three daughters of Eberhard, each of whom received a share of her father's library.

Evidence from charters of the ninth century also sustains the contention of a limited diffusion of the knowledge of Latin among the laity. A Frankish document of 834 is subscribed by eight laymen.[85] It is highly significant, moreover, that there are signs in the ninth century even of the writing and circulation of books in the vernacular. Paschasius Radbertus, the author of the famous treatise *De corpore et sanguine Domini,* which precipitated the eucharistic controversy in the Middle Ages, says in the preface to the first edition, dedicated to Warin, abbot of Corvey, in 831, that he had composed it in a popular style and intended it for the general public.[86] A line in one of Paschasius' early poems is an indication that books in the vernacular (*romana lingua*) were not unknown.[87]

We turn now to the fourth and fifth generations of Carolingian princes following Charlemagne. If we can believe a tale told by the author of the *Chronicon Salernitanum,* Louis II, the son of Lothar I, must have had a very good knowledge of Latin. The scene of the story is Benevento, famous in the days of King Louis for its men of learning, the wisest and best of whom was Hilderic. One day—so the story goes—Louis II called in his notary and ordered him to draw up a letter and dispatch it to a designated place. Now, for reasons unknown, the notary that day completely forgot about the matter. On the morrow, when the king's command again came to his mind, he could not for the life of him remember what it was that he was supposed to write; whereat he was greatly perturbed. In great distress he hastened to Hilderic and told this man of God his tale of woe. Hilderic sought divine aid by prayer in the Church of the Virgin, and the substance of the forgotten letter was revealed to him. On his return to the notary, he said, "Quick about it, sit down, and write." *Quid plura?* Greatly relieved and rejoicing, the notary went back to his king. Louis, when he heard the letter read to him, was astonished. "Confess, now," he said, "and speak truly, for this letter is not of your own making. What man dictated these words?" But when he heard the notary's confession, the king was even more astonished; and calling Adelchis, the prince of Benevento, he said to him, "I should, in truth, like to know who in this city is more learned in the liberal arts than all the rest." Then Adelchis named several, but Hilderic was not among them. And the king said, "Know you not Hilderic?" "Forsooth," Adelchis replied, "I know him, but hold him in great contempt; for he sings not our praises as do the others." Thereupon Louis turned to the court and told those present all that had happened. And from that day forth, Hilderic, the man of God, was held in high esteem by all.[88]

According to this story, Louis II must have been very well educated, since he could distinguish between the ordinary style of the notary and the more correct and elegant language of the scholar, Hilderic. The anecdote of the *Chronicon Salernitanum* cannot, however, be accepted without reservation.[89] It is, moreover, doubtful whether Louis II was able to write. The Gospel MS of Cividale, referred to above, contains among other signatures the names of Louis and his wife, Ingelberga: "✕ lodohicus imp. ingelberga regina." According to Bethmann,[90] the entire entry is written in one hand; it cannot, therefore, be the autograph of both the emperor and the queen. It may be that the entry was written by Ingelberga and that Louis II then added his mark, since it is possible that Ingelberga could write.[91] Whether or not she could write, it is probable that she could at least understand Latin. Irmingard, the daughter of Louis II, and wife of Boso of Provence, seems also to have had some acquaintance with Latin. She had been "instructed in sacred letters" by a certain teacher named Anastasius, and apparently she had learned enough to enable her to read the Scriptures.[92]

Lothar II was praised by Rhabanus Maurus for his zeal in knowledge and learning and his keenness of mind; we may assume, therefore, that he was able to understand Latin, and perhaps to read it."[93] His wife, Teutberga, may also have been able to read Latin,[94] and his daughter, Bertha, the wife of Adalbert of Tuscany, was evidently a woman of some culture, or charm at least. She is pictured as having drawn men to her by the sweet flow of her speech, but perhaps the vernacular rather than Latin is referred to.[95]

According to one authority, there can scarcely be any doubt that the sons of Ludwig the German received some training in Latin letters.[96] Regino of Prüm tells us that Carloman was "well instructed in letters."[97] Charles the Fat "was not entirely without interest in learning, as is shown by his relations with Saint-Gall, from whose library he occasionally borrowed books."[98] The oldest catalogue of the library of Saint-Gall records in a marginal note the loan of a volume of sermons of Gregory the Great to Charles;[99] and the catalogue of the books which the abbot Grimald (d. 872) gave to Saint-Gall makes mention of a lectionary which Grimald's successor, Harmot, presented to the emperor Charles the Fat on the latter's request.[100] Charles was therefore undoubtedly able to understand Latin and perhaps to read it; nevertheless, it seems that he was unable to write.[101] Ricarda, the wife of Charles the Fat, must have received some education since she, too, borrowed books from the library of Saint-Gall.[102]

Louis the Stammerer, the son of Charles the Bald, probably received a better education than any of his cousins. His instructor in Latin letters was Joseph, who had been trained at Saint-Martin-de-Tours and who at one time had been chancellor to Pepin II of Aquitaine.[103] That Louis derived profit from his studies seems to be indicated by the fact that he obtained part of the library of his father.[104]

It would interest us very much to know what provisions, if any, were made by the later Carolingian princes for the education of the laity. The royal court school started by Charlemagne did not suddenly disappear at his death; it still functioned under Louis the Pious even though its glory had departed.[105] Under the princes of the next generation the situation was worse. Dümmler presents a gloomy picture of the cultural conditions in the Germany of that time:

No evidence whatsoever has come down to us from the time of Ludwig the German of the existence of a court school for the instruction of laymen such as Charles the Great had founded; and we must therefore assume that this salutary arrangement, which Louis the Pious already had permitted to fall into decay, was not renewed by Ludwig. The learned readers at the royal court who are mentioned by Rhabanus Maurus, are to be found only in ecclesiastical circles; laymen who have an interest in scholarly studies disappear completely in the time following, and the secular magnates display interest only in feats of arms.[106]

Wattenbach expresses a view which is slightly more optimistic:

As to Dümmler's contention that the court school for laymen was no longer in existence already under Ludwig the German, it must be admitted that we have no express mention of it. Nevertheless, I incline to believe that provision of some sort was made for the instruction of the young men commended to the king's care.[107]

The fact that there were learned men at Ludwig's court means, it is true, that it was not impossible for noble laymen to acquire a knowledge of Latin letters; but there were probably not a great many who availed themselves of the opportunity. As Kirn has remarked, "there can hardly have been very many laymen in Germany at this time who were able to write."[108] The same statement can undoubtedly be applied to France, especially after the time of Charles the Bald. At his court, literature and learning received a fair amount of attention, and even a court school existed,[109] but after the conclusion of his reign darkness seems to descend. As we approach the year 900, the light of secular learning north of the Alps is almost extinguished.

There are two other aspects to the problem of lay education in the ninth century which deserve brief consideration here. First, probably very few laymen felt any need or desire to acquire a knowledge of Latin letters; and second, it became constantly more difficult for laymen to obtain a liberal education, even if they so desired. North of the Alps there were no schools save those of the Church. The Church, moreover, had always been somewhat reluctant to admit laymen to its schools lest they bring worldly ideas with them. As far back as the sixth century, Caesar of Arles in his *Regula ad virgines* warned against the introduction into nunneries of girls who came only to be educated.[110] The abbots who met at Aachen in 817 for the purpose of furthering monastic reform decided among other things that "no school ought to be held in any monastery except for the *oblati*."[111] If we can trust our authority, a similar decree was adopted (at Mainz) in 976, with reference to episcopal or cathedral schools.[112]

It would be unfair and inexact, however, to say that the Church universally and officially adopted a policy against the education of laymen. Much depended on the attitude of the individual churchmen who conducted the schools. Saint Liutberg of Halberstadt, for example, instructed girls in the Psalms and in "hand work" and then permitted them to return home or to go wherever they wished.[113] According to Trithemius, a late and not very reliable authority, Rhabanus Maurus did not bar laymen from attending his school at Fulda, and many men of secular life came to hear him. He was thus the first German, says Trithemius, to hold a public school.[114] The monastery of Saint-Gall also admitted laymen into its school. We are told that Notker Balbulus (d. 912) educated boys who were to inherit their paternal estates, in other words, laymen, as well as those who were to enter the Church;[115] and his successor, Tutilo, taught music to the sons of the nobility in a place designated by the abbot.[116]

Notes to Chapter II

[1] See the seventeenth canon of the Third Council of Tours (813), which reads: "ut easdem homilias quisque aperte transferre studeat [episcopus] in rusticam Romanam linguam, aut Theotiscam, quo facilius cuncti possint intelligere quae dicuntur."—Cited from *Gallia Christiana* (Paris, 1715–1865), XIV, 34; cf. Dalton, tr., *History of the Franks*, Intro., I, 168, n. 1.

[2] Molinier, *Les sources de l'histoire de France*, I, 50, no. 169.

[3] *Vita S. Urbani*, I, 2: *AA. SS.*, January, III, 105 (all references to the *AA. SS.* are given according to the edition published by Victor Palm, edited by J. Carnandet; Paris, 1863 ff.) : "Hujus itaque S. Urbani vita quamvis omnigenis virtutibus plena fuerit, nullo tamen illius temporis hominum studio est tradita litterarum monimento; eo quo usque ad tempora Caroli Magni, propter persecutiones gentium, et intestina etiam bella Regum, vix possent in Galliis inveniri qui in Grammatica essent sufficienter instructi."

[4] *Ibid.*, 106.

[5] Pp. 4 f.

[6] *Annales d'histoire économique et sociale*, I, 18.

[7] *Revue bénédictine*, XLVI, 165.

[8] In support of his contention, Pirenne emphasizes (1) that cursive does not reappear until early in the thirteenth century, when economic, social, and cultural developments had again reached a stage which called for a more general and common ability in the art of writing, and (2) that in medieval Ireland, where education and letters were throughout confined exclusively to the clergy, a cursive form of writing was never adopted.—*Acad. des inscr. et belles-lettres, Comptes rendus*, 1928, 178–179.

[9] Pirenne, *Annales d'hist. écon. et sociale*, I, 18.

[10] Redlich, *Urkundenlehre* . . . , 108. Cf. also the statement of P. Kirn (*Archiv für Urkundenforschung*, X [1928], 132): "Die Karolinger unterschreiben nicht mehr persönlich, *weil sie nicht schreiben können*. Sie vollziehen nur ein vorgezeichnetes Monogram." (The italics are my own.)

[11] See Giry, *Manuel* . . . , 715–717, and the examples there given: "Signum X inlustri viro Pippino majorem domus. Signum X Carolomanno gloriosissimo rege." On Pepin cf. also M. Manitius, *Geschichte der lateinischen Literatur des Mittelalters*, I (1911), 245.

[12] See the illustration in Giry, *op. cit.*, fig. 40, 717.

[13] *Ibid.*, 717.

[14] C. H. Beeson, *A Primer of Medieval Latin* (Chicago, 1925), 158, n. 35.

[15] The subscription in the documents of Louis the Pious is usually "Signum (monogr.) Hludowici (*parfois* domni Hludowici) serenissimi augusti (*ou* imperatoris augusti)." Lothar I also uses a monogram. See Giry, *op. cit.*, 722–723.

[16] Because the validity of a royal document did not depend upon the personal subscription of the king, many of the documents of Charlemagne, Louis the Pious, and Lothar do not even contain the monograms of these kings. Their validity is established by the seal and the subscription of the chancellery. (See

Giry, *op. cit.*, 720, 722, 723.) The validity of a private document, too, gradually came to depend no longer on the personal signature or even the personal mark (cross or monogram) of either its author or witnesses. The reason for this development is, of course, to be found in the increasing inability on the part of laymen to write. Cf. Redlich, *op. cit.*, 95.

[17] From the letter of Freyculf to the empress Judith, in which he dedicates to her the second part of his *Chronicle* or *Universal History: MGH. Epist.*, V, pt. 1, 319, 8, "quis nobilior imperatorum aut sapientior in divinis seculariumve disciplinis Hludowico caesare invicto?"

[18] *Vita Hludowici*, chap. 19 (*MGH. SS.*, II, 594, 34): "Lingua graeca et latina valde eruditus, sed graecam melius intellegere poterat quam loqui; latinam vero sicut naturalem aequaliter loqui poterat."

[19] See E. Dümmler, "Beiträge zur Geschichte des Erzbisthums Salzburg," *Archiv für Kunde österreichischen Geschichtsquellen*, XXII (1860), 282–283, 289; cf. B. Simson, *Ludwig der Fromme*, I, 39 and n. 4.

[20] *Vita Hludowici*, chap. 19: "Sensum vero in omnibus scripturis spiritalem et moralem, nec non et anagogen optime noverat. Poetica carmina gentilia quae in iuventute didicerat, respuit, nec legere, nec audire, nec docere voluit." Cf. also A. Kleinclausz (*L'empire carolingien, ses origines et ses transformations* [Paris, 1902], 325, n. 1), who objects to the interpretation commonly put on this passage (by Fauriel, Ampère, Ebert, Simson, and others), namely, that Louis the Pious destroyed the collection of old barbarian songs which Charlemagne had ordered made. In Kleinclausz' opinion (and he says that Kurth, *Hist. poétique des Merovingiens*, 55 and n. 2, agrees with him), Theganus meant simply that Louis came to dislike the pagan classics. Without attempting to enter more deeply into the controversy, I may say that I have accepted the interpretation of Kleinclausz for the following reasons: (1) the crux of the problem lies in the word *gentilia;* and although *gentilia* may mean pagan in the sense of *old heathen* (Germanic), I think it more probable, i.e., more conformable to the usage of that time (cf. Du Cange, *Glossarium . . .*, under *gentiles*, 1 and 2), that it here means pagan in the sense of *profane* (classical); (2) I do not see how this passage can in any way imply any sort of destruction: the strongest term Theganus uses is *respuit*, and this, it seems to me, merely means that the classical literature was repugnant to him.

[21] See the interesting remarks in the *Vita S. Odonis* (written by his disciple, the monk John), I, 23 (Migne, *PL*, 133, 53): "Fuit isdem vir [Euticius, i.e., Benedict of Aniane, as is clear from the following; cf. Migne's note] temporibus Ludovici magni imperatoris, charus videlicet regi, omnibus quia amabilis. Nam cum esset laicus, et peregrinis studiis eruditus, deserens ea unde superbire solet humana fragilitas, totum se dedit beatorum Patrum regulis et institutionibus; ex quibus nempe auctoritatibus diversas consuetudines sumpsit, unoque volumine colligavit. Deinde non multo post monachus est effectus: et in tanto amore apud regem habitus, ut intra palatium illi construeret monasterium."

[22] *MGH. SS.*, I, 336, 4: "reginam pulchram nimis, nomine Judith, et sapientiae floribus optime instructam. . . ."

[23] *De imagine Tetrici*, vv. 192–208 (*MGH. Poet. Lat.*, II, 376), and *Carm. ad Judith* (*ibid.*, 378–379).

[24] *Carm. in honorem Hludowici*, III, 497–501 (*MGH. SS.*, II, 511).

[25] See the dedicatory letters in Migne, *PL*, 109, 539, and 635.

[26] *MGH. Epist.*, V, pt. 1, 319. Cf. also Specht, *Geschichte des Unterrichtswesens* ... , 285.

[27] *Hist. littéraire de la France*, XII, 78; Ravaisson, *Rapports sur les bibliothèques des départements de l'ouest* (1841), 120 and 361.

[28] *Op. cit.*, 237.

[29] In a genealogical table of the Carolingians (*Tabulae ex codice Steynveltensi: MGH. SS.*, III, 215, 10) Pepin is listed as "Pippinus rex Aquitaniae ebriosus." Cf. E. Dümmler, *Geschichte des ostfränkischen Reiches* (2d ed.; Leipzig, 1887–1888), I, 18.

[30] *Ibid.*, I, 18.

[31] *Ibid.*, III, 55.

[32] See the dedicatory verses of the grammar which Clemens wrote for the young Lothar (*MGH. Poet. Lat.*, II, 670):

> "Pauca tibi, Caesar, de multis, magne Hlothari,
> Iure tuus Clemens saepe legenda dedi,
> Caetera quo valeas per te penetrare sophiae
> Calle velut veterum, scita profunda virum."

Cf. Dümmler, *op. cit.*, I, 396.

[33] See the letter sent with the *Homiliae in evangelia et epistolas* (Migne, *PL*, 110, 135): "ut haberetis quod in praesentia vestra tempore veris et aestatis, si vobis ita placeret, horis competentibus legeretur." Further, the preface to the *Expositio super Jeremiam* (*ibid.*, 111, 795): "... ut habeatis illud legatisque, ... " Similarly, the dedication of the *Commentariorum in Ezechielem libri XX* (*ibid.*, 110, 495): "... ut habeatis illud, et simul cum vestris eruditis doctoribus examinantes, ... " See also on the same page the letter of Lothar to Rhabanus, requesting that a commentary on Ezekiel be sent him, and closing with the following curious sentence, which shows the emperor in the rôle of patron: "Duas tibi epistolas misi, quarum una est legenda tantum, haec vero altera et legenda, et in libro operis tui anteponenda." One would like to know just what was in the other letter.

[34] *Epist.*, 108 (*MGH. Epist.*, VI, 93). This letter offers no direct evidence of the king's knowledge of Latin, but contains an interesting reference to a monk who was employed for a time either in the royal chancellery or else as Lothar's personal secretary: "in officio condendarum epistolarum perseveraret."

[35] *MGH. LL.*, I, 239–240.

[36] *De litterarum studiis apud Italos* ... , 10; cf. also B. Simson, *Jahrbrücher des fränkischen Reichs unter Ludwig dem Frommen* (Leipzig, 1874–1876), I, 237, n. 3.

[37] Migne, *PL*, 112, 1089: "... cogitavi quod haec simul cum caeteris in unum volumen coaptarem, et vobis ad legendum ..."; *ibid.*, 1091: "Tu autem, sapientissime rex, in omnibus bene eruditus."

[38] Migne, *PL*, 111, 9: "feci libenter quod petistis, et ipsum opus vobis ... transmisi: ut, si Serenitati Vestrae placuerit, coram vobis relegi illud facia-

tis; et si aliquid in eo dignum emendatione repertum fuerit, cum vestris saga-
cissimis lectoribus, prout ratio dictat, illud emendare curetis."

[39] *MGH. Epist.*, V, 468, 33: "Quod etiam opusculum tibi, rex nobilissime
Hludowice, . . . postquam consummaveram, ad legendum et ad probandum di-
rexi; . . . si quid autem aliter per te vel eos, quos tecum habes peritissimos
lectores, positum repereris, ignoscas imperitiae meae atque fragilitati, . . . "

[40] *Ad Hludowicum regem in persona cuiusdam presbiteri, MGH. Poet. Lat.*,
II, 410.

[41] *Epistola ad Grimaldum* (chaplain at the court of Ludwig the German),
MGH. Epist., V, 542, 21: "De quibus [sc. artibus] tamen aliquantisper enu-
cleatius domino regi quaedam colligere cogitavi et inter alia ludi nostri dicta
ceu quoddam coraulium dare." Cf. Dümmler, *Ostfr. Reich.*, II, 418. If the work
was ever written, it has not, so far as I know, been preserved.

[42] *Gesta Karoli*, II, 11 (*MGH. SS.*, II, 754, 22): "sapientia singularis, quam
acutissimo fretus ingenio scripturarum assiduitate cumulatiorem reddere non
cessabat." A. J. Grant, *Early Lives of Charlemagne* ("The King's Classics
Series"; Boston, 1907), 128, incorrectly refers this passage to Louis the Pious;
cf. Dümmler, *Ostfr. Reich.*, II, 418.

[43] Published in Migne, *PL*, 125, 957: cf. Dümmler, *Ostfr. Reich.*, II, 418, who
cites still other examples of a similar nature, showing Ludwig's interest in
theological or exegetical problems.

[44] *DGQ* (6th ed.), I, 221–222.

[45] For this and for the following, see Wattenbach, *DGQ* (6th ed.), I, 221 ff.,
and Dümmler, *Ostfr. Reich.*, II, 417 ff.

[46] First by Schmeller in his edition of the *Muspilli* (Munich, 1832), which
has not been available for this study.

[47] W. Wackernagel, *Geschichte der deutschen Litteratur* . . . (2d ed.; Basel,
1879–1894), I, 71.

[48] See K. Müllenhoff and W. Scherer, *Denkmäler deutscher Poesie und Prosa
aus dem VIII–XII Jahrhundert* (3d ed., rev. by E. Steinmeyer; Berlin, 1892),
II, 30, 36, and esp. Steinmeyer's note, p. 40: ". . . ob sie [die erhaltene Nieder-
schrift] von Ludwig dem Deutschen herrührt, lässt sich nicht entscheiden, hat
aber geringe wahrscheinlichkeit."

[49] See the letter of Freyculf to Judith (*MGH. Epist.*, V, 319, 13): "Sin
autem de prole, nonne mundi gloria et hominum delectatio Karolus? qui ele-
gantia corporis ac moribus optimis seu agili prudentiae studio inmaturam
vincendo propriam superat aetatem, ut videatur avus eius non obisse, sed potius,
detersa caligine somni, novum inlustrare orbem, siquidem in nepote inmortale
ipsius ingenium una cum nomine decor et virtus splendeant." In general, cf.
Kleinclausz, *op. cit.*, 385, n. 2.

[50] See the dedication of Heiric's *Vita S. Germani* (*MGH. Poet. Lat.*, III, 429,
5): "illud vel maxime vobis aeternam parat memoriam, quod famosissimi avi
vestri Karoli studium erga inmortales disciplinas non modo ex aequo repraе-
sentatis, verum etiam incomparabili fervore transcenditis."

[51] See the *Libellus de imperatoria potestate*, written about 950 (*MGH. SS.*,
III, 722, 2): "Cum haec ita geruntur, Romani pontifices semper per oratores

litteras mittebant invitatorias ad Carolum Calvum regem Francorum, invitantes eum clam. Et quia *erat in litteris quasi philosophus,* rogabant illum supervenire," etc. Heiric of Auxerre thinks that the words "felicem . . . rempublicam, si vel philosopharentur reges vel philosophi regnarent" are seeing their fulfillment under Charles.—*MGH. Poet. Lat.,* III, 429, 1.

[52] See the *Versus ad Karolum Calvum,* attributed to John Scotus Erigena, published by A. Mai, in *Auctores classici* (Rome, 1828–1836), V, 447:

"Cui [sc. Karolo] lux interior donavit mentis acumen,
Quo divina simul tractans humana gubernet,
Vere subsistens rex atque theologus idem."

Cf. Dümmler, *Ostfr. Reich.,* III, 55, n. 2.

[53] M. Bouquet, *HF* (= *Recueil des historiens des Gaules et de la France;* Paris, 1870–1874), VII, 701 e: "Si nos in Dei Sanctorumque ipsius servitio mors praeoccupaverit, Eleemosynarii nostri, secundum quod illis commendatum habemus, de eleemosyna nostra decertent: et libri nostri, qui in thesauro nostro sunt, ab illis, sicut dispositum habemus, inter S. Dionysium et S. Mariam in Compendio et filium nostrum dispertiantur."

[54] Cf. Wattenbach, *DGQ* (6th ed.), I, 299–300, and Dümmler, *Ostfr. Reich.,* III, 55 and n. 2. See also below, p. 33, concerning Nithard.

[55] Charles's connection with the work of Freyculf has already been mentioned. See further the letter of Lupus of Ferrières to the young king (*Epist.,* 93: *MGH. Epist.,* VI, 83, 15): "Imperatorum gesta brevissime comprehensa vestrae maiestati offerenda curavi, ut facile in eis inspiciatis, quae vobis vel imitanda sint vel cavenda." According to Dümmler (*Ostfr. Reich.,* III, 55, n. 4), this treatise was not a "lost" work written by Lupus himself, as Kleinclausz (*op. cit.,* 387 and n. 1) and Desdevizes du Dézert (in his edition of Lupus' letters, *Epist.,* 74) suppose, but rather an epitome of Sextus Aurelius Victor's *De vita et moribus imperatorum Romanorum.*

[56] Freyculf sent Charles a copy of Vegetius, *Epitoma rei militaris;* see the dedicatory letter in C. Lang's edition (1885) of Vegetius. Cf. also Dümmler, *Ostfr. Reich.,* I, 404, n. 4, and Wattenbach, *DGQ* (6th ed.), I, 219, n.

[57] Three of these are extant; the fourth, now lost, is noted by Mabillon, *De re diplomatica,* 43.

[58] See W. Erben, *Die Kaiser- und Königsurkunden des Mittelalters in Deutschland, Frankreich und Italien* (Erben-Schmitz-Redlich, *Urkundenlehre* . . . , I; Munich and Berlin, 1907), 159 and n. 2. Cf. P. Kirn, *Archiv f. Urkundenforschung,* X (1928), 133 and n. 2.

[59] *Versus ad Karolum Calvum,* in Mai, *op. cit.,* V, 436: "Orans, ac legitans libros, manibusque laborans." Cf. Specht, *Geschichte des Unterrichtswesens,* p. 285.

[60] Jonas, bishop of Orléans (d. 843), dedicated to Pepin the treatise *De institutione regia* (written in 834). The letter to Pepin which Jonas sent along with his treatise concludes with the following tantalizing remarks: "Restant praeterea plura quae vestrae celsitudini charitate dictante scribenda forent, ni veritus fuissem et modum epistolarem excedere, et vestrae dignationi quoquo modo oneri esse: quae quia hic praetermittuntur, in sequentibus ex oraculis

divinis et sanctorum Patrum dictis congesta capitulatim ponuntur. *Quae si legere, aut ab alio vobis adminiculante,* quam profutura sint satis dici non potest" (Migne, *PL,* 106, 284). The words italicized have three possible meanings: either (1) that Pepin could read well enough by himself, but might prefer to have someone read to him; or (2) that he was able to read only with difficulty, and therefore needed someone to help him along and explain things to him; or (3) that it was necessary for someone to translate the Latin into the vernacular for the king. As indicated above, I have preferred the meaning suggested under (2). I find it difficult to accept the third interpretation in view of what we know about the court of Louis the Pious; and as for the first meaning suggested, I believe that Jonas would not have used the word *adminiculare* if he had meant simply that Pepin could read his treatise himself in private but might prefer to have it read aloud in his presence. *Adminiculare* is synonymous with *auxiliari;* cf. Du Cange.

[61] Ebert, *Geschichte der latein. Literatur des Mittelalters . . . ,* II, 170 ff.

[62] Count Rotharius founded the monastery of Charroux in Poitou in the reign of Louis the Pious and provided it with a library (Theodulfus, *Carmina,* 50, v. 10). But whether the books were his own or whether he purchased them for the purpose, cannot be established. If he gave his own library, then we may suppose that he was able to read, like some other nobles of the ninth century.

[63] Nithard wrote his work at the request of Charles the Bald and dedicated it to this prince; cf. Molinier, *Les sources . . . ,* I, 229, no. 750.

[64] *Ibid.,* I, 250, no. 812. Cf. Manitius, *op. cit.,* I, 442, and Jourdain, *Mém. de l'Inst. Nat. de France: Acad. des inscr. et belles-lettres,* XXVIII, pt. 1, 89.

[65] *Ibid.,* 443. On Dhuoda's style see esp. W. Meyer, *Nachrichten der Gesell-schaft der Wissenschaften zu Göttingen,* phil.-hist. Klasse, 1908, 59.

[66] See Dhuoda's words (cited according to the edition of E. Bondurand, *Le Manuel de Dhuoda* [Paris, 1887], chap. 70, 231) : "Finita sunt hujus verba libelli, quae, ut valui, animo libenti dictavi, et utiliter in tuam specie tenus formam transcribere jussi." This passage seems to have the meaning which I have given it in my text; but it can also mean that Dhuoda herself wrote out a first draft, which she then had transcribed in the more legible hand of a clerk.

[67] The material in the book is, in fact, drawn directly from the writings of many of the Church fathers, Saint Augustine, Gregory the Great, Isidore of Seville, Gregory of Tours, and Alcuin; and the work contains also traces of Prudentius, Sedulius, Fortunatus, and Donatus. Cf. Manitius (*op. cit.,* 443–444), and Becker (*Zeitschr. f. röm. Phil.,* XXI [1897], 93 and 99), who believes that Dhuoda relied upon her memory in using her sources, for she wrote the treatise at Uzès, away from home, and it is therefore doubtful whether she had access to her books.

[68] Manitius (*op. cit.,* 443) finds it significant that Dhuoda's book shows not a single trace of Vergilian influence.

[69] *Liber manualis,* Prolog., 51: "Licet sint tibi multa aderescentium librorum volumina, hoc opusculum meum tibi placeat frequenter legere, et cum adjutorio omnipotentis Dei utiliter valeas intelligere."

[70] *Ibid.,* chap. 7, 70: "Admoneo te etiam, o fili mi V. pulchre et amabilis, ut

inter mundanas hujus saeculi curas, plurima volumina librorum tibi acquiriri non pigeas, ubi de Deo creatore tuo[rum] per sacratissimos doctorum magistros aliquid sentire et discere debeas, plura atque majora quam supra scriptum est." Further, chap. 8, 72: "Lege volumina ortodoxorum Patrum, et quid sit Trinitas invenies." Again, chap. 50, 199: "Et, ut tali emulatui adhaerere valeas, fili, secundum admonitionem meam, et tua in Christo adcrescente voluntate, frequenter debes legere, frequenter orare."

[71] *De institutione laicali libri tres, Praefatio,* in Migne, *PL,* 106, 121–124: "Dilecto in Christo Mathfredo Jonas in Domino perpetuam salutem. Tuae nuper strenuitatis litteras suscepi, quibus meam extremitatem communefecisti, ut tibi citissime et quam brevissime scriberemus qualiter te caeterosque qui uxorio vinculo ligantur, vitam Deo placitam ducere oporteret. [Jonas therefore has written this treatise] ut in eo quasi in quodam speculo te assidue contemplari, qualiterque conjugalem vitam honeste ducere debeas, *ejus crebra lectione valeas instrui.* [Further, Jonas begs the count] imo *pro te caeterisque, quibus studii fuerit,* id cum charitate suscipere, et pia devotione amplecti. Et *ne ob sui prolixitatem taedio esset legentibus,* id tribus libellis distinxi: videlicet ut primus et ultimus omnibus generaliter fidelibus, medius autem magna sui ex parte conjugalem vitam ducentibus specialiter conveniret. *Moneo interea tuam experientissimam sagacitatem,* et erga Christi famulatum devotionem humillimam, *ut hoc crebro legas, aut tibi legi facias:* eisque quibus animo est magis aliena carpere, quam fraterno affectu diligere, non facile prodas. Si quid vero in hoc opere secus quam debui congessi, per Dominum mihi humiliter peto ignosci. Si quid autem *in eo legentes, sive audientes,* sibi profuturum inesse cognoverint, non mihi, sed Deo, mecum gratias agere meminerint." (Italics are mine.)

The words, *aut tibi legi facias,* might possibly be construed as a reflection on Matfrid's ability to read Latin independently; but I cannot induce myself to believe that they were so intended by the writer. Jonas is merely suggesting another possibility: he himself seems not to doubt that the count was able to read.

Dümmler (*Ostfr. Reich.,* III, 651) says that the count belonged to that small handful of laymen under Louis the Pious (including Dhuoda, Eberhard of Friuli, and Heccard or Ekkard, founder of the priory at Perrecy) who took an interest in things intellectual. The other passages in Dümmler which treat of Count Matfrid (*ibid.,* I, 25, 42 f., 52–54, 57, 67–70, 91, 97, 99 f., 119) are concerned with Matfrid's political movements and importance. Molinier (*Les sources*..., I, 233, no. 759) and Wattenbach (*DGQ,* I, 265, n. 3) led me to the letter quoted above. B. Simson (*Ludwig der Fromme,* I, 381 ff.) has some interesting remarks on Jonas of Orléans and his literary activities, but gives no further pertinent information on Count Matfrid. I have not been able to consult the older general references given by Dümmler (*Ostfr. Reich.,* III, 650, n. 4) to Bähr, *Karol. Literat.,* 393–394, and [Wiener] *Jahrb. f. väterl. Gesch.,* I, 178; but I doubt that these would yield anything additional. As far as I know, therefore, the passages here cited from Jonas' letter are the only known references to Matfrid's intellectual interests.

[72] The material here offered is drawn for the most part from E. Bishop's article, "A Benedictine Confrater of the Ninth Century," in his collection of essays entitled *Liturgica Historica*, 362–369 (previously published in the *Downside Review*, July, 1892). The will has been published in the old collection of Pérard, *Recueil de pièces curieuses servant à l'histoire de Bourgogne* (Paris, 1664), 25 ff., and more recently in the *Bulletin de la Société de l'histoire de France*, 1855–1856, 189 ff., and also in M. Thévenin's *Textes relatifs aux institutions privées et publiques aux époques mérovingienne et carolingienne* (Paris, 1887), no. 71.

[73] The last-mentioned, perhaps Isidore's *Etymologiae*, or, as Bishop suggests, the *Pseudo-Isidorean Decretals?* Compare the accounts of Bishop (*op. cit.*, 363–365) and P. Lejay ("Catalogues de la bibliothèque de Perrecy, XIe siècle," *Revue des bibliothèques*, VI [1896], 228), who prints this part of the will, and points out (*ibid.*, n. 4) that there are traces of Heccard's library in two eleventh-century catalogues of the library of Perrecy, a priory dependent on the Benedictine abbey of Fleury-sur-Loire, which was founded by Heccard.

[74] Cf., in this connection, Müllenhoff, *Zeitschr. f. deutsches Altertum*, XII (1865), 292.

[75] Cf. Bishop, *op. cit.*, 364, and Müllenhoff, *op. cit.*, 292.

[76] In his will he tells his executors to "return the books belonging to the monastery of St. Benedict at Fleury, which are kept in that little hutch at Sigy, in my closet, . . ."—Bishop, *op. cit.*, 365.

[77] At least two. Heccard's will mentions "istos libros qui fuerunt germani mei Bernardi, i.e., canones paenitentiales, liber Ambrosii de misteriis" (cf. Lejay, *op. cit.*, 228).

[78] Most of the books are left to ecclesiastical institutions or clerical friends, but there are also the following gifts to lay persons: the copy of the Salic code to a namesake, Heccard, son of Heccard; the Burgundian code and the book on military art to a lay friend, Gerbaldus; and the book on medicine to Teutberga, the wife of Lothar II.—Bishop, *op. cit.*, 363–364.

[79] E. Favre, "La famille d'Evrard, marquis de Frioul dans le royaume franc de l'ouest," in *Etudes d'histoire du moyen âge dédiées à Gabriel Monod* (Paris, 1896), 157.

[80] Specht, *op. cit.*, 237 and n. 1. Specht gives a reference to Dümmler, "Fünf Gedichte des Sedulius Scottus an den Markgrafen Eberhard von Friaul," *Jahrbuch f. väterländische Geschichte* (Wien, 1861), I, 178 ff., which I have not been able to consult.

[81] Migne, *PL*, 112, 1554 ff.: "Et quia praedicti fratres [who have recently returned to Rhabanus from a journey to Rome, in the course of which they enjoyed Eberhard's hospitality] nobis retulerunt vos expetere opusculum nostrum in laudem crucis Christi dudum confectum, ex vestro verbo rogantes ut illud vobis transmitterem, voluntarie feci quod rogabant, et praeterito anno per nuntium Gagauzardum ad nos venientem, et id ipsum expetentem, opusculum vobis transmisi, deprecans ut habeatis illud, et coram vobis legere faciatis, . . ." The rest of the letter is a diatribe against Gottschalk, "who has been defiling the air of Friuli with his pernicious doctrine of predestination."

[82] The text of the will mentioning the individual legacies in books is in L. d'Achery, *Spicilegium* (nov. ed.; Paris, 1723), II, 877. I have not deemed it necessary to transcribe here the list of Eberhard's books. Léon Maître, *Les écoles épiscopales et monastiques en Occident avant les universités (768–1180)* (2d ed.; Paris, 1924), 189–190, has reprinted this part of the margrave's will, but not with accuracy; he fails, for example, to include among the books left to Berengar, the *Gesta Francorum* mentioned in d'Achery's edition. The will is also cited, but not quoted, by Th. Gottlieb, *Ueber mittelalterliche Bibliotheken* (Leipzig, 1890), nos. 798, 372. E. Bishop, *Liturgica Historica*, 366–367, has several general remarks upon Eberhard and his library, and cites an article by Dom Wilmart, in the *Revue bénédictine*, XXVIII, 341–377, esp. 365–366. One example of Eberhard's library still survives, the *Regina Psalter* (Vatican MSS Reg. 11) written in late uncial and capital script, with corrections in Merovingian minuscule. It was among the volumes bequeathed to Eberhard's son, Eberhard, from whom it passed into the abbey of Cysoing between Lille and Tournai, a monastery founded by the family.

[83] It is interesting to note that the psalter which she used was equipped with a commentary ("psalterium cum sua expositione . . . , quem Gisla ad opus suum habuit"). I believe that we are justified in accepting this statement as an indication of Gisela's ability to read, especially in view of the fact that she was brought up at the Frankish court.

[84] Particularly worth noting among the books left to Unroch is a "librum rei militaris" which is probably the copy of Vegetius that Bishop Hartgar of Lüttich had presented to Eberhard (see the poem of presentation, in *MGH. Poet. Lat.*, III, 212; cf. Dümmler, *Ostfr. Reich.*, I, 404, n. 4, and Wattenbach, *DGQ* [6th ed.], I, 174). In view of Berengar's historical importance it seems worth while to note here the books which were bequeathed to him: "Berengarius aliud psalterium volumus ut habeat cum auro scriptum, et librum de civitate Dei sancti Augustini, de verbis Domini, et gesta Pontificum Romanorum, et gesta Francorum, et libros Isidori, Fulgentii, Martini Episcoporum, et librum Ephrem, et Synonyma Isidori, et librum glossarum et explanationis et dierum."

[85] Thévenin, *op. cit.*, nos. 71, 88, 100, 100 *bis*.

[86] ". . . ideo sic communius volui stylo temperare subulco."—Migne, *PL*, 120, 1260. The literal meaning is that "even a swineherd may read." Was the original version written in the vernacular?

[87] "Rustica concelebret romana latinaque lingua." Petit Radel, *Recherches sur les bibliothèques anciennes*, 61; Dümmler, *MGH. Poet. Lat.*, III, 45, and his article in *Neues Archiv*, IV (1879), 301.

[88] *Chronicon Salernitanum*, chap. 122: *MGH. SS.*, III, 534: "Ut retro traham stilum, tempore quo Samnitibus Lodoguicus saepedictus praeerat, triginta duobus philosofis illo in tempore Beneventum habuisse perhibetur; ex quibus illorum unus insigne, cui nomen fuit Ildericus, inter illos degebat, et non solum liberalibus disciplinis aprime imbutus, set etiam proba virtute deditus; cuius facta minutatim omittimus pandere, set quamvis exigua omnimodis non praetermittam. Dum idem Lodoguicus quadam die notarium suum vocasset et ei praecepisset, quatenus epistolam comeret eamque quodam loco dirigeret, ille

notarius verba augusti oblitus est. Die vero altera recordatus est re quae ei praeceperat; set nequibat mente redire, qualiter ei intimaverat; unde non exiguum exinde angustiatus est. Postremum ad virum Dei Ildericum properavit, adiciens: 'Mi pater, praecepit mihi augustus heri, quatenus iuxta morem epistolam comerem, ego autem oblitus sum dictis illius, et quid faciam nescio; tantum te enixius exoro, ut mihi auxilium inpendas.' Cui philosophus Christi dixit: 'Et quomodo scire potero quod auribus non ausi, dicente Domino: *Nemo scit hominum quae sunt hominis, nisi spiritus hominis qui in ipso est?*' [I Cor., 2: 11] Ad haec notarius: 'A Deo et eius genitrice optines.' Idem vir Dei Ildericus statim Dei genitricis ecclesiam est ingressus, et indesinenter sanctam Dei genitricem eiusque natum exflagitavit, ut secreta re suo servo intimaret. Ilico domum suum habiit, set praedictum virum flentem reperit, eumque consolari coepit et adiecit: 'Sede, cito scribe.' Set dum ille cum stupore resideret, ei praecepit, quomodo scribere et qualiter verba distinguere, in illo ordine quemadmodum augusti ei depromserat. Cumque iuxta morem augusto epistolam ille notarius cum magno gaudio detulisset eamque legisset, in hunc modum verba depromsit: 'Veritatem mihi dicito; qualis fuit vir ille qui hanc epistolam indicavit?' Cui notarius: 'Confiteor, domine, quia dictis tuis oblitus fui, et quid agere nesciebam; quapropter perrexi ad virum Dei Ildericum eique omnia intimavi. At ille ilico ecclesiam est ingressus; set dum paulisper ibidem moraret, ad me est reversus, et omnia quae cernis mihi studenter indicavit.' Statim augustus mirari coepit, et principem Adelchisum acclamavit, et in verbis talia promit: 'Volueram veraciter agnoscere, quis in hac urbe liberalibus disciplinis super omnes est deditus.' At princeps coepit nominare ceteri sapientes, verum virum Dei Ildericum omisit. Rex ait: 'Numquid non scis Ildericum?' Cui princeps: 'Veraciter scio, set eum exosum habebam, eo quod non ei adolatoria verba sicuti ceteri exibebam.' Quapropter rex omnia suis optimatibus enodavit; ab illo die magnam reverantiam ei videlicet optulerunt."

[89] Wattenbach, *DGQ* (7th ed.; Stuttgart, 1904), I, 485.

[90] *Neues Archiv*, II (1877), 116.

[91] There still exists in the Biblioteca Pubblica at Piacenza a psalter written on red parchment which Ingelberga is alleged to have written with her own hand. See Ch. Cahier, *Nouveaux mélanges d'archéologie, d'histoire et de littérature sur le moyen âge: Bibliothèques* (Paris, 1877), 95, n. 1. Cahier, however, fails to state whether he had seen the MS himself, or whether he is merely relying upon Valery (*Voyages historiques, littéraires et artistiques en Italie* [Paris, 1838], IX, p. xxv), whom he cites as authority. This supposition is of doubtful validity, however, because the catalogue of the books which the abbot Grimald gave to the library of Saint-Gall lists a "psalterium optimum glossatum, quod ipse Grimaldus Notingo Brixiensi [should be Veronensi?] ep. primum; post vero Engelbirge regine dedit, et per Richbertum magistrum aliud restituit." See also Weidmann, *Geschichte der Bibliothek von St. Gallen seit ihrer Gründung um das Jahr 830 bis auf 1841* (St. Gallen, 1841), 397. Weidmann remarks (*ibid.*, n. 570) that, according to J. von Arx (*Zusätze zur Geschichte des Cantons St. Gallen*, I, 16), this psalter given to Ingelberga "is undoubtedly the famous MS still preserved in Lombardy."

[92] Flodoard, *Hist. Remensis eccl.*, III, 27 (*MGH. SS.*, XIII, 550, 10), reports that Hincmar of Rheims wrote a letter to Irmingard: "Irmingardi, coniugi Bosonis incliti viri, pro rebus ecclesiarum Dei, quam audierat [sc. Hincmarus] *sufficienter litteris sacris imbutam ab Anastasio quodam didascalo;* unde petit, ut, qui eam dedit scire, det bonum velle et posse atque perficere; monens, ut hortetur virum suum, timere Deum et eius custodire mandata. De rebus etiam ecclesiasticis, quas, sicut audierat, ab ecclesiis abstractas suis hominibus diviserat, *ut ostendat illi ex scripturis sanctis,* quam grave iudicium proinde sit a Deo prolatum." Cf. Dümmler, *Ostfr. Reich.*, III, 122 and n. 3.

[93] *Tractatus de anima* (Migne, *PL*, 110, 1109): "Cum nobilitatis vestrae ingenium aviditatemque multa sciendi et copiosa investigandi perspiciam, sensus etiam vestri perspicaciam quo apprime sublimitas vestra floret demirer, statui, pro ingenioli mei parvitate, quoddam de manu deputare." This treatise is sometimes incorrectly held to have been dedicated to Lothar I, but Dümmler (*Ostfr. Reich.*, I, 404, n. 4) has shown that it was offered to Lothar II. Rhabanus also sent Lothair II several other books, including a copy of an abridged Vegetius, to which he added comments on the customs and practices of the Franks; cf. Wattenbach, *DGQ* (6th ed.), I, 219, n., and C. Lang's edition (1885) of Vegetius, p. xxviii.

[94] The will of Count Heccard records the gift to her of a book on medicine (Bishop, *Liturgica Historica*, 364; see above, note 78).

[95] Bertha is thus described in an epitaph inscribed on her tomb (probably in the eleventh century), published by Dümmler in his edition of the works of Liutprand of Cremona (in the "In usum scholarum" series; Hanover, 1877), 167:

> "Partibus ex multis multi comites veniebant,
> Mellifluum cuius quaerere colloquium."

I cite this item of information merely as an interesting aside. It would be uncritical to take these words as serious evidence of a knowledge of Latin on the part of either Bertha or the counts who came to hear her. Cf. Dümmler, *Ostfr. Reich.*, III, 673, n. 3.

[96] H. Gerdes, *Geschichte des deutschen Volkes und seiner Kultur im Mittelalter* (Leipzig, 1891–1908), I, 653: "Es kann nicht zweifelhaft sein, dass auch noch seine [Ludwigs des Deutschen] Söhne eine litterarische Bildung erhielten."

[97] *Chronicon*, ad a. 880: *MGH. SS.*, I, 591, 14: "Fuit vero iste praecellentissime rex litteris eruditus. . . ." Cf. Dümmler, *Ostfr. Reich.*, III, 139, and n. 3.

[98] Dümmler, *Ostfr. Reich.*, III, 291.

[99] Weidmann, *op. cit.*, 368 and n. 363. According to Wattenbach, *Das Schriftwesen im Mittelalter* (3d ed.), 575, n. 4, this catalogue has also been published by G. Scherer, *Verzeichnis der Incunabeln der Stiftsbibliothek von St. Gallen* (St. Gallen, 1880), 233 ff.

[100] Weidmann, *op. cit.*, 397: "Lectionarium optimum, quem petenti imperatori Karolo dedit domnus Harmotus et pro eo alterum reposuit"; cf. also, *ibid.*, nn. 564 and 565.

[101] Once more I cite an entry from the Cividale Gospel MS: ". . . domno Karolo imperatore. domno liuttuardo episcopo." Bethmann (*Neues Archiv,*

II, 116) informs us that both names are written in one hand, and suggests that the Italian endings point to the bishop, Liutward of Vercelli, the imperial chaplain and chancellor (who, I may add in passing, was also a borrower from the library at St. Gall; see Weidmann, *op. cit.*, 373 and n. 395, 385 and n. 487).

[102] See Weidmann, *op. cit.*, 369 and n. 368, 372 and n. 388.

[103] Joseph was the author of the *Historia translationis SS. Ragnoberti et Zenonis*. He identifies himself as follows (d'Achery, *op. cit.*, II, 133): "Ego Joseph peccator, sacerdos omniumque servorum Christi ultimus, quondam autem Aquitanorum Regis Cancellarius, nunc inclyti Regis Hludovici liberalium litterarum etsi immeritus praeceptor," etc. Cf. Wattenbach, *DGQ* (6th ed.), I, 300, n. 1.

[104] See Bouquet, *op. cit.*, VII, 701 e.

[105] Cf. B. Simson, *Ludwig der Fromme*, II, 254–255.

[106] Dümmler, *Ostfr. Reich.*, II, 434.

[107] Wattenbach, *DGQ* (6th ed.), I, 222, n. 2.

[108] *Archiv f. Urkundenforschung*, X (1928), 134.

[109] Cf. Dümmler, *Ostfr. Reich.*, III, 55–56.

[110] Migne, *PL*, 67, 1108, chap. 5: "Nobilium filiae sive ignobilium, ad nutriendum aut docendum, penitus non accipiantur."

[111] *MGH. LL.*, Sect. II, *Capit. regum Franc.*, I, 346, 34: "Ut scola in monasterio non habeatur, nisi eorum qui oblati sunt."

[112] Specht, *op. cit.*, 34, n. 2, who gives a reference to the collection of V. F. Gudenus, *Codex diplomaticus anecdotorum res Moguntinas illustrantium* (Frankfort and Leipzig, 1747–1758), I, 355, which I have not been able to check.

I say, "if we may trust our authority," because Specht gives two other references which are not pertinent. One is to the *Regula canonicorum* (*ca.* 750) of Chrodegang, bishop of Metz, in d'Achery, *op. cit.*, I, 574. But the passage does not refer to laymen; it speaks only of the waywardness of boys in general and the dangers to discipline arising therefrom. The precautions which Chrodegang advises show clearly that he was not thinking of boys who were to return to the world: "Quapropter in hujuscemodi custodiendis, et spiritaliter erudiendis, talis a praelatis constituendus est vitae probabilis frater, qui eorum curam summa gerat industria, eosque ita arctissime constringat, qualiter ecclesiasticis doctrinis imbuti, et armis spiritalibus induti, et ecclesiae utilitatibus decenter parare, et ad gradus ecclesiasticos quandoque digne possint promoveri." The other reference—to canon 135 of the decrees of the council of Aachen in 816 (Specht refers to Sirmond, *Conc. Gall.*, II, 398; I have used Mansi, *Sacr. conc.*, XIV, 240)—is simply a verbatim repetition of the passage referred to above and quoted in part. The council of Aachen, in other words, embodied in its decrees this part of Chrodegang's rule.

[113] *Vita S. Liutbirgae* (written *ca.* 870, soon after the saint's death): *MGH. SS.*, IV, 164, 8: "puellas eleganti forma transmiserat [Saint Ansgar], quas illa [Saint Liutberg] et in psalmodiis et in artificiosis operibus educaverat, et edoctas libertate concessa seu ad propinquos, sive quo vellent, ire permisit." Cf. Specht, *op. cit.*, 281.

[114] See the *Vita B. Rhabani Mauri*, I (Migne, *PL*, 107, 82–84), which is a discussion of Rhabanus' importance in the history of education in general, and therefore chiefly concerned with the education of ecclesiastics. Though Christ and the Gospel were the end of wisdom and learning, nevertheless Rhabanus gave his pupils a broad foundation in the liberal arts. From our point of view, the most interesting passage is the following (*ibid.*, col. 84): "Denique, sicut in superioribus est dictum, primus omnium apud Germanos publicam monachorum scholam tenuit, in qua non solum claustrales, sed plures etiam saecularis vitae homines habuit auditores."

[115] Ekkehard, *Casus S. Galli*, chap. 16 (*MGH. SS.*, II, 142): "[Notker] filios autem aliquorum, qui patrum beneficia habituri erant, ad se sumptos severe educaverat." Cf. Gerdes, *op. cit.*, I, 681.

[116] *Casus S. Galli*, chap. 3 (*MGH. SS.*, II, 94): "Nam et filios nobilium in loco ab abbate destinato fidibus edocuit."

Chapter III

ITALY (From *ca.* 900 to *ca.* 1300)

DURING THE MIDDLE AGES, it is often said, there were more educated laymen in Italy than in any country north of the Alps.
This statement is, generally speaking, true, but it needs modification and interpretation. If we are to understand and evaluate correctly the cultural level of the medieval Italian laity, we must first
of all make a clear distinction. We must differentiate between *professional* laymen, as teachers, lawyers, notaries, and physicians,
whose business in life made it necessary for them to be educated,—
or, in other words, to have a knowledge of Latin letters,— and
nonprofessional laymen, the nobility and upper classes in general,
whose education was the result either of personal inclination or
of unusual circumstances. In the north of Europe those professions
or occupations which in Italy were in the hands of the first-men-
tioned class, either did not exist at all or not on so large a scale, or
else they were in the hands of the clergy. Consequently, the gen-
eralization that there was more education among the laity of Italy
than among that of northern Europe is true by virtue of Italy's
unique class of professionally educated laymen. Is it also true by
virtue of the existence of a rather large group of learned nonprofessional laymen among the upper classes of society? Before pro-
ceeding to a discussion of this question, it may be well to adduce
some evidence concerning the knowledge of Latin by the first or
professional class. Although their existence is a fact universally accepted by scholars, and their knowledge of Latin an obvious truth,
nevertheless a few particulars seem worthy of attention here.

The professionally educated laity of Italy may be divided into
three groups: first, grammarians, whose chief occupation was
teaching and whose instruction consisted of Latin grammar and
rhetoric; second, jurists, including all those for whom a knowledge
of law was essential, notaries, lawyers, and judges; and third, those
of the medical profession, teachers, students, and practitioners.

In the north of Europe the teachers of grammar were almost
without exception churchmen, and instruction in Latin letters could
not be had except in the schools of the Church. In Italy, however,

conditions were different. Here could be found, in addition to the cathedral and monastic schools, private schools founded and conducted by laymen.[1] Further, in Rather's *Praeloquia* we find vivid evidence of how much more varied the lay classes were in Italy as compared with those in Germany and the Low Countries, and a remarkable understanding of social relations and perception of social distinctions. We find this contrast pointed out again, and at almost the same time, by the abbot William of Saint-Bénigne in Dijon, who was an Italian called into France by the Cluniac movement for monastic reform. His biographer, Rodolf Glaber, relates his astonishment at discovering the depth of ignorance into which the laity of Burgundy and Normandy were sunk, compared with the laity in Italy, and his pity over their inability to read the Psalter and other service books of the Church.[2]

The number of private teachers in medieval Italy seems to have been fairly large. The *Chronicon Salernitanum* tells us that in the time of the emperor Louis II (840–870) there were thirty-two *philosophi* at Benevento, the most famous among whom was Hilderic, a man thoroughly versed in the liberal arts.[3] Giesebrecht believes that *philosophus* is here synonymous with *doctor liberalium artium,*[4] and that most of these thirty-two men must have taught in private schools. Whether or not they were laymen, however, is another question. Hilderic later became a monk at Monte Cassino, and very likely many or most of these *philosophi* were ecclesiastics. Pertz[5] defines *philosophi* as *clerici* or *monachi,* drawing attention to a passage from Liutprand of Cremona (d. 972) in which the word *philosophare* clearly means *to become* or *to live as a monk.*[6] Nevertheless, we ought not to exclude the possibility that some of the Beneventan *philosophi* were laymen, for two reasons : the first, that *philosophus* is elsewhere used in the general sense of *doctor* or *magister scholarum,* and refers, after all, primarily to intellectual rather than to social status;[7] and the second, that we know from other sources that there were numerous private teachers in Italy who were laymen.

William of Aversa was famous as a grammarian long before he became a monk, and earned great honor and riches by his teaching.[8] Both Peter Damiani (d. 1072)[9] and Lanfranc (d. 1089) had been lay teachers and had founded schools in various places before they entered the Church. We may also mention Papias, the most famous

---

[1] Superior figures refer to notes on pp. 74–81.

of all the Italian grammarians of the eleventh century; Irnerius
of Bologna, who was a teacher of the arts before he turned to law;
and finally, in the twelfth century, Burgundius, whose epitaph describes him as "a doctor of doctors, a model of teachers, and the authority of poets."[10] These three teachers remained laymen throughout their lives. In most of the Italian sources of this period a definite
distinction is made between teachers who were clerics and those
who were laymen. The *Necrologium* of Modena, for example, records the death of two men named John; one of them is described
as *presbyter magister,* whereas the other is listed simply as *magister.*[11] It is needless to give here further examples of this kind.[12]

Davidsohn reports that the Florentine documents of the eleventh
century designate a number of laymen as *magistri,* in other words,
as teachers, primarily of grammar; and that, as the population in
and around Florence grew, by the twelfth century even the small
towns and villages in the vicinity had their lay teachers.[13] We can
be reasonably sure that the men known simply as *magistri* were
laymen, because great care was taken not to omit mention of even
the lowest ecclesiastical rank.[14] To many of these men teaching was
merely a means of obtaining a livelihood;[15] and some of them, like
William of Aversa, may have acquired a modest fortune by it.

In Italy, law and medicine, even more than teaching, were in
the hands of the laity; and a knowledge of Latin was regarded as
an indispensable preparation for both professions.[16] We may take
it for granted that all the municipal judges, the lawyers, and the
notaries had been educated in Latin letters in greater or less degree. Romuald, a barrister of Salerno, was interested in the literary
work of Alphanus, the learned monk of Monte Cassino who later
became archbishop of Salerno.[17] The fact that most of the Italian
notaries were laymen is so well known that it needs no more than
mention here. Almost every Italian city had its group of professional scribes,[18] who were to be found even on the islands of Dal-
matia.[19] The study of medicine also presupposed a knowledge of
Latin letters. Guarimpertus, for example, a doctor who was contemporary with Peter Damiani, is called "very learned in letters."[20]

We turn now to the more interesting and disputed question of
the extent of Latin learning among the Italian nobility and upper
classes in general, that is, among the nonprofessional laity. Giesebrecht believed that the *majority* of the Italian noblemen *usually*

received a liberal education.[21] This belief, which became widely accepted among scholars, has been severely attacked by A. Dresdner in a vigorous *excursus* which it seems well to insert here in full.[22]

Wilhelm von Giesebrecht, in his well-known and excellent dissertation, *De litterarum studiis apud Italos*, attempted to prove that in the tenth and eleventh centuries the upper classes in Italy as a rule received the benefit of a liberal education. After Giesebrecht, this opinion seems to have been generally accepted.[23] We wish to examine it anew.

One fact, it is true, is certain beyond the shadow of a doubt. A lay learning [or culture] did flourish in Italy; its bearers, the well-known *magistri grammatici*, can be identified in large numbers. The question, therefore, is whether we must accept only the existence of this class of laymen who were learned by reason of their profession, or whether we can postulate a liberal education for the upper classes of society in general. For, in and by itself, the existence of a professional class of learned men by no means proves the existence of lay education in general, since this professional class depended upon certain conditions then prevailing. The *magistri* were the instructors of a large proportion of the young men studying for the priesthood; in addition, they taught also those who, for their part, wanted to become learned professional men. The business activities open to these *magistri*, by means of which they earned their livelihood, were not inconsiderable. Notaries and lawyers were needed in great numbers; the services of the *grammatici* were required for diplomatic negotiations and in public affairs of all sorts; and on many an occasion the ability to hammer out verse may also have been a commodity in demand. In the eleventh century, a liberal education was likewise the prerequisite for the study of medicine.[24] But there is no reason therefore to assume without more ado that these *magistri* were also the instructors of the young noblemen.[25]

I examine first the evidence upon which Giesebrecht bases his contentions.

(1) Rather, *De cont. can.*, I, 22 (*Opera*, 362): "pone quemlibet nobilium scholis tradi, quod ubique hodie magis fieri ambitu videtur episcopandi quam cupiditate Domino militandi." This passage evidently means: formerly the noble youths attended the schools because of a desire to serve God, that is, in order to become ecclesiastics; now the end they have in view is merely the obtaining of a bishopric. This statement, therefore, proves rather that the *nobiles iuvenes* were wont to attend the schools only if they wished to take up an ecclesiastical career.[26]

In (2) and (3) we are offered remarks by a Frenchman and a German respectively. Milo Crispinus says in his *Vita Lanfranci* (*Lanf. Opera*, Paris, 1648, 6; in Fitting, *Anfänge*, 19) that his hero "eruditus est in scholis liberalium artium et legum saecularium ad suae morem patriae. . . . Meminit horum Papia."[27] And Wipo in a famous passage of the *Tetralogus* (V, 195 ff.: *SS.*, XI, 251) says:

"Moribus his dudum vivebat Roma decenter,
His studiis tantos potuit vincire tyrannos;
Hoc servant Itali post prima crepundia cuncti,
Et sudare scolis mandatur tota iuventus. . . ."

A certain generality of expression is peculiar to both passages: in Wipo this is evident to the point of manifest exaggeration,[28] and comes suspiciously close to empty verbiage, "his studiis tantos potuit vincire tyrannos," whereas the Frenchman by "patria" may have meant Pavia, whose high level of culture was famous far and wide.[29] An exact knowledge of the pertinent conditions in Italy cannot be assumed for either. *Per contra*, if we stop to consider that it was most unusual for a layman of that time in either France or Germany to have received a liberal education and, further, that Wipo and Milo had heard of the large number of learned men in Italy who were laymen, then it seems quite natural that they should have misunderstood these conditions, so strange to them, and that they were thereby led astray in their remarks. But we can by no means consider these passages as valid proofs of the customary, or rather prevalent, education of the upper-class Italian laymen, which is usually taken for granted.[30]

On the other hand, a remark of Damiani (*Opusc.*, LVIII, 3: *Opera*, III, 800), which Giesebrecht, by the way, has not used, does make for difficulties. Damiani here says of a layman named Boniface: "quia tu in saeculo non imum obtines locum, nec potes prorsus effugere, ut . . . aliquando de litteratoriae disciplinae studiis aliquid non attingas." This Boniface has been held to have been a jurist, and I, for my part, also regard him as such. But the passage is noteworthy, even at that; it suggests, we admit, the possibility that individual laymen of prominence did acquire some sort of education. Nevertheless, I believe that no decided significance should be attached to these words. For there are actually no valid reasons for assuming a liberal education among the upper classes. Giesebrecht and Wattenbach, it is true, believe that the singular development of Italian literature, in which a great deal of liberal learning suddenly becomes manifest after a long period of sterility and barbarism, can only be explained by just this assumption. But it seems to me that the existence of a professional class of learned laymen in itself suffices to explain this development. These men preserved intact that store of liberal knowledge which disappears temporarily from before our eyes, only to reappear, suddenly, but by no means spontaneously. I cannot, in this phenomenon, see any basis for assuming a liberal education among laymen in general.

Per contra, several facts speak most definitely against the existence of such an education; and in view of the meagerness of the pertinent evidences in the sources, these notices deserve a double consideration.

1) William, in his *Vita Bened. Clus.*, 10 (*SS.*, XII, 206), tells of a certain *Wilhelmus miles Allobros* who is called *moribus et genere haud ignobilis*, that he became a monk and engaged in disputations in Latin, "cum esset laicus et litterarum penitus ignarus, coepit tamen cum illis ita agere verbis Latinis, ac si doctus fuisset inter grammaticos tempore ineuntis aetatis." Here, therefore, we find the view that the *laicus*, as such, is a stranger to education. And that this opinion is applied to a foreigner means nothing, for the Italian author undoubtedly proceeded in his remarks on the basis of his own national concepts.

2) From the opposite end of the peninsula, from Rossano, the birthplace of Saint Nilus, we hear that Gregory, a *vir nobilis* "cum numquam didicisset

litteras, ita psallebat et cantabat," etc. (*Vita S. Nili,* 35; *AA. SS.,* Sept., VII, 282). This particular nobleman, therefore, had not received any liberal education.

3) Romuald, as it is well known, came from a prominent Ravennese family; nevertheless it is said of him: "quia saeculum idiota reliquerat" (*Vita S. Rom.,* 4; Damiani, *Opera,* II, 432). Not until later did he acquire any education (chap. 50, *ibid.,* 470).

4) A remark of Rather which has been discussed above, that is, the passage in *De cont. can.,* I, 22, seems to allow the conclusion that the sons of the nobility attended schools only to become ecclesiastics, but a passage in the biography of Saint Peter of Perugia (cf. *supra,* 176),[31] shows definitely that to attend school and to become an ecclesiastic were regarded in the main as being one and the same thing. This sort of attitude could hardly have been prevalent if it had been the regular, or even simply a rather frequent, custom among a large and distinguished part of the population to attend the schools.

Finally, if the nobles and the propertied classes had regularly received a liberal education,—say as far as the reading of Vergil and Horace,—we should certainly expect to find at least some further traces of such an education, especially in view of the large amount of the extant narrative and documentary source material. But absolutely no such traces are to be found.[32] More than one prince and nobleman found his panegyrist; but none of these says anything about the education [or culture] of their heroes. Liutprand says of King Hugh that he loved and honored the philosophers;[33] but he does not add that the king was a philosopher. Donizo does not neglect to call attention to the linguistic abilities of Mathilda and the musical knowledge of Bishop Tedald of Arezzo; but beyond that, he says nothing about a liberal education of any of the margraves of Tuscany. On those rare occasions, however, when we do obtain some information concerning the cultural level of men of rank, a liberal education is disavowed for them, and that, in part, in terms which indicate that this condition was the rule among laymen.

Naturally, I do not say that there were no exceptions to this rule. It is certainly true that special circumstances or individual personal inclinations did occasionally lead a nobleman to busy himself with matters of learning. But that is not the core of the problem. If its upper classes in general had actually received a liberal training, Italy would, in this respect, assume an even more remarkable position among the nations of the Middle Ages than the one which is nevertheless ascribed to her in view of the existence of her professional class of learned laymen. But I can discern no cogent grounds for such an assumption.

Dresdner's attack on Giesebrecht's interpretations needs revision as much as the latter require modification. From a reconsideration of the evidence, it will become apparent that neither one of them is entirely accurate.

(1) The statement of Rather of Verona ("Pone quemlibet nobilium scholis tradi; quod ubique hodie magis fieri ambitu videtur episcopandi, quam cupiditate Domino militandi")[34] in my opinion

proves nothing whatsoever concerning the education of laymen. As Dresdner has suggested, it seems to mean that whereas young nobles had formerly gone to school in the desire to serve God by entering the Church, now many of them did so only in order to obtain a good living. Giesebrecht's interpretation of this passage is entirely too loose and deserves the criticism it has received. On the other hand, it is difficult to accept Dresdner's statement that the passage proves that "the *nobiles iuvenes* were wont to attend the schools only if they wished to take up an ecclesiastical career." The passage proves nothing of the kind. The fact is that both of our authorities were nodding. Dresdner apparently failed to note that Giesebrecht advised his readers to continue further in the paragraph from Rather; and Giesebrecht might have used his evidence to much better advantage. Rather[35] goes on to inveigh against the evils resulting from the advancement to ecclesiastical offices of men without proper qualifications, in violation of canon law. In such promotions, says Rather, whenever the Scripture passage from John, 10:1, is read ("He that entereth not by the door into the sheepfold, but climbeth up some other way, the same is a thief and a robber"), those laymen who have some knowledge of letters ("hi ex saeculari-bus, qui non penitus sunt litterarum expertes") cannot help but draw the conclusion that their priest or prelate is a thief and a robber, since he has entered the sheepfold (the Church) not by the door, but by some other way (i.e., not canonically). Surely we cannot dismiss this passage as irrelevant by saying that the laymen to whom Rather refers were the professionally educated class. The phrase "qui non penitus sunt literarum expertes" is hardly applicable to men whose business demanded more than a passing knowledge of Latin. To me it seems more probable that Rather was thinking of those nonprofessional, ordinary laymen who had received at least an elementary education, and who were thereby enabled to understand the Vulgate and apply the gospel lesson to their own day. To my mind this passage lends strong support to the contention that there was in tenth-century Italy a class of nonprofessional laymen, noblemen probably, who had at least a fair knowledge of Latin.[36]

(2) In the *Vita B. Lanfranci,* chap. 5 (Migne, *PL,* 150, 39), Milo Crispin (Crispinus; d. *ca.* 1150) says of his hero: "Hic igitur homo ... nobili ortus parentela, ab annis puerilibus eruditus est in scholis

liberalium artium et legum saecularium ad suae morem patriae."
Dresdner suggests that the passage may mean either that Lanfranc
received a good training in the liberal arts *as was customary in
Pavia* (Lanfranc's "patria"), or that Lanfranc was instructed in
the liberal arts *and* secular law, a combination quite customary in
Italy. These two interpretations are certainly possible, but so is
Giesebrecht's, that, following the custom of noble youths *in general*, Lanfranc also received good training in grammar and law.
My own belief is that this is what Milo meant when he wrote the
words. Dresdner's other objection to this passage, that Milo probably had no exact knowledge of conditions in Italy, deserves consideration but is, after all, hypothetical. We may assume, for the
sake of argument, that Milo never visited Italy, since all we know
of him is that he was descended from an illustrious Norman family
and that he was cantor at Bec;[37] even so, it is still possible that he
had received accurate information from someone who had been in
Italy. Nor is it necessary to accept Dresdner's belief that in the
latter event Milo misinterpreted his information. Dresdner's assumption rests, in the final analysis, upon his opinion that Milo's
statement, as interpreted by Giesebrecht, is incompatible with other
evidence. We are not ready, however, to accept the contention that
the general trend of the evidence is against a rather widespread
cultivation of Latin letters among the Italian nobility.

(3) We come now to Wipo's famous statement (*Tetralogus*, vss.
190–198: *MGH. SS.*, XI, 251) :

> Tunc fac edictum per terram Teutonicorum,
> Quilibet ut dives sibi natos instruat omnes
> Litterulis, legemque suam persuadeat illis,
> Ut cum principibus placitandi venerit usus,
> Quisque suis libris exemplum proferat illis.
> Moribus his dudum vivebat Roma decenter,
> His studiis tantos potuit vincire tyrannos :
> Hoc servant Itali post prima crepundia cuncti,
> Et sudare scholis mandatur tota iuventus :
> Solis Teutonicis vacuum vel turpe videtur,
> Ut doceant aliquem nisi clericus accipiatur.

Dresdner assumes that Wipo, like Milo, had no exact knowledge of
conditions in Italy, and believes that Wipo also probably misunderstood his informants concerning lay learning in Italy. I believe that
Dresdner overlooked the probability that Wipo wrote these lines

on the basis of personal observations. There is good reason to believe that Wipo did visit Italy.[38] Although these lines are manifestly an exaggeration, they cannot be dismissed lightly as "empty verbiage."

(4) In his tract *De vera felicitate et sapientia* (*Opusc.*, LVIII, 3: Migne, *PL*, 145, 833: *Opera*, III, 880), Peter Damiani addresses his lay friend Boniface, a *vir prudentissimus*, thus:

> Sed quia tu in saeculo non imum obtines locum, nec potes prorsus effugere, ut aut saecularis eloquii cum colloquentibus verba non conferas, aut aliquando de litteratoriae disciplinae studiis aliquid non attingas, hac tibi discretione utendum est; ut in saecularibus quidem te velut hebetem reddas, in spiritualibus vero studiis omnes tuae mentis nervos exerceas: in illis te praebeas negligentem, in his autem omnino vivacem.

I agree with Dresdner that "no decided significance should be attached to these words"; yet I cannot approve of the argument by which he arrives at this opinion, namely, that there are no other valid reasons for assuming that the upper classes in Italy generally received a liberal education. If Boniface was actually a jurist, as Dresdner believes, then the passage is significant only in respect to the education of professional laymen. In other words, it is not specific for lay culture or education in general, excluding the professional classes. Stated simply, Damiani's words mean: If a jurist wants to make any headway whatsoever in his calling, he must have a good knowledge of Latin letters; but lest he lose true happiness and wisdom, he must not become too much attached to his liberal studies, but rather give his heart and mind to studies divine.

Dresdner continues his discussion by citing examples which seem to argue definitely against the existence of a liberal education among laymen in general. He points out, first, that in those rare passages where information concerning a layman's state of culture is given, we are usually told that he had *not* received a liberal education; and second, that this information implies the existence of a general condition of ignorance among the Italian laity.

1) In his *Vita Benedicti abbatis Clusensis*,[39] William, a monk of Chiusa and a disciple of the abbot Benedict, tells the story of a certain Burgundian (?) knight (*Miles Allobros*), also named William, who came to Chiusa and who, "although he was a layman and entirely ignorant of letters, nevertheless held forth learnedly *in*

Latin, as if he had been instructed by grammarians in the days of his youth."

Willelmus nomine, moribus et genere haud ignobilis .... Qui ab eodem patre, necnon et Herimanno cardinali, sancti praeconii viro et eruditissimo, visitatus, post sacram unctionem sanctaeque eucharistiae perceptionem, cum esset laicus et litterarum penitus ignarus, coepit tamen cum illis ita agere verbis Latinis, ac si doctus fuisset inter grammaticos tempore ineuntis aetatis.

This passage is evidence of the most pliable kind. Are we to believe from it, as Dresdner does, that laymen were as a matter of course ignorant of Latin letters? It is possible that the author used the phrase *litterarum penitus ignarus* as a descriptive synonym of *laicus,* but this interpretation is not necessarily the right one.[40] To me it seems rather to be a mention of a certain layman, and a non-Italian layman at that, who was ignorant of Latin letters. It should be noted also that the episode is recorded as a miracle, and is therefore open to suspicion. If we accept the story as it reads, however, two explanations are possible: either the phrase *litterarum penitus ignarus* is an expression of pious exaggeration; or the knight referred to may have received in his youth an elementary education, the substance of which was actively recalled to his mind by his religious experience.

2) The *Vita S. Nili* (abbot of Grotta-Ferrata, d. 1005), chap. 35 (*AA. SS.* [ed. novissima], Sept., VII, 282), tells us that George (whom Dresdner inaccurately calls Gregory), a nobleman of Rosano, "though he had never learned letters, nevertheless sang and chanted hymns and psalms so well that all who heard him were astonished and stupefied" ("Et quod mirum, erat, cum nunquam didicisset litteras, ita psallebat et cantabat psalmos et hymnos, ut mirarentur et obstupescerent omnes, qui audiebant...").[41] Dresdner is obviously correct in saying that this is an example of a nobleman who had not received a liberal education. But in what way does it prove that illiteracy was the rule among the upper classes? Clearly, the tale is told for purposes of edification; and the explanation is probably that George, uneducated though he was, had heard the hymns and psalms so often that he knew them by heart.

3) Peter Damiani gives us a similar example. In his *Vita S. Romualdi* (abbot of Camaldoli, d. 1027), chap. 4 (Migne, *PL*, 144, 959: *Opera,* II, 432), he tells us that when Romuald forsook the world to become a monk, he had not yet learned letters: "Romual-

dus autem, quia saeculum idiota reliquerat, aperto psalterio, vix suorum versuum notas syllabatim explicare valebat."[42] It would be no more far-fetched to assume that Romuald's illiteracy was noted here because it was unusual than to consider his ignorance as indicative of a general condition among laymen, as Dresdner does.

4) Dresdner maintains that the sons of noblemen attended school only in order to become ecclesiastics, and that generally speaking going to school and becoming an ecclesiastic were regarded as the same thing. In addition to the passage from Rather, he calls upon, as evidence, the following passage in the *Vita S. Petri* (abbot of Monte Caprario, near Perugia, d. 1007) : ". . . quique cum solummodo sex annorum esset, etiam invitis parentibus litteras coepit discere scholarum utpote prudentus clientulus. Quid plura? Sacris ab infantia eruditus litteris, collum jugo Dominici supposuit servitii, etc."[43] We need not stop to debate the validity of Dresdner's conclusion, because his source itself is questionable. If he had consulted the Bollandist edition of the *Vita* by Pinius, he would have discovered that the *Vita* exists in two different versions, and that he had used the later and less reliable version, that by Mabillon.[44] A comparison of the two versions proves conclusively that the author of Mabillon's text had before him the older text, that printed by the Bollandists, when he wrote. As a matter of fact, neither of the two *Vitae* can be considered a source of the highest credibility.[45] If the statement of either concerning Peter's education is to be accepted, it should be that of the earlier version, which runs thus (chap. 1, 110) :

Petrus, ex provincia Tusciae in Castro Agello, qui a Perusia civitate fere sex millibus distat, ortus est. *Suos non ignobiles habuit parentes, qui puerum Petrum e prima in humanis studiis instruxerunt; sed ipse sacris insistens*, thesaurum illum absconditum invenit, quapropter, venditis omnibus, emit agrum, ac sese in ministerio Ecclesiae mancipavit, atque per gradus ad sacerdotium pervenit.

This older account makes Dresdner's position untenable since it provides a definite example of noble parents who were interested in giving their son a liberal education. There is no evidence that the author saw in this fact anything strange or unusual.

In discussing the general state of culture in Italy in the first half of the tenth century, Giesebrecht (*op. cit.*, 12) directs attention to a passage in the *Carmen panegyricum Berengarii*,[46] written between

916 and 924, which is noteworthy for its sweeping implications. In
the prologue to his poem the author addresses himself thus:

> Quid vanis totiens agitas haec tempora dictis,
> Carmina quae profers si igne voranda times?
> Desine; nunc etenim nullus tua carmina curat;
> Haec faciunt urbi; haec quoque rure viri.[47]

Naturally, these words should not be taken too literally. We must
make allowance for poetic exaggeration and note that the generality
of the statement makes it impossible to determine its exact value for
us. The author may have been a layman, or he may have been a
cleric; the most that can be said is that he seems to have been a
schoolmaster at Verona.[48] Nevertheless, his words seem to indicate
a comparatively high degree of culture in the society of which he
was part. There must have been a fairly large group of educated
people in a society of which the poet says that no one will bother
to read his work because everybody else is busy writing the same
sort of thing. Dresdner has overlooked this illuminating passage.

Another significant passage, overlooked by both Giesebrecht and
Dresdner, is contained in the *Vita S. Joannis Laudensis,* written by
an anonymous monk of Avellino who was a contemporary and disciple of John, the author of the life of Damiani (1026–1106).[49] In
speaking of John's studies, the author says:

> Nempe cum litterarum januam acris ut puto ingenii puer transmeasset,
> atque ad floribundos liberalium artium domus pervenisset, quos incaute trac-
> tando multa, proh dolor! hominum millia non modo vulnerata, sed ad gehen-
> nam usque irremediabiliter sunt demersa; ille, ut coeleste animal, intus et
> undique oculatus, tam circumspecte a noxiis secernebat utilia, ut nulla, Domino
> custodiente, animam sauciaret laesura.[50]

Even if we allow for pious exaggeration by the author, we must
admit that the acquisition of a liberal education is not represented
as being at all extraordinary. The *Vita* goes on to tell of the many
schoolmates of John who were interested in the salacious stories of
the profane authors, and of John's refusal to take delight in such
things. Perhaps these boys were preparing for a professional career,
but nothing in the passage obliges us to accept such an interpretation. John seems to have proceeded from the elements of grammar
to the liberal arts quite as a matter of course. There is no mention
of preparation for a particular career, and John had evidently not
yet decided upon a monastic life. F. Neukirch, to whom I owe this

reference, believes that John "studied the liberal arts in his youth, as the sons of the Italian noblemen were regularly accustomed to do."[51] This statement is doubtless too sweeping, but it seems permissible to consider the passage quoted as an indication of the fact that a liberal education for the sons of Italian noblemen was not altogether unusual.[52]

To sum up: I do not believe that the evidence justifies the conclusion of Giesebrecht that the greater part of the upper classes in Italy as a rule received a liberal education or training in Latin letters. Yet neither can I accept the dictum of Dresdner that as a general rule, with a few exceptions, the nonprofessional upper classes were devoid of education. In the first place, the existence of so many learned professions in Italy deserves more consideration than Dresdner has given it, for it implies that educational opportunities were open to laymen of all sorts.[53] Concerning Italian education in this period, Taylor has written thus:

... there is evidence of the unintermitted existence of lay schools, private or municipal, in all the important towns, from the eighth century to the tenth, the eleventh, and so on and on. These did not give religious instruction, but taught grammar and the classic literature, law and the art of drawing up documents and writing letters. ... In Italy there never ceased to be schools conducted by laymen for laymen, where instruction in matters profane and secular was imparted and received for the sake of its profane and secular value, without regard to its utility for the saving of souls.[54]

We must remember that there were men in Italy who, according to a well-known passage, stood in the market places and offered wisdom and learning at a price to anyone who might wish to buy.[55] Perhaps most of those who hearkened to the cry of the teachers became teachers themselves or entered some other profession, but we should not forget the potentialities inherent in this situation with respect to nonprofessional education for laymen. In the second place, I believe that the exceptions to his rule are more numerous than Dresdner supposed. There are a number of instances which seem to prove the existence of a group of cultivated men among the upper classes who had received the benefits of a liberal education to a greater or less degree. This evidence we shall now consider in some detail.

In Lower Italy we meet with educated laymen who knew both Latin and Greek. Sergius I, duke of Naples in the ninth century, was so well versed in both languages that he could translate from one into the other rapidly and easily.[56] It is not surprising that such a man should be interested in books and libraries. We are told that he presented to the episcopal library at Naples three copies of Josephus.[57] The two sons of Sergius I were also thoroughly at home in Greek and Latin. This was natural in Athanasius, who entered the Church and became bishop of Naples;[58] it is more noteworthy in Gregory, his brother, a layman, who is described as expert in both tongues.[59] This tradition of culture was maintained by the rulers of Naples in the tenth century. Duke John (926–968) seems to have had a good knowledge of Latin letters, and the same is probably true of Theodora his wife and Marinus his co-ruler. The Duke "encouraged translation from Greek into Latin, and showed interest in learning by collecting books and having many MSS copied."[60]

There is evidence of similar conditions in other centers of southern Italy. We may infer from the story of Louis II and his notary that Adelchis, prince of Benevento, had some knowledge of Latin letters;[61] and it is hard to believe that Adelchis was the only educated prince of his line. Adelrad, a noble lord of Salerno and a Bendictine *confrater,* and John, a public official of Salerno, the two men who encouraged the monk John to write the *Vita S. Odonis,* must also have had some training in Latin.[62] At the end of this same tenth century John Philagathos, a hellenized Italian, was a teacher of the young Otto III.[63] From this time on, all information with respect to educated laymen and lay libraries in South Italy fails us until the twelfth century, when Normans ruled the South. But Giesebrecht has suggested that the relations of Alphanus (monk of Monte Cassino, later archbishop of Salerno, d. 1086) with Gisulph, prince of Salerno, and Guido, his brother, would seem to prove that these two laymen had received some sort of literary education.[64]

It has been suggested by Hagenmeyer,[65] and by Yewdale,[66] who follows him, that Bohemond learned to read and write Latin. They base their contention on a document containing a grant to the Genoese, dated at Antioch, July 14, 1098, which has the following subscription:

X Signum mei Boamundi, qui hanc chartam donationis fieri iussit, firmavi et testes firmare rogavi.

X Signum episcopi Adriani.

X Signum Roberti de Surda Valle.

✗ Signum Roberti de Anza.

✗ Signum Rodulfi Rufi.

✗ Signum Boelli de Carrato.

Hagenmeyer[67] says the use of the first person proves that the first entry of the subscription, both the cross and the words which follow, was written by Bohemond himself. He thinks, moreover, that the other entries were made by the hands of those whose names are recorded, four of whom were evidently laymen, followers of the prince of Antioch. It is difficult to agree with Hagenmeyer, both because of the absence of the word *subscripsi* and because of the presence of the cross or *signum*. The most that can be safely argued is that the mark (✗) was in each instance made *manu propria*. Such a conclusion, however, neither proves nor disproves that these men had a knowledge of Latin. Nevertheless, we can be sure that some Norman noblemen of Lower Italy were not without a degree of education. The outstanding example is the anonymous author of the *Gesta Francorum,* who was a layman of the lesser nobility from southern Italy, and very probably a Norman.[68]

The private documents written in Italy in this period contribute some illuminating information to our subject. There are still many ninth- and tenth-century documents which bear the personal signatures of the contracting parties. In documents of the later period, autograph signatures are rarer because it became the custom for the notary to write the entire document, including the subscription.[69] This fact, while proving nothing conclusive about ability or inability to write on the part of the contracting parties, is probably indicative of a decline in the level of lay culture.[70]

One of the most interesting pieces of documentary evidence is found in a deed of 945 by which Alberic, prince and senator of the Romans, and other members of his family gave to the monastery of Saint Andrew the Apostle and Saint George in Rome, certain properties in perpetuity. The remarkable subscription to this document[71] runs in part as follows:

✗ Albericus Princeps atque omnium Romanorum Senator huic a die presentis donationis cartula de suprascriptis immobilibus locis et familiis cum eorum pertinentiis facta a me cum meis consortibus in suprascripto Monasterio in perpetuum, sicut superius legitur, *manu propria subscripsi,* et testes qui subscriberent rogavi.

Signum ✗ *manu* suprascripta Marozza nobilissima femina donatrice qui supra *lra* ✗ *n.*[72]

Signum **X** *manu* suprascripta Stephania nobilissima femina donatrice qui supra *lra* **X** *n*.

X Berta nobilissima puella huic a die presentis donationis [etc., as above], *manu propria subscripsi*, et testes qui subscriberent rogavi.

(Sergius, bishop of Nepi, subscribet, *manu propria*.)

X Constantinus in Dei nomine nobilis vir huic a die presentis donationis [etc., as above], *manu propria subscripsi*, et testes qui subscriberent rogavi.

[Among the witnesses, we find these two:]

X Benedictus in Dei nomine Consul, et Dux in hanc a die presentis donationis de suprascriptis omnibus [etc., etc.], sicut superius legitur, rogatus ab eis *testis subscripsi, et traditam vidi.*

X Johannes nobili viro in hanc cartulam [etc., etc.], rogatus ab eo *testis subscripsi,* et traditam vidi.

The subscription shows, it is true, as Gregorovius[73] has pointed out, that some of the women of the Roman nobility were probably unable to read or write. Marozia and Stephania apparently had to put their marks to the document because they were ignorant of letters. Gregorovius, however, has drawn attention only to the dark side of the picture. The subscription also shows that some of the leading Roman laymen of the time had some knowledge of Latin. Alberic himself, as well as his kinspeople, Constantine and Bertha, signed the document *manu propria*. It is possible that the two lay witnesses, Benedict, *consul et dux*, and John, a noble Roman (the sons respectively of Stephania and Theodora III), also signed in person, although this is not probable because of the absence of the phrase *manu propria*.

Another significant document is the eleventh-century (1063) grant by Bishop Wolmar of Reggio to the nuns of Santo Tommaso, which contains the following subscription:

> *Ego Wolmarus Episcopus subscripsi.*
> *Bernardus Archidiaconus subscripsi.*
> *Argicardus Archipresbiter subscripsi.*
> *Albertus Prepositus, et Custos subscripsi.*
> *Joannes Scolarum Magister subscripsi.*
> *. . . . . . nericus Clericus subscripsi.*
> *Eurardus Subdiaconus subscripsi.*
> *Everardus Acolitus . . . .*
> *Romanus subscripsi.*
> *Ubertus Comes subscripsi.*
> *Tetelmus interfui.*[74]

Although Redlich[75] warns us not to accept too readily the genuineness of seemingly *bona fide* signatures, nevertheless it seems fairly safe to assume that these are actually the signatures of the parties named. If the assumption is correct, the subscription affords evidence of two or three Italian laymen, nonprofessionals, who could write their own names and even something more, for the *subscripsi* and *interfui* are probably by the same hands as the names. The hypothesis that the signatures are real autographs is supported by several considerations.

(1) Redlich's warning, which will be discussed more fully in its appropriate place, applies chiefly to documents written north of the Alps.

(2) Apparently we have here a document the validity of which is established not by the signature or name of a notary, but by the personal subscriptions of the author and his witnesses. It is significant that no notary or scribe is mentioned throughout the document.

(3) Since there is no reason to believe the contrary, we may assume that the signatures of the ecclesiastics and professionals (note *Joannes Scolarum Magister*) are autographs; such men were undoubtedly able to write. Therefore, since Romanus and Count Hubert subscribe in exactly the same manner, it may be reasonable to assume that their signatures are also autographs. And if the explanation of the fact that Tetelmus records only his presence (*Tetelmus interfui*) is perhaps a legal one, his signature also is probably personal.

(4) Finally, it is to be noted that Muratori (*loc. cit.*) used the word *autograph* in speaking of the document. It is possible that he used the word loosely in the sense of *original,* but he may have meant to indicate thereby that the document was actually an autograph, and the signatures genuine.[76]

In Tuscany of the eleventh century we have a distinguished example of lay learning in the person of the countess Mathilda.[77] Not only could she speak the three important vernaculars of continental Western Europe;[78] she was equally at home in the language of learning.[79] In the words of Nora Duff, Mathilda

could converse fluently in four different languages, and could correspond in Latin with the great men her contemporaries; she wrote her letters herself without the aid of a clerk. She helped to foster and develop the love of learning; she herself was well versed in jurisprudence, and one of her greatest pleasures was in collecting manuscripts and mastering their contents.[80]

Although it is impossible to cite an exact passage in support of Miss Duff's statement concerning Mathilda's activity in writing, nevertheless there can be no doubt about her ability to write. She seems until shortly before her death to have been in the habit of signing her own documents. Her subscription consists of a large cross in the four corners of which she wrote "Matilda Dei gratia si quid est subscripsi" in large and rather awkward majuscule letters which clearly reveal the hand of the great countess herself rather than that of a trained scribe.[81] By way of contrast, her adopted son, Guido Guerra, was unable to write, and in using the same form of subscription he could only make the cross, if that much, and had to have a scribe add his name.[82] Overmann thinks it probable that all the princes of the house of Canossa from Thedald (d. 1012) on were able to write, since all, except Gottfried of Lorraine, sometimes use the formula *subscripsi* in their documents.[83] This conjecture is plausible but, as Overmann admits, no definite conclusions can be reached until the documents have received a more thorough paleographical study.

Some very interesting bits of information concerning lay Italian culture in the twelfth century are contained in the accounts of Frederick Barbarossa's relations with the Lombard communes. We learn that Frederick spoke in German when addressing his Italian subjects. For example, Romuald tells us that Frederick's German address at Venice in July, 1177, was translated into the vernacular (*vulgariter*) by Christian, archbishop of Mainz.[84] Since, therefore, it would seem that the emperor's speeches were usually translated into Italian,[85] we may reasonably assume that there were not many laymen in Italy in this period who could understand spoken Latin. Commenting on the fact that Frederick was unable to use Latin when addressing the Roman senate in 1155, Gregorovius says:[86] "Since the greater number of the senators were no longer able to speak Latin, the emperor of the Romans may have comforted himself with the thought of their ignorance." Although the Italians took great pride in their ability to make speeches, most of them were doubtless limited to oratorical displays in the vernacular.[87] This does not necessarily mean, however, that they were unable to understand or to read Latin. According to Romuald,[88] the Latin sermon of Alexander III, given at Venice in July, 1177, was translated into German for the benefit of the emperor. Could the Italian laymen who were present understand the Latin address? Probably some, at least, could do so. We must remember that Latin was still the language of business in twelfth-century Italy, and hence the ordinary businessman undoubtedly had a smattering of Latin letters.[89] A reading knowledge of Latin among the laity was probably not at all uncommon in this period. Cahier directs attention to a MS of the letters of Saint Jerome which was copied in 1157 at the request of several women of Modena; their names are given at the end of the MS.[90]

In general it would seem that lay culture in Italy was steadily diffused in the twelfth century. The comparatively high level of this culture is strikingly reflected in the historiography of the period. Whereas in the north of Europe history was still written exclusively by ecclesiastics, much of the history written in Italy, especially toward the close of the twelfth century, came from the pens of laymen. We need not consider this at great length, because all these lay historians seem to have been professional men to whom a knowledge of Latin was an indispensable part of their equipment.[91] The most notable example, perhaps, is that of the two Morenas, father and son. The elder, Otto Morena, who began the *Historia Friderici I*,[92] was born at Lodi about 1100 and saw the destruction of his native city by the Milanese in 1111. In charters written by himself he is styled "judex ac missus." He became consul or podestà in 1147. After a few years as a citizen of Milan he returned to his native city, and was henceforth an imperial partisan. His son Acerbus was also a podestà in Lodi, and an imperial *judex* in Lombardy. He was with Frederick in Italy in 1167, where he died of fever. Amid all this political activity Acerbus found time to continue his father's history. It is apparent from his writing that he was more lettered than his father; he was acquainted with Lucan's *Pharsalia,* Suetonius' *Lives of the Caesars,* and especially the works of Sallust.

It is significant that there are signs in the historiography of this period of a tendency toward popularization. Many authors express a desire to make their works intelligible to a literate lay public.[93] A good example of this tendency is afforded by Godfrey of Viterbo. In his *Memoria seculorum*[94] he expresses the hope that those who have been wasting their time on fables and stories of dubious worth will now turn their attention to his own comprehensive and useful treatise; and he addresses his *Speculum regum*[95] to Henry VI and his court.[96]

Considered as a whole, the cultural achievements of the Italian nobility from the ninth to the end of the twelfth century are not to be despised, especially when we remember that the clergy of medieval Italy were often ignorant and illiterate.[97]

The most brillant center of lay culture, however, was to be found in the South, in Norman Italy and Sicily, where, as Professor Haskins has written, "within its limits, the intellectual movement at the court of King Roger and his son had many of the elements of a renaissance."[98] The conqueror of Sicily, the great Count Roger (d. 1101), was in all probability illiterate; he and his companions were primarily warriors. By the twelfth century, however, there developed an interest in letters among the Norman laity of southern Italy and Sicily which is truly remarkable. Roger II, the first king of Sicily (1130–1154), received an education which far surpassed that usually given to the princes of Western Europe in this age.[99] He learned to read and write not only Latin but Greek as well, as is evident from the personal subscription of his documents.[100] Very probably he also understood Arabic, like his son William the Bad and his grandson William the Good.[101] The Saracen, Edrisi, who under the king's direction compiled the famous geographical treatise still commonly known as *King Roger's Book,* said that he was incapable of describing his patron's knowledge of the exact and technical sciences.[102] From Roger II to Frederick II, the Sicilian monarchs are without exception praised as highly educated men. William I is described by Aristippus, his minister, the Latin translator of the *Meno* and *Phaedo* of Plato, as a king whose equal in culture cannot be found.[103] His philosophic mind, catholic tastes, and patronage of scholars are praised also by Eugene the Emir, a learned Saracen who translated the *Optics* of Ptolemy from Arabic into Latin.[104] William II's knowledge of letters is vouched for by Peter of Blois, who had been one of the king's teachers. According to this authority, although William had learned the rudiments of composition and verse-making, he was not so good a scholar as Henry II of England, being more inclined to courtly amusements than to study.[105] He was not so much interested in higher learning as his father had been, but even so he was able to read and write Arabic.[106] Tancred (1190–1194) was as literate as his predecessors.

While he was still count of Lecce he seems to have signed his documents with his own hand;[107] and Peter of Ebulo tells us expressly that Tancred learned Greek letters during his enforced stay at the Byzantine court.[108]

Among the upper classes of the laity a knowledge of letters seems to have been rather widely diffused in Sicily. In his researches into the documents of the Sicilian court, Kehr found that the following men made their subscriptions by personal signatures: Admiral Majo; his brother, Admiral Stephen, the victor of Negroponte, and Stephen's fellow officer, Salernus; Count William of Marsico; a count Simon; and the vice-chancellor, Matthew.[109] Some of these men had probably received clerical training, as had Matthew, and perhaps also Majo, who was the author of a commentary on the Lord's Prayer, but many had probably learned letters with no professional end in view. Kehr says that where laymen have subscribed *manu propria,* their signatures are seldom made in neat minuscules, but are generally in large but awkward characters, indicative of hands more accustomed to the sword than to the pen.[110]

Notes to Chapter III

[1] R. L. Poole, *Illustrations of the History of Medieval Thought and Learning* (2d ed.; London, 1920), 71–72.

See the remarks of Rather of Verona, *Synodica ad presbyteros et ordines caeteros,* chap. 13 (Migne, *PL,* 136, 564; in Rather's *Opera,* ed. Petrus et Hieronymus fratres Ballerini, Verona, 1765, 419): "De ordinandis pro certo scitote, quod a nobis nullo modo promovebuntur, nisi [1] aut in civitate nostra, [2] aut in aliquo monasterio, [3] vel apud quemlibet sapientem ad tempus conservati fuerint, et litteris aliquantulum eruditi, ut idonei videantur ecclesiasticae dignitati." Cf. Giesebrecht, *De litt. studiis . . .,* 14.

[2] *Vita Guilelmi,* chap. 14; Migne, *PL,* 142, 709.

[3] Chap. 122 (*MGH. SS.,* III, 534).

[4] He says (*De litt. studiis . . .,* 15–16): "Philosophia enim, utpote rerum humanarum scientia, illa aetate plerumque opponitur theologiae, et philosophi sive sapientes nominantur ii, qui philosophiam, i. e. artes liberales docent." In support of this statement, Giesebrecht cites the following evidence: (1) Henricus Septimellensis, who at the end of the twelfth century, following the example of Boethius, wrote an *Elegia de diversitate fortunae et philosophiae consolatione,* in which he pictures Philosophy with the seven liberal arts in her retinue:

"Hanc phronesin dictam septena cohors comitatur,
Praebuit officium cuilibet illa suum."

(from Leyseri, *Historia poetarum et poematum medii aevi,* 476); (2) Richer, to whom *philosophia* has a somewhat wider significance, embracing all studies, both human and divine (*MGH. SS.,* III, 620), and to whom *sapientes* and *scholasticus* have the same meaning; (3) Thietmar, who uses the terms *philosophus* and *scholarum magister* interchangeably (*ibid.,* 833, 847); (4) Peter Damiani, who uses the phrase "grandiloqua tumentium philosophorum gymnasia" (*Opera omnia,* III, 111).

[5] *MGH. SS.,* III, 534, n.

[6] *Antapodosis,* V, 21 (*MGH. SS.,* III, 333): "Cumque dies adveniret optata, cunctis de palatio iuxta morem egressis, Stephanus et Constantinus facta congressione super patrem irruunt, eumque de palatio civibus ignorantibus deponunt, et ad vincinam insulam, in qua coenobitarum multitudo phylosophabatur, tonso ei, ut moris est, capite, phylosophandum transmittunt."

[7] G. Waitz (*MGH. SS.,* III, 919) defines *phylosophus* as *scholasticus magister scholarum, monachus doctus.*

[8] See Giesebrecht, *op. cit.,* 16 and nn. 2 and 3, for this and for the following examples; and cf. H. O. Taylor, *The Medieval Mind,* I, 251.

[9] See F. J. Raby, *History of Christian-Latin Poetry* (Oxford, Clarendon Press, 1927), 251.

[10] "Doctor doctorum, schema magistrorum, dogma poetarum" (see Fabricius, *Bibl. med. et inf. latin.,* under *Burgundius*).

¹¹ L. Muratori, *Antiquitates Italicae medii aevi* (Milan, 1738–1742), III, 726, 727.

¹² Giesebrecht (*op. cit.*, 17) has compiled a long list of references to both *presbyteri magistri* and simple *magistri*.

¹³ R. Davidsohn, *Geschichte von Florenz* (Berlin, 1896 ff.), I, 807.

¹⁴ Giesebrecht (*op. cit.*, 17) cites from Affò, *Storia di Parma*, II, 338, a certain "Ingo acolitus et magister scolarum" (eleventh century).

¹⁵ See Rather of Verona, *Praeloq.*, I, xvi: Migne, *PL*, 136, 178 (*Opera*, 39): "multi enim lucri ambitu, tegenda silentio vendunt loquendo." Cf. Giesebrecht, *op. cit.*, 17 and n. 3.

¹⁶ H. O. Taylor, *The Medieval Mind*, I, 251, and the remarks of H. Niese, in his article, "Zur Geschichte des geistigen Lebens am Hofe Kaiser Friedrichs II," *HZ* (= *Historische Zeitschrift*, Munich), 108 (1912), 479–480.

¹⁷ See Peter the Deacon, *De viris illustribus Casinensibus*, chap. 19: Muratori, *SS. rer. Ital.*, VI, 34; cf. Giesebrecht, *De litt. studiis* . . . , 39.

¹⁸ See esp. Redlich, *Urkundenlehre* . . . , 16, 21. By the thirteenth century the notaries in many of the towns were organized into guilds (*ibid.*, 223).

¹⁹ *Ibid.*, 216: "Auf den dalmatischen Inseln, dem Zufluchtsort der Romanen bei der Eroberung der Kroaten im 7. Jahrhundert, erhielt sich spätrömisches Urkunden- und Schreiberwesen in Nachwirkungen bis ins 12. Jahrhundert. Hier finden wir Laien als Schrieber, gleich den alten *tabelliones*."

²⁰ Damiani, *Opusc.*, XLII, 5: Migne, *PL*, 145, 671 (*Opera*, III, 697): "Dicam quod mihi Guarimpotus [*sic*] senex, vir videlicet honestissimus, apprime litteris eruditus ac medicus, retulit."

²¹ See esp. his statements (*op. cit.*, 18 and 19): "Iam vero inde a saeculo decimo manifesta extant testimonia, his studiis [sc. liberalibus] non modo clericos, sed etiam *maiorem partem* laicorum, qui nobili loco nati erunt, vacasse," and ". . . constat, iam ex longo tempore *in morem* abiisse, ut nobiles iuvenes doctorum scholas peterent."

²² *Kultur- und Sittengeschichte der italienischen Geistlichkeit im 10. und 11. Jahrhundert* (Breslau, 1890), 373–377.

²³ Cf., e.g., Wattenbach, *DGQ* (5th ed.; Berlin, 1885–1886), I, 293; Neukirch, *Damiani*, 6; Vogel, *Damiani*, 5.

²⁴ Cf. Dresdner, *op. cit.*, 214 [i.e., a discussion of medicine in the tenth and eleventh centuries and its relations to the liberal arts]. This connection, moreover, explains the following remark of Damiani: "Guarimpotus senex, vir videlicet honestissimus, apprime litteris eruditus ac medicus." *Opusc.*, XLII, 5 (*Opera*, III, 697).

²⁵ The existence of a professional class of learned men is also sufficient to explain two passages in Rather (*De contemptu canonum*, I, 22, and *Praeloq.*, I, 32: *Opera*, 362, 39) which speak of learned laymen.

²⁶ I am at a loss for an explanation of how Giesebrecht (19) was able to draw from this passage the conclusion: "iam ex longo tempore in Italia in morem abiisse, ut nobiles iuvenes doctorum scholas peterent." Giesebrecht's conclusion proves absolutely nothing if it is supposed to refer to ecclesiastics; if it aspires to a general validity, it is incorrect.

[27] That Lanfranc receives a legal and general liberal education in the first place is nothing striking: he becomes a scholar [i.e., a professionally learned man].

[28] Which both Giesebrecht and Ozanam have admitted.

[29] Unless the phrase "ad suae morem patriae" refers in the final analysis to something entirely different, namely, to the connection customary in Italy between the *artes liberales* and the study of jurisprudence.

[30] The fact that Benzo, II, 3 (*SS.*, XI, 613), very pompously calls Nicholas, the *magister sacri palatii*, "adornatus praeciosissimis gemmis phylosophorum," means very little, especially since the phrase does not refer to a knowledge of the Greek language. Cf. note 52 below.

[31] On p. 176 Dresdner says: "Indeed, attending school was probably regarded outright as a distinguishing mark of the ecclesiastical class, so that the entrance of the abbot Peter (d. 1007) of Monte Caprario near Perugia into this class is reported simply by saying that against the wishes of his parents he began to study the liberal arts." See *Vita S. Petri Perus.*, chap. 1: Mabillon, VI, 1, 761.

[32] It is necessary to go back into the eighth century for such evidence: Romuald (d. 787), the son of the prince of Benevento, was "grammati pollens, mundana lege togatus" (*MGH. SS.*, III, 483).

[33] Liutprand, *Antap.*, III, 22 (*MGH. SS.*, III, 316).

[34] *De cont. can.*, I, 22 (Migne, *PL*, 136, 511: *Opera*, 362).

[35] *Ibid.* (Migne, *PL*, 136, 512: *Opera*, 362–363).

[36] Cf. Giesebrecht's comment on this passage (*op. cit.*, 19, n. 1): "Quod de nobilibus maxime interpretandum esse videtur. Vulgus enim haud dubie litterarum plane erat imperitum."

[37] See *Hist. litt. de la France*, XII, 333; and Molinier, *Les sources* ..., II, 57–58, nos. 1199, 1202, 1203.

[38] In his official capacity as court chaplain, Wipo must have accompanied Conrad II to Italy at least in 1036, and, if he became Conrad's chaplain before 1026, then also in this year; cf. G. H. Pertz, "Ueber Wipo's Leben und Schriften," *Abhandlungen, Akademie der Wissenschaften* (Berlin, 1851), 215–216.

[39] Chap. 19 (*MGH. SS.*, XII, 206). The *Vita* was written after the abbot's death in 1091.

[40] Dresdner's interpretation would be more acceptable if the author had said, "cum esset laicus et igitur litterarum penitus ignarus," or, "cum esset laicus, coepit tamen cum illis ita agere verbis Latinis, ac si clericus fuisset et doctus inter grammaticos."

[41] We may accept this story with some confidence since, according to Carnaudet, the unknown author of the *Vita*, perhaps Bartholomew, third successor to Saint Nilus, was a contemporary of the saint. See *ibid.*, 260.

[42] Cf. also chap. 50 (*ibid.*, 996: *Opera*, II, 470): "Unde postea vir sanctus [i.e., Romualdus] totum psalterium, et nonnulla prophetarum cantica luculenter exposuit, et licet corrupta grammaticae regula, sanum tamen sensum ubique servavit."

⁴³ Mabillon, *AA. SS. ord. S. Bened.* (Venice ed.), Saec. VI, 1, 647; (Paris ed.), VI, 1, 761.

⁴⁴ See Pinius' prefatory remarks, *AA. SS.* (ed. novissima), July, III, 108, and 111, note c. The reader may, for example, compare the opening sentence of the version given by the Bollandists (quoted below) with the opening sentence of the version printed by Mabillon: "Temporibus Ottonis secundi Imperatoris, fuit quidam vir egregiae, venerabilisque vitae Petrus nomine ex Perusino Comitatu, ex Agelione videlicet pago, qui sex fere millibus distat a Perusina civitate, ex nobili Vintioliorum familia ortus, Dei per omnia plenus gratia, qui a primaevo suae aetatis tempore, justitiae callem ingrediens Deo devotum pectus gerebat; quique, etc." These words certainly give the impression of a greater distance in time between writer and event than do the words of the Bollandists' *Vita.*

⁴⁵ Pinius says of the *Vita* which he published (*AA. SS.*, July, III, 109–110): "Atque haec quidem, non nisi remote et oblique ad S. Petrum, proxime vero ac directe ad monasterium pertinentia, cujus ipse primus Auctor ac moderator extitit, visum nobis est non negligere hoc loco, sed typis committere, ne vel in illis, in satis mediocri rebus ejus gestis ad posteritatem transmissis monumentis, minus recte meriti de ipso alicui videamur."

I give but one example of the author's disregard for accurate historical details (110): "Petrus abbas, Imperatorem [sc. Ottonem] adiit (quisquis ille fuerit sive II, sive III, hujus nominis, hoc parum refert)."

⁴⁶ First edited by Valesius, Paris, 1663; in the *MGH. SS.*, IV, 189–210. The best edition is Dümmler's, under the title *Gesta Berengarii imperatoris. Beiträge zur Geschichte Italiens im Anfang des 10. Jahrhunderts* (Halle, 1871), which was not available. Cf. Wattenbach, *DGQ* (6th ed.), I, 311, n. 3.

⁴⁷ *MGH. SS.*, IV, 191.

⁴⁸ Wattenbach, *DGQ* (6th ed.), I, 312.

⁴⁹ See the remarks of Suyskenus in *AA. SS.* (ed. novissima), Sept., III, 147–148.

⁵⁰ Chap. 2, *ibid.*, 161.

⁵¹ F. Neukirch, *Das Leben des Petrus Damiani* (Göttingen diss., 1875), 6–7.

⁵² I would draw attention here to a passage in Benzo, *Ad Heinricum IV Imperatorem*, II, 3 (*MGH. SS.*, XI, 613, 44), which mentions a certain Nicholas, *magister sacri palatii* (at Rome), who was "adornatus *praec*iosissimis gemmis phylosophorum," and not "*graec*iosissimis" as Dresdner writes it (375, n. 2). The passage therefore does not refer to a knowledge of the Greek tongue; and it means very little with respect to knowledge of Latin, since this Nicholas was probably a professonal in the first place.

⁵³ According to Otto of Freising (*Gesta Friderici*, II, 13: *MGH. SS.*, XX, 397), liberal studies in Italy were open even to those of the "mechanical arts": " . . . inferioris conditionis iuvenes vel quoslibet contemptibilium etiam mechanicarum artium opifices," etc.

⁵⁴ *The Medieval Mind*, I, 249.

⁵⁵ Cf. Rather, *Praeloq.*, I, xvi (Migne, *PL*, 136, 178: *Opera*, 39).

[56] See the *Vita Athanasii* (bishop of Naples and son of Sergius, d. 872), *MGH. SS. rer. Langob.*, 441: "Cum autem ad virilem pervenisset aetatem, litteris tam Graecis quam Latinis faborabiliter eruditus est, ita ut, si casum librum Graecis exaratum elementis in manibus sumeret, Latine hunc inoffense cursimque legeret et Latinos libros Greco expedite sermone rimaret."

[57] Johannis, *Gesta episcoporum Neapolitanorum* (*MGH. SS. rer. Langob.*, 434): "Dedit etiam in eiusdem episcopii bibliothecam tres Flavii Iosepi codices." Cf. E. A. Lowe, *The Beneventan Script: A History of the South Italian Minuscule* (Oxford, 1914), 54 and n. 6; Lowe suggests that the MSS were probably Latin translations.

[58] See the *Gesta episc. Neapol.* (*MGH. SS. rer. Langob.*), 433–434.

[59] *Vita Athanasii, loc. cit.:* " ... vir per omnia strenuus ut genitor et in Greco Latinaque lingua peritissimus." Lowe (*op. cit.*, 54, n. 5) evidently misunderstood the passage just quoted, and therefore incorrectly took Gregory to be the father of Duke Sergius. Their relationship, however, was just the opposite; cf. *Gesta episc. Neapol.*, 434.

[60] Lowe, *op. cit.*, 55. The evidence for these statements is taken from a MS (Bamberg E III 14, fol. 193) first published by Waitz in Pertz's *Archiv*, IX (1847), 692; reprinted by Lowe, *op. cit.*, 82–83, and by B. Capasso, *Monumenta ad Neapolitani Ducatus historiam*, I, 339–340. See also O. Hartwig, "Die Uebersetzungsliteratur Unteritaliens in der normannisch-staufischen Epoche," *Zentralbl. f. Bibliothekswesen*, III (1886), 164; Manitius, *Gesch. d. latein. Lit. des Mittelalters*, I, 529–531.

[61] *Chronicon Salernitanum*, 122: *MGH. SS.*, III, 534. See above, Chap. II.

[62] See the *Vita S. Odonis* (Migne, *PL*, 133, 43); and cf. E. Sackur, *Die Cluniacenser in ihrer kirchlichen u. allgemeingeschichtlichen Wirksamkeit bis zur Mitte des elften Jahrhunderts* (Halle, 1892–1894), I, 112 and n. 2.

[63] V. Rose, *Hermes*, VIII (1874), 46; Hartwig, *op. cit.*, 223; F. Tocco, *L'eresia nel medio evo* (Florence, 1884), 387; Salvioli, *L'instruzione pubblica in Italia nei primi secoli del medio evo* (Florence, 1895), n. 87.

[64] *De litt. studiis ...*, 39. See Peter the Deacon, *De viris illustribus*, chap. 19 (Muratori, *SS. rer. Ital.*, VI, 34–35).

[65] *Die Kreuzzugsbriefe aus den Jahren 1088–1100* (Innsbruck, 1901), 310, n. 16.

[66] *Bohemond I, Prince of Antioch* (Princeton, 1924), 7.

[67] *Op. cit.*, 156.

[68] This opinion, first expressed by Bongars, who discovered the text of the *Gesta* in the sixteenth century, was reasserted by Sybel in 1841 and is now generally accepted. See Molinier, *Les sources ...*, II, 280–281, no. 2115; Thurot, *Revue historique* (1876), I, 67–77; Hagenmeyer, *Forschungen*, XIV, 155–175, and his *Anonymi gesta Francorum et aliorum Hierosolymitanorum* (1890); Beatrice A. Lees, *Anonymi gesta* (Oxford, 1924); and Bréhier, *Histoire anonyme de la première croisade* ("Les classiques de l'histoire de France en moyen âge"; Paris, 1924), pp. ii–iii.

[69] Redlich, *op. cit.*, 213: "Die Signa waren ja ohnedies regelmässig vom Schreiber gemacht worden, wenn jetzt die Beweiskraft auf den Notar allein

überging, bedurfte es überkaupt keiner Unterschriften oder Handzeichen von Aussteller und Zeugen."

[70] Redlich, *op. cit.*, 25.

[71] The document is published by G. Marini; *I papiri diplomatici* (Rome, 1805), 157 f., no. 100. I have omitted the names of ecclesiastics and notaries and avoided needless repetition.

[72] The abbreviation *lra n* probably stands for *litteras nesciens* or *nescientis;* cf. Marini, 321, n. 3 to no. 100.

[73] *History of the City of Rome in the Middle Ages*, III, 258 and n. 2.

[74] Muratori, *Antiquitates* . . . , II, 780.

[75] *Op. cit.*, 37 ff.

[76] When Muratori published this volume of the *Antiquitates* in 1739, the original was still preserved at Reggio by the nuns of Santo Tommaso.

[77] Of educated Italian women of the tenth century, the Lady Imiza, with whom Gerbert corresponded, seems to have been a rare example. See *Epistolae Gerberti*, ed. Havet (Paris, 1889), nos. 4 and 22. She probably dwelt at Pavia, since she was a close friend of Pope John XIV, former bishop of Pavia.

[78] See the passage from the *Vita Mathildis* published by Muratori (*SS. rer. Ital.*, V, 392): "Teutonicam, Francigenam, et Lombardicam optime novit linguam," and Donizo's lines in his *Life of Mathilda* (II, 42–43: *MGH. SS.*, XII, 380):

> "scit Theutonicam bene linguam,
> Haec loquitur laetam quin Francigenamque loquaelam."

[79] *Vita Mathildis* (Muratori, *SS. rer. Ital.*, V, 396): "Fuit etiam scientiarum studio dicata, et liberalium artium grandis bibliotheca sibi non defuit." Donizo's *Vita*, II, 20, ss. 1364 ff. (*MGH. SS.*, XII, 405):

> "Tempore nocturno studiosius atque diurno
> Est sacris psalmis ac officiis venerandis
> Relligione pia satis haec intenta perita.
> . . . .
> Nullus ea presul studiosior invenietur,
> Copia librorum non defuit huicve bonorum;
> Libros ex cunctis habet in artibus figuris."

[80] *Mathilda of Tuscany: la Gran Donna d'Italia* (London, 1909), 6–7; cf. also 78–79.

[81] An excellent photographic facsimile of a document of the year 1106 is given by F. Steffens, in his *Lateinische Paläographie*, no. 64 in the first edition, no. 87 in the second. Cf. A. Overmann, *Gräfin Mathilde von Tuscien* (Innsbruck, 1895), 215–216.

[82] The scribe's subscription is given by Overmann, *op. cit.*, 216: "Ego rogante vice ejus scripsi quia scriber nesciebat."

[83] *Ibid.*, 214–215.

[84] Romuald, *Annales*, ad a. 1177 (*MGH. SS.*, XIX, 453, 47): ". . . imperator, deposito pallio, de suo faldestolio surgens, cepit in lingua Teotonica concionari, Christiano cancellario verba sua vulgariter [i.e., according to the editor, W. Arndt, *italice*] exponente."

[85] Rahewin reports (*Gesta Friderici*, IV, 3: *MGH. SS.*, XX, 445, 42) that at Roncaglia, in 1158, Frederick spoke "per interpretem," and he means probably an Italian rather than a Latin interpreter.

[86] *Op. cit.*, IV, 535 n.

[87] See Rahewin's account of the congratulations offered to Frederick Barbarossa after his speech of November 14, 1158, at Roncaglia (*Gesta Friderici*, IV, 4: *MGH. SS.*, XX, 446, 19): "surgentesque unus post unum, sicut eius gentis mos est, seu ut principi suum quisque manifestaret affectum et propensiorem circa eum devotionem, *seu ut suam in dicendo peritiam, qua gloriari solent, declararet,*" etc.

[88] *Annales*, ad a. 1177 (*MGH. SS.*, XIX, 453, 9).

[89] See H. Niese, *HZ*, 108 (1912), 479, and Davidsohn, *op. cit.*, I, 807, who says: "in anderer Art wäre es denn aucht nicht erklärlich, wie von ihnen kaufmännische Unternehmungen in weiter Ferne hätten ausgehen können, was durchaus ein gewisses Masz an Kenntnissen zur Voraussetzung hatte." Cf. also H. Pirenne, *Ann. d'hist. écon. et sociale*, I, 14 and n. 2.

[90] *Nouveaux mélanges d'archéologie, d'histoire et de littérature sur le moyen âge. Bibliothèques* (Paris, 1877), 96, n. 4. Cahier cites as reference Valery, *Voyages en Italie . . .*, IX, p. i, which is not available.

[91] See esp. B. Schmeidler, *Italienische Geschichtsschreiber des XII. und XIII. Jahrhunderts: ein Beitrag zur Kulturgeschichte* (Leipzig, 1900), 12–13, 35, 38 f.; but also Giesebrecht, "Zur mailandischen Geschichtsschreibung im zwölften und dreizehnten Jahrhundert," *Forschungen zur deutschen Geschichte*, XXI (1881), 299–339, especially 301, and Wattenbach, *DGQ*, II, 323.

[92] See the edition by F. Güterbock, *MGH. SS.*, n. s., VII.

[93] Schmeidler, *op. cit.*, 24.

[94] *MGH. SS.*, XXII, 105.

[95] *Ibid.*, 21.

[96] See Schmeidler, *op. cit.*, 24–25.

[97] The most important references may be found in Dresdner's oft-mentioned work, especially 175 ff. An illuminating example, omitted by Dresdner, is found in the poignant observation of Atto, cardinal of the title of St. Mark, writing to the canons of his church in the time of Gregory VII (A. Mai, *Scriptorum veterum nova collectio*, VI, 2, 60): "Scio dilectissimi fratres, quod duae causae sunt ignorantiae vestrae: una quod aegritudo loci extraneos qui vos doceant hic habitare non sinit, alia quod paupertas vos ad extranea loca ad discendum non permittit abire: quibus compellentibus causis factum est ut paenitentiale romanum apocrythum fingeretur, et rusticano stilo; ut illi qui authenticos canones nesciunt, et litteras non intelligunt, in his fabulis confidant; atque tali confidentia sacerdotium, quod eos non decet, arripiant; et caeci duces cum sequacibus suis cadant in foveam."

[98] *Studies in the History of Mediaeval Science* (Cambridge, 1924), 190.

[99] Cf. E. Caspar, *Roger II (1101–1154) und die Gründung der normannisch-sicilianischen Monarchie* (Innsbruck, 1904), 38.

[100] See K. A. Kehr, *Die Urkunden der normannisch-sicilischen Könige* (Innsbruck, 1902), 177 and nn. 1 and 2; and cf. Caspar, *op. cit.*, 38 and n. 1.

[101] Cf. E. Curtis, *Roger of Sicily and the Normans in Lower Italy* (New York, 1912), 310–311, and the statement of Caspar, *op. cit.*, 38: "Aus der Geistesrichtung und Bildung, die Rober später als König an den Tage legte, geht klar hervor, dass arabische Einflüsse bei seiner Erziehung sehr wesentlich beteiligt waren." Cf. Gregorovius, *Siciliana* (London, 1914), 157.

[102] Cf. Caspar, *op. cit.*, 443–444, and W. Cohn, *Das Zeitalter der Normannen in Sizilien* (Bonn, 1920), 94.

[103] See the prologue to the *Phaedo* tr. in *Hermes*, I (1866), 386–389; and cf. Haskins, *Studies . . .* , 165–166.

[104] See Eugene's eulogy of the king in the *Byzantinische Zeitschrift*, XI (1902), 451; cf. Haskins, *op. cit.*, 142–143.

[105] See Peter's letter to Walter, the archbishop of Palermo, *Epist.*, 66 (Migne, *PL*, 207, 198): "Nam cum rex vester bene litteras noverit, rex noster longe litteratior est. Ego enim in litterali scientia facultates utriusque cognovi. Scitis, quod dominus rex Siciliae per annum discipulus meus fuit, et qui a vobis versificatoriae atque litteratoriae artis primitias habuerat, per industriam et sollicitudinem meam beneficium scientiae plenioris obtinuit. Quam cito autem egressus sum regnum, ipse libris abjectis ad otium se contulit palatinum."

[106] See Hartwig, *op. cit.*, III, 178.

[107] Kehr, *op. cit.*, 176, n. 4.

[108] "Exul quam didicit, littera graeca fuit." Quoted by Kehr, *op. cit.*, 176, n. 4, from the edition of Peter's works by E. Hinkelmann (Leipzig, 1874).

[109] *Op. cit.*, 180.

[110] *Ibid.*

Chapter IV

GERMANY (FROM *ca.* 900 TO *ca.* 1300)

IN GERMANY the darkest period in the history of lay learning followed the death of Charles the Fat (887), the last of the direct and legitimate heirs of Charlemagne east of the Rhine. If Arnulf of Carinthia, the successor of Charles the Fat, had any intellectual interests, it is hard to discern them. The sources tell us nothing except that he once took a Gospel MS from the library at Fulda which he later restored at the urgent entreaty of Abbot Huggi.[1] His son, Ludwig the Child, probably received some sort of instruction from Adalbero, bishop of Augsburg.[2] Conrad I also may have been able to read or at least understand Latin, for Arnold of St. Emmeran tells a story about him similar to the one about Arnulf, how Conrad took from the monastery at Regensburg a beautiful Gospel MS (a gift from King Arnulf), and was induced to return it by a sickness which the patron saint visited upon him.[3]

Whether Arnulf, Conrad I, or Henry I should receive the unenviable distinction of being the first German king who was unable to read and write, we cannot say with certainty. Henry I, like the rest of the lay members of the Liudolfinger family, seems to have been quite illiterate.[4] His wife, Mathilda, however, was exceptionally well educated. The oldest biography of the queen says that she had been sent to the monastery of Herford not to become a nun, but to be educated.[5] Although Widukind, on the contrary, says she learned letters after her husband's death, nevertheless her interest in learning is revealed in another statement of his, that she "instructed all the servants and maids of her household in various arts, and also in letters."[6] A picture which one of Mathilda's pious biographers has drawn of her is worth repeating here: "When the glorious queen learned from the letter that her beloved son [Duke Henry of Bavaria, d. 955] had departed this life, a pallor appeared on her face and a cold tremor ran through all her limbs, and she buried her face in the book which she was holding in her hands."[7] The same author tells us that she often visited the school for nuns at her own foundation in Nordhausen, in order to supervise personally the studies of the inmates.[8]

Otto the Great apparently did not learn to read and write in his youth, but, according to Widukind, after the death of Queen Edith in 946, he set to studying, and was so successful that he was able to read and understand books with ease.[9] This interest in letters, however, was probably not acquired until after his marriage to Adelheid in 951; for at a synod held in Ingelheim in 948, the papal letters had to be translated into German for the benefit of the two kings present, Otto I and Louis IV, d'Outre-mer,[10] of France. Notwithstanding Widukind's statement, Otto I seems never to have become very proficient in Latin. In the *Casus S. Galli* Ekkehard tells how Otto II translated a Latin letter into the Saxon vernacular for his father's benefit.[11] Although he could speak both French and Slavic as well as his native Saxon,[12] Otto I was unable to speak Latin. His speech to the Romans in 962 at the council which deposed John XII, was translated from German into Latin by Liutprand of Cremona.[13] The cultural interests of the empress Adelheid are revealed in her friendship and correspondence with the learned Gerbert.[14] Ekkehard tells how one day she came upon Otto II as he was reading a tirade of Ekkehard's against Sandrati, a monk of St. Maximin, and found him so dissolved in laughter that she asked the reason why. In answer he handed her the tract and begged her to read for herself, for "she was very learned in letters."[15] We may well believe that she was a diligent and serious reader.[16]

The education of Otto II seems to have been entrusted chiefly to Volcold, a cleric, afterwards bishop of Meissen.[17] Ekkehard II, Palatinus, and Bruno of Cologne are also named as his teachers,[18] but these notices probably deserve little credence.[19] Richer boasts of Otto that he was a man of great talents and so distinguished in the liberal arts that he could use with skill the principles of formal logic, and formulate his own opinions about the merits of philosophical discussions.[20] The early German kings seem to have had an inveterate habit of borrowing books, for Otto II, like his predecessors Arnulf and Conrad I, is charged with removing books from the library at St. Gall, some of which he later returned at the request of Ekkehard.[21] Theophano, the Byzantine princess whom Otto married, was a very cultivated woman, as we might expect.[22] She brought with her to Germany the learned John of Calabria, who later taught Greek to her son, Otto III; and she herself is said to have assisted in his education.[23] It is probable that he even

advanced beyond the trivium, for the book which Bernward of
Hildesheim, another of his teachers, used for his instruction in
arithmetic is still preserved at Hildesheim.[24] He was regarded as
a veritable philosopher.[25]

Later, Otto III himself called to his court the great Gerbert, whose student
he wished to be regarded. He so far surpassed his contemporaries in learning
that flatterers called him one of the wonders of the world. In Otto III the
inclination to studies was so strong that his duties as ruler suffered in conse-
quence. It would seem further that a court school was again inaugurated at
the court of Otto III, for, according to Gerbert, many scholars gathered there.[26]

Henry II, last of the Saxon emperors, having been destined in
his youth to an ecclesiastical career, naturally received a liberal
education, first at Hildesheim, and later under Bishop Wolfgang
at Regensburg.[27] There is abundant evidence to show that Henry II
could read Latin with ease;[28] and as a book collector he has a distinguished reputation. When he founded his favorite see, the bishopric
of Bamberg, he endowed the cathedral with a magnificent library.
The nucleus of this collection was the books which he inherited
from Otto III,[29] supplemented by the books which Henry had received from his teacher.[30] The most notable MSS, however, which
the emperor gave to Bamberg were from Italy, for in 1022, when
on his campaign into Lower Italy, Henry II acquired a remarkable
collection.[31] Although a dignified and learned ruler, Henry II loved
to play practical jokes upon members of his entourage, especially
if he could ridicule their ignorance. Two of these jokes, it is related,
were played upon Bishop Meinwerk of Paderborn. In one the king
changed the words "famulis et famulabus" in the missal which the
bishop used in public worship to "mulis et mulabus," and roared
with laughter when Meinwerk inadvertently so read the service.
Equally pertinent is the other prank he played upon Meinwerk,
which is related in the following chapter. "Miratus autem imperator multiplicem episcopi erga cultum Dei devotionem, experiri
proposuit, si sinceriter ex Deo esset, eius intentionem; et ascitis
notariis scribi fecit litteris aureis in scedulis : *'Meinwerce episcope,
dispone domui tuae; morieris enim quinta die.'* " When the paper
was dropped down on the bishop through the ceiling, as he was sitting at table, he naturally regarded it as the death summons from
on high; but after a momentary fright he recovered his senses and
made ready for his death as befitted a true man of God.[32]

Kunigunde, the wife of Henry II, could read Latin, and, if our
authority is to be trusted, was also able to write. The *Vita S. Cunegundis* says[33] that she was always to be seen either reading or listen-
ing to someone else read, and that she herself instructed her niece,
Uta, the first abbess of Kaufungen, Kunigunde's own foundation,
in profane letters. The author of the *Vita* even included a letter to
the nuns of Kaufungen which the queen is supposed actually to
have written herself.[34] It is impossible, however, to credit this statement. Aside from the fact that the testimony is very late, at this
early date the Danish court could have offered no opportunity for
such an education. Steindorff merely says that Kunigunde was frail
of body and somewhat "simple" in character.[35]

Two generations later, cultural conditions in Denmark had
changed from those in the time of Canute the Great. King Svend
Estridsen of Denmark (1047–1076), from whom the historian
Adam of Bremen learned much pertaining to the history of the
Norse peoples, was possessed of extraordinary learning for a layman; so much, in fact, that he won the commendation of Pope Gregory VII.[36]

In summary, of the five kings of the Saxon house only one, Henry
I, seems to have been entirely illiterate. Otto the Great made a
creditable but belated attempt to acquire the rudiments of the
language of learning, and his successors, Otto II, Otto III, and
Henry II, had a very good knowledge of Latin. What can we say
of the rest of the German laity, that is, of the upper classes, since
the illiteracy of the masses can be taken for granted?

Gerdes believes that in general there was but little formal training for laymen in Germany.

Nevertheless [he continues], there are numerous indications that among the
upper classes a liberal education was more common than is generally supposed. During the first part of the Middle Ages conditions in this respect seem
to have been better under the kings of the Saxon house than in the centuries
following, in which the nobility devoted itself exclusively to the service of
arms. This was due, in part, to the fact that the customs and the traditions of
Carolingian times still exerted some influence; in part, to the fact that the
cultural awakening of the tenth century made itself felt also among the laity.[37]

He sees an indication of rather widespread lay education and culture in the fact that "in addition to the Latin literature which was
intended for ecclesiastics, the tenth century produced also a litera-

ture which was popular in nature and which directed itself exclusively to laymen," such as the *Modus Ottinc,* glorifying the deeds of Otto I, the *Modus Liebnic,* and the *Mendosa Cantilena.*[38] Many of these poems seem to have been written for laymen because of the secular nature of their contents. Wattenbach thinks that in the days of Otto the Great, under the influence of the emperor's brother, Bruno of Cologne,

> a court school was again called into existence, as in the days of Charlemagne, even though it differed in some respects because there were now better facilities for obtaining the elements of an education in many other places. But those sons of noble lineage who were still sent to the court after the manner of old, were hardly left without any instruction whatsoever.[39]

We must be careful, however, not to read too much into the evidence. Wattenbach himself admits that we cannot assume the existence of a permanent and regular educational organization.[40] Dümmler flatly denies that there was anything comparable to the Carolingian court school at the court of Otto the Great;[41] and Kleinclausz objects to the exaggerated picture of the so-called "Ottonian Renaissance" which is drawn by certain German historians, especially Giesebrecht and Lamprecht,[42] and reminds us that Otto I, and even Otto II, were men of war rather than patrons of letters.[43] Specht, on the other hand, insists that under the Ottos, as in the days of Charlemagne, "it again became customary for the children of the nobility to learn Latin and the art of reading, and it was almost regarded as a disgrace if a nobleman was unable to understand and apply the books of law."[44] He bases his contention in the first place on the characterization of Herimann, bishop of Toul (d. 1026), in the *Gesta episcoporum Tullensis:* "domnus Herimannus, nobili Agrippinensium gener procreatus, litterarum studiis, *ut decet nobilibus,* adprime eruditus."[45] Since the *Gesta,* however, seem to have been written early in the twelfth century,[46] it is probable that these words are more applicable to conditions in that period than to the days of the Ottos. Specht also cites as evidence the well-known complaint of old Count Udalrich of Ebersberg (d. 1029) concerning the neglect of the study of law among the noble youth of his day. Formerly, he says, things were very different. The early German noblemen were able to read the laws of their kings, and even his own generation considered it disgraceful not to be able to do so, but now the modern generation neglects the legal instruction of its sons, with regrettable consequences.[47] Since the chronicle referred to is contemporary and fairly trustworthy, written probably shortly after 1048,[48] Udalrich's words deserve consideration. Naturally, they do not mean that all the old count's contemporaries could read Latin; the large amount of literature written in the vernacular, and especially the numerous translations from Latin into German, indicate that Latin was an unknown tongue to many German laymen.[49] The most important implication in Udalrich's remarks is that illiteracy seems to have increased in the late tenth and early eleventh centuries in Germany. This may very well have been true as a general rule, but there were exceptions which deserve brief consideration.

It probably happened occasionally that boys who acquired a liberal education because they intended to become ecclesiastics, for one reason or another never entered the Church. Certainly a number of learned laymen in the Middle Ages were noted for their piety and religious zeal as well as for their wisdom. Such a layman was Duke Wenzilaus of Bohemia (d. 939), famous for his goodness and piety, who went to Budec to learn letters.[50] Another learned layman, a contemporary of Udalrich, was Count Henry of Stade (d. 1016), the founder of Rosenfeld; he, too, was well educated, and so zealous a Christian, besides, that he thrice dedicated himself to the service of the Virgin, each time having to redeem his vow by the gift of books and ornaments to the Church.[51] Count Ansfrid, a powerful magnate of Erisia (d. 1010), who later in life was made bishop of Utrecht, "was of so studious a nature that he was taunted by some senseless fellows with leading the life of a monk."[52] His case is doubly interesting because it shows the existence among the laity of a group who considered studious pursuits to be unbefitting a man of the world. Ekkehard of St. Gall records that there were "day" students in the school there who received instruction for the purpose of qualifying themselves to handle their property, and who were without thought of becoming clerics.[53] Another educated layman of the late tenth and early eleventh centuries was Hugo, an Alsatian nobleman, the father of Leo IX. He is described by Wipert as "most fluent both in his native tongue and in Latin."[54] Helvide, the mother of Leo IX, was also, according to the same authority, skilled in both languages.[55]

Throughout the Middle Ages a knowledge of liturgical Latin

seems to have been more common among women than among men. Most often, however, their knowledge was probably elementary, and limited to a reading of the Psalms.[56] This is illustrated by a story concerning Mathilda, the sister of Burchard of Worms. When her brother asked her to become abbess of a nunnery which had recently lost its head, Mathilda objected, saying: "Do you forget, holy father, that I have lived all my life among those of the world, and that I know nothing about the duties of this office? Except for the Psalter, I am entirely ignorant of books."[57] However, we occasionally hear of noblewomen who had more than a rudimentary knowledge of Latin. Hedwig, the niece of Otto I and daughter of Duke Henry of Bavaria, passed her days after the death of her husband, Burchard of Bavaria, in reading the Latin poets with Ekkehard II of St. Gall. According to a highly improbable story, she is said to have been betrothed as a young girl to the emperor of Byzantium and to have been instructed in Greek by chamberlains whom that ruler sent to the West. She is also said to have taught Greek to her son, Burchard, and to have given him a copy of Horace.[58]

In sharp contrast both to the last rulers of the Saxon house and to his own successors, Conrad II, the first emperor of the Salian house, was wholly illiterate.[59] He did not even know the letters of the alphabet,[60] even though one of the foremost prelates of the realm, Burchard of Worms, was in charge of his education.[61] It is recorded of Conrad's wife, Gisela, that she had copies made of Notker's German translation of the Psalms and Job,[62] but whether or not she knew any Latin remains an unanswered question. At any rate, she saw to it that her son, Henry III, received an excellent education.[63] Bishop Bruno of Augsburg and, later, Egilbert of Freising supervised the training of the young prince, but the principal instructor seems to have been Almeric, a monk of Pavia, and future abbot of Farfa.[64] It is probable that Wipo, Conrad's chaplain, also had some part in Henry's education.[65] It is clear that Henry acquired not only a good knowledge of Latin but also genuine literary tastes. In the *Chronicon Novaliciense* Henry is described, in contrast to the illiterate Conrad II, as "well steeped in the knowledge of letters."[66] There is evidence of his patronage of letters and learning in the many works written for him or dedicated to him.[67] There has been preserved for us indirectly one of the emperor's orders for the copying of a number of books which he wanted.[68] Finally, the *Annales Augustenses* tell us that under Henry III's encouragement and patronage, learning, literature, and the arts flourished exceedingly.[69] One unfortunate aspect of Henry III's intellectual superiority over most of the laymen of his time was that it alienated him from the German nobility, who considered ability to read almost a disgrace.[70] Henry III's wife, Agnes of Poitou, the daughter of the cultured William V of Aquitaine, was undoubtedly a woman of education. We know that she was able to read;[71] and her patronage of letters and correspondence with learned men seem to indicate that her cultural interests were as broad as those of her husband.[72]

Henry IV received an education as good as that of his father and perhaps better. Ebbo, in his *Life of Otto of Bamberg*, tells us that "the emperor had been so well instructed that he was thoroughly able by himself to read and understand letters no matter from whom they had come."[73] Herbord, a later biographer of the same bishop, who was a favorite companion of Henry IV, goes even further and says that the emperor was so well educated that he could both read and write his own letters.[74] Since Herbord, however, doubtless used Ebbo's *Vita* as his source, we cannot accept without question his statement concerning Henry's ability to write.[75] As often as his affairs permitted, the emperor took time to chant or read the Psalms in the company of Otto, with the result that his Psalter became quite soiled and worn from use.[76] Ekkehard of Aura gives us a broader picture of the cultural life at Henry's court:

After the manner of his father, the emperor was desirous of attaching to himself clerics and especially those of great learning. These he provided for handsomely; and kept them at work, at times in chanting the Psalms, at times in reading or collating, or else in personally studying with himself the Scriptures and the liberal arts.[77]

Henry IV was indeed a learned king, whose reputation was known afar.[78]

It is a striking fact that history has left no definite information concerning the personality and character of Henry V.[79] Next to nothing is known about his education. Undoubtedly Henry V was less fortunate in his rearing than his father, a circumstance probably attributable to the disquieting and disturbing effects of the investiture struggle. The last of the Salian kings, however, was certainly not altogether without cultural interests, and it is probable that he had at least a fair knowledge of Latin. At his request Ekkehard of Aura wrote a history of the Frankish empire from the time of Charlemagne down to his own day, and sent the king a recension of his *Chronicon* with the following prefatory remark: "I pray that it may be found not unworthy, I shall not say of your imperial eyes, but at least of the readers at your court."[80] We cannot safely argue merely from this passage that Henry V was able to read Latin, but at least the mention of "readers" (*lectores*) at his court indicates the presence there of an educated group. Furthermore, in 1110 when Henry V was making ready to go to Italy, he took care to provide himself not only with men of arms, but also with men of learning, as was befitting an Emperor of the Romans.[81] Among the scholars who went with him was David the Scot, whom the emperor commissioned to write the official history of the campaign. We learn from Ekkehard that "David, therefore, upon the king's command, wrote the full story of this expedition and its events in three books, *in the simple style of the Gesta, which differs in almost no respect from ordinary speech; having in mind in this undertaking the interest of lay readers, and persons of moderate learning, whose minds could grasp these things.*"[82] It is a reasonable conjecture that the chief of the lay readers for whose benefit David wrote his account in "the highly simple style of the *Gesta*" was the emperor himself. It is also safe to assume that Ekkehard's plural is not mere rhetoric but refers to a fairly large group of German laymen in this period who were able to read and understand simple, straightforward Latin narrative.[83]

This highly significant passage from Ekkehard seems to have been entirely overlooked by the authorities. In discussions of the general state of lay culture and learning in Germany under the Salian kings, the stock reference is usually to Wipo's exhortation to Henry III in which he contrasts the cultural condition of Italy "where all the youths are sent to sweat in the schools" with that in Germany, where "people deem it useless and unseemly to instruct anyone who does not intend to become a cleric." He urges the young king to issue an edict that every rich man should have his sons instructed in letters and in law.[84] Wipo has doubtless exaggerated the state of affairs in both countries in order to drive home his point, but there is no reason to doubt the general implication of his statement that there was little learning or desire for learning among the German nobility of the early Salian period. Probably when parents resolved on an education for their son, most often the decision meant that the boy was destined for an ecclesiastical career. This is vividly illustrated in the *Life of Theodoric* (1007–1087), abbot of St. Hubert at Liège. Theodoric's mother, herself wholly ignorant of letters,[85] became convinced in a dream that her son was destined for the Church, and thereupon determined to have him educated, against the will of her husband, who was equally resolved that the boy should be a soldier and layman like himself.[86] The battle over the boy's future was long and grievous; as often as his mother secretly sent him to school, his father had him brought home again. In the end, since some evil always befell Theodoric when he was brought home, the mother won out, and he was educated to become a monk.[87]

It might also happen, however, as has been mentioned above, that a boy trained for an ecclesiastical career would for some reason fail to enter the Church. An example is afforded in Frederick II, count palatine of Saxony (d. 1088). His mother, Agnes of Weimar, was a woman of unusual culture, "who had been well educated at Quedlinburg, both in letters and in various arts, after the manner of the ancients."[88] She and her husband, Count Frederick I, had three sons, who were provided for as follows: Adalbert was to enter the Church, and was sent off to Halberstadt to become a canon (later he became archbishop of Bremen); Dedo was to succeed his father, and was therefore sent to win his spurs under King Henry III; and Frederick was sent to Fulda, evidently with the monastic life in view.[89] When Dedo died without heirs, however, young Frederick was recalled and made count palatine.[90] Count Frederick II, therefore, was extraordinarily well educated for a layman; his learning made a great impression on his contemporaries. According to our chronicler, "he had been so well educated at Fulda that he could, by himself, read and understand letters sent to him, and could even correct the chaplains when they made errors in the service."[91] The secular life apparently did not destroy his love of books. He acquired "a library composed of Gregory's *Moralia,* a passional, and not a few other valuable codices," the whole of which he ordered to be given to the church at Goseck in 1075, when he was held captive in Italy by Henry IV and despaired of his life.[92] The evidence at our disposal, however, does not permit us to regard Count Frederick as typical, but rather as a striking exception to the general rule of illiteracy. There were probably not many German noblemen of Henry IV's generation who could read Latin. The ordinary nobleman of higher rank doubtless kept a cleric at his court to take care of his correspondence, to translate the letters received, and to answer them.

In his *De bello Saxonico,* Bruno tells a fantastic tale of a certain Saxon nobleman of high rank (*quidam de familiaribus regis,* whose name he intentionally withholds) whom Henry IV wished to get rid of. The nobleman was sent, therefore, on a mission to the "king" of Russia, and at the same time a letter was dispatched posthaste to the Russian court asking the "king" to do away with the coming guest by any means he might see fit to use. By chance the letter fell into the hands of the intended victim, who "without delay broke the seal and ordered his cleric to disclose the contents to him."[93] Despite the incredibility of this story, which is a manifest calumny of Henry IV, there is no reason to doubt the cultural condition indicated in the reading of the letter. The same condition is revealed in *Ruodlieb,* the oldest German medieval romance, written by a monk of Tegernsee in the first half of the twelfth century (*ca.* 1130).[94] When Ruodlieb, away from home in the service of a foreign king, receives letters from his mother and the lords whom he has served at home, he, too, must have his letters read to him by a cleric.[95]

All in all, there seems to have been little desire for learning and culture on the part of the German laymen of the eleventh century. An outstanding exception is the Alsatian, Manegold, but the fascinating story of this famous teacher and his interesting family belongs to the history of French rather than German culture. It is hard to accept Wattenbach's contention of the existence of a court school for laymen in the reign of Henry III.[96] The great master of German medieval historiography seems to have erred in this matter, for, on the basis of our limited evidence, it would appear that the court at this time trained young men only in military affairs.[97] We occasionally find authorities stating that the cultural level was higher among women than among men.[98] The evidence adduced is the story of Marianus Scotus of Regensburg (d. *ca.* 1088),[99] who is said to have copied many small books and psalters which he distributed freely to the needy widows and poor clerics of his native city.[100] This passage, however, hardly proves more than we have already indicated above, that a knowledge of liturgical Latin was probably commoner among women than among men; it comes, moreover, from hagiographical literature, and may be open to doubt.[101]

The level of lay culture seems to have been somewhat higher in the last decades of the Salian period. One striking bit of evidence comes from the closing years of the eleventh century. The contemporary *Life of Erkanbert,* founder and first abbot of the monastery of Frankenthal, near Worms, who died in 1132 at the age of fifty-three, tells us that Erkanbert, along with many other noble youths, had studied under Abbot Stephen of Limburg on the Hardt, quite clearly without any definite intention at first of entering the Church. Though he had a natural bent for learning, his studies profited him but little as a layman. To the disgust of his mother, he spent his time in the company of clerics, and finally, after a severe illness, he left the world and entered upon a religious life. Of great importance to us is the pronouncement of Erkanbert's teacher, Stephen of Limburg, on the subject of education: ". . . a knowledge of letters is in no way detrimental to one who intends to become a knight, although it is of greater profit to one who intends to forsake the world."[102] We may assume, therefore, that Stephen's instruction of the noble youths entrusted to him included some study of letters. This fact, together with the passage from Ekkehard cited above,[103] indicates an increasing knowledge of Latin among the German nobility of the early twelfth century.

We find an interesting example of a learned layman of this period in the annals of Polish history. Zbignew, the bastard son of Wladislaw of Poland, began to study letters in Cracow after he had already reached maturity, and later was sent for further education to a monastery in Saxony by his stepmother, Judith, Wladislaw's second wife, the sister of Henry IV and the widow of Solomon of Hungary.[104] The purpose of this step—to prevent Zbignew from attempting to claim a share in his father's inheritance—was frustrated, for political intriguers rescued him from the monastery, and he remained a layman throughout his life. The influence of Zbignew's education is seen in his use of effective rhetoric in addressing the Poles at Breslau in 1098, exhorting them to support his half-brother against the machinations of Zetheus (also

Ziethec, Sieciech), count palatine and favorite of Wladislaw.[105] The fact that Zbignew acquired a liberal education, however, is to be attributed to political intrigue rather than to an interest in learning on the part of his parents or himself.[106]

Hungary also contributed a learned layman to the twelfth century, in King Coloman, whose love of letters won for him the surname Könyves, or the Bibliophile. According to the *Chronicon Polonorum* for the year 1107, he was the most learned king of Europe in his day.[107]

There seems to be no evidence concerning the education of Lothar of Supplinburg.[108] It is quite probable that he was illiterate, and very likely the same thing was true of Conrad III, the first Hohenstaufen ruler. It would appear that Conrad was rather simple-minded.[109] He had a typically lay attitude toward higher learning, marveling greatly at the seeming logic of false syllogisms, and expressing with naïveté an opinion that scholars seemed to lead a jolly life.[110] Frederick Barbarossa is pictured to us a serious student of Scripture and history,[111] but notwithstanding his pompous utterances concerning Roman law, the emperor had small knowledge of Latin.[112] He had not received a liberal education.[113] All his famous speeches were delivered in German. We possess the text of his speech to the delegates of the Lombard communes at Roncaglia on November 14, 1158; but although it is recorded by Rahewin in Latin and embellished with bits of Roman law and a quotation from Sallust, it was actually delivered in German and then translated to the delegates.[114] Similarly, in his speech to the Roman Senate in 1155 the emperor must have spoken through an interpreter,[115] as he did later during the negotiations at Venice in July, 1177, with Alexander III, and the deputies of the Lombard cities. We are expressly told that here Frederick addressed the assembly in German which Christian, archbishop of Mainz, then translated into Italian.[116] At the time of the same negotiations, Alexander III delivered a sermon in Latin, on the feast of St. James (July 25); when he noticed that the emperor was trying very hard to understand his words, the pope ordered the archbishop of Aquileia to translate the sermon clearly into German for the emperor's benefit.[117] Although the emperor was himself illiterate, he recognized the value and importance of learning,[118] not only for clerics and scholars,[119] but also for laymen, at least for the ruling class; for

Otto of St. Blaise informs us that Frederick I took care that all his children received an education.[120] This statement receives confirmation in the training of Henry VI, whose education was entrusted chiefly to Conrad of Querfurt, later his chancellor, and to Godfrey of Viterbo, who dedicated to Henry his *Memoria seculorum*.[121] The character and extent of Henry's learning are noted by contemporaries; he was not only well versed in ecclesiastical and secular law,[122] and skillful in his use of the Latin language,[123] but even "more learned than the learned," in the somewhat extravagant words of Gervase of Tilbury.[124] Many other contemporaries, as Toeche has pointed out,[125] wrote in praise of his culture. Among their number we find the anonymous monk of St. Salvador, at Anchin, who continued the *Chronographia* of Sigebert of Gembloux,[126] Hermann of Niederaltaich,[127] and finally, the emperor's old tutor, Godfrey of Viterbo.[128]

Philip of Swabia can also be numbered among the educated kings of medieval Germany. Destined in his youth for an ecclesiastical career,[129] he had naturally been well trained in letters.[130] Even later in life he was still able to recite Scripture readings and liturgical responses, and he enjoyed the company of clerics and poor scholars.[131] There is no direct evidence that Otto IV had a knowledge of Latin letters,[132] but it is probable that he could understand simple Latin when it was read to him. Gervase of Tilbury dedicated and sent to him the *Otia imperialia* because he "deemed it fitting to present to the king's ears a book whose tales would serve to refresh and revive the royal mind in hours of weariness."[133] Finally, in the person of Frederick II, we reach what is undoubtedly the high point in the history of culture and learning among medieval rulers.

Before attempting to arrive at any conclusions concerning the cultural level of the German nobility in the twelfth century, it may be well to consider the general statements of two German scholars on this subject. Friedrich Philippi writes thus:[134]

[The contention] that the cultural level of the German nobility of the twelfth century was an extraordinarily low one, is an assumption which receives no support whatsoever from the sources. That the art of writing was not very widespread is incontrovertible; even the poet Hartmann von der Aue was not able to write. On the other hand, the art of reading and above all a mastery of the most important foreign languages, that is, Latin and French, must be taken for granted for the members of the nobility in the twelfth century.[135] The rudiments of Latin were indispensable to them if they were to follow with complete

understanding the ecclesiastical services, and they had need of French in order
to become acquainted with the courtly literature of the time. This does not
mean to say that the noblemen had mastered these languages so thoroughly
as to be able to express themselves fluently either orally or in writing. At any
rate, so thorough a mastery is more probable in reference to French than to
Latin; but in general they could undoubtedly understand books and documents written in the foreign languages.

This statement seems to me to err in two respects. First, Philippi
has exaggerated the low level of culture among the German nobility before the twelfth century; secondly, he himself has probably
painted too glowing a picture of conditions in general, especially
of the prevalence of the knowledge of Latin. The evidence cited by
Schultz probably represents more the ideal than the actual fact,
except in such instances as that derived from the *Ruodlieb,* where
the information is incidental.

Gerdes presents a more detailed but too bright picture of the
state of culture among German laymen during the Hohenstaufen
period in general:[136]

In spite of the decline of the schools of learning in Germany, the education
of laymen made decided advances during the twelfth and thirteenth centuries.
In the old days it had been customary for the nobility to give a liberal training
also to some among those of its sons who remained laymen. But, for the most
part, the young noblemen grew up without a formal education. Over against
the seven liberal arts of the clerics, there were set up the seven accomplishments of the knight: riding, swimming, the use of the bow and arrow, boxing,
hunting or hawking, chess, and writing verses (*equitare, natare, sagittare,
cestibus certare, aucupari, saccis ludere, versificare*). But from the time of
Frederick I on, it seems, it again became the general custom among the nobility
to give also to those sons who were not intended for an ecclesiastical career the
benefits of a formal education. The cause for this change is perhaps to be
found in the general cultural advance of the class of knights (*Ritterstand*)
which took place throughout Western Europe. The knight had to be a well-bred
man, and even his education should not fall short of that of the cleric. Toward
the middle of the twelfth century, as the court life became fuller and richer
along with the rise of the knight, the German nobility began to take part also
in literary activities. If a knight wished to maintain his high position, he had
to cultivate the arts of poetry and song, and without some measure of training
in letters this was well-nigh impossible. Many knights, therefore, attended the
schools of learning in their youth, learnt Latin, and French more or less; read
books, like the clergy, though not, of course, the learned theological and philosophical treatises, but poems, written either in the mother tongue or else in
French. Still, a knowledge of Latin must have seemed very desirable to many
a nobleman, since the laws were still for the most part written in Latin.

There is plenty of evidence that a large part of the German nobility received a training in letters. Most of the *Minnesänger* and the epic poets of this time were laymen of noble birth. Without literary training, the composition of poetry according to the rules of art was very difficult. The poet had to be able to read and write, at least. It is true that Wolfram von Eschenbach was not able to do either, but in this respect he must undoubtedly be looked upon as a rare exception. We may assume that many well-known laymen possessed literary training; for some it is expressly mentioned. We often meet persons with a liberal training in the towns also, as is proved by the notices in the city charters.[137] Even the merchants in the towns were not able to dispense with reading and writing unless they were willing to be entirely dependent upon a scribe, even on their business trips.

Many noblemen sent their sons to episcopal or monastic schools. We hear repeatedly of several German schools that they were attended by young noblemen who remained laymen. In Austria, at the time of the Babenberger, it seems to have been customary for the prospective knight first to attend a monastic school before he entered the service of a lord as his page. For this reason, the Austrian nobility was later noted for its literary culture. Rich noblemen, especially those of princely rank, even sent their sons to attend the University at Paris. This is true also for Denmark....[138]

Even the common man may not have had too much difficulty in obtaining a liberal education; for everywhere in Germany in the time of Caesar of Heisterbach[139] (*ca.* 1230) there were schools, not dependent on the Church, in which instruction could be obtained even by an adult.

The beginnings of a general *Volksschule* may be seen already in the thirteenth century. The congregation of the parish appointed the teacher, who for the most part also held the office of sexton of the church. His business was to instruct the children in reading, writing, and religion. Still, we may reasonably assume that arrangements of this sort were not made everywhere, least of all in the rural districts.

Gerdes' characterization, like most such generalizations, is done in strokes which are too broad. The question of the prevalence of a knowledge of Latin among the German laity in the Hohenstaufen period cannot be answered by such a simplified, all-inclusive description of conditions, especially in view of the complexity of the cultural pattern during this period. Two facts, however, stand out fairly clearly. One is that education in the more limited sense, that is, instruction in reading and writing, began to occupy the attention of laymen more and more. Confined, perhaps, in the early part of the period to the courts of the nobility, the interest in education gradually penetrated more deeply into the lower strata of German society, and finally resulted in the rise of a new type of school, primarily in the towns, which was intended chiefly for the instruction of the laity in secular subjects.[140] The other fact to be noted is that education was no longer solely dependent upon the Latin language; the vernacular began to come into its own. The chief cultural achievement of Germany in the twelfth and thirteenth centuries was the creation of a literature written in the vernacular whose representatives were, almost without exception, laymen.[141] This condition, however, does not imply either a widespread interest in or knowledge of Latin and Latin letters among the laity. In fact, there is some reason to suppose that there was a wider diffusion of Latin learning among the laity in the last years of the Salian dynasty than in the Hohenstaufen era.

Let us consider a few examples which may throw some light on conditions in the Hohenstaufen period. An interesting one is that of Bernhard von der Lippe (1140–1224). As a boy he attended the cathedral school of Hildesheim, apparently with the intention of pursuing an ecclesiastical career.[142] On the death of his older brother, however, Bernhard left the Church to succeed his father, and became a man of the world and a warrior of some renown. He seems not to have progressed very far in his studies, or else in his secular life to have forgotten what he had learned, for in later life when he returned to the Church as a Cistercian monk at Marienfeld, probably soon after 1197,[143] he set about learning letters anew.[144] Another prominent layman of this period, who, we know, was unable to read or even to understand Latin, was Otto of Wittelsbach, who assassinated Philip of Swabia. His illiteracy is revealed in Arnold of Lübeck's account of the events leading up to the regicide. Philip had planned to give his daughter Beatrice to Otto in marriage, but changed his mind, according to Arnold, because of a streak of cruelty in Otto's character. When Otto then fixed his choice upon Gertrude, the daughter of Henry of Silesia, he asked Philip for a letter of recommendation, and since Philip professed to be willing, Otto promptly produced such a letter, already drawn up and needing only the signature. Taken aback, Philip resorted to deceit, telling Otto to return later, when he would give him the letter properly endorsed and sealed. Otto, on his return, noticed a blot on the letter and suspected, correctly, that the contents had been tampered with. Thereupon he ordered an attendant to open it and explain the meaning of the altered reading.[145]

On the other hand, undoubtedly some of the nobility possessed a knowledge of Latin. Henry the Lion seems to have been able at least to understand Latin when it was read to him. According to the *Annals of Stederburg,* Henry in his old age "ordered the manuscripts of the early chronicles to be collected and put together [literally, written together], and to be read out loud to him, and in this way he passed many a sleepless night."[146] Since the earliest chronicles in the German language were not written until after the death of Henry the Lion, we may assume that the works to which he listened were in Latin.[147] Henry's knowledge of Latin, however, was probably not very great. He seems to have been dominantly German in his cultural as well as in his political attitudes, and eager to raise the vernacular to the dignity of a literary language. To his patronage we owe the earliest extant piece of Low German prose, and the first prose work of a scientific nature in either High or Low German, the *Lucidarius,* an encyclopedia of the contemporary knowledge in theology, philosophy, astronomy, geography, and natural science in general.[148] The oldest preface to this treatise shows clearly the important rôle played by Henry in having this monument of German prose composed. It also gives us fine insight into the character of the great duke, who insisted that the work be written not in rhyme as the chaplain wished, but in straightforward German prose: he wanted no fiction, but only the pure substance of Latin knowledge.[149]

Arnold of Lübeck reveals a remarkably high level of culture among the Danish nobility of the late twelfth century:

They have made no little progress also in the knowledge of letters; for the nobles of the land send their sons to Paris, not only to raise the level of the clergy, but also for instruction in secular matters. There they become steeped in both the literature and the language of that land, and interest themselves not only in the arts, but also in theology. Having by nature a ready tongue, they are found to be not only subtle in dialectical arguments, but also prove themselves good canonists and lawyers in transacting eccleciastical business.[150]

This condition of affairs seems to be confirmed in a passage from Arnold of Stade which tells of two sons of a brother of Count Adolf of Holstein who returned home in 1246 after having spent two years abroad, presumably studying in Paris.[151] Finally, we may point to a certain Gilbert, leader of a band of German mercenaries in the employ of Ezzelino, whom Roland of Pavia describes as being "laudably learned."[152]

During the Hohenstaufen period, as in the preceding age, the customary education for women of rank consisted chiefly in learning to read the Psalter.[153] This sort of education was common, it is quite clear,[154] but of course one infers that it meant only a very limited knowledge of Latin. A broad training in Latin letters was still considered an unusual and notable achievement for a woman, as we can see from the comments of Vincent of Prague concerning the learning of Judith, the daughter of Ludwig of Thuringia and wife of Wladislaw of Bohemia. Vincent considers a good knowledge of letters and especially of the Latin language to be the crowning adornment of a young woman of noble rank.[155]

Since it is not within the compass of this study to include any general discussion of educational theory and practice, the vast literature, primary and secondary, dealing with the new educational institutions which began to appear in the late thirteenth century, the parish or municipal schools, will not be considered here. It will be valuable, however, to note the educational program of one of the earliest of these schools, the *Stadtschule* of Breslau, organized in 1267, which testifies to the continued significance of Latin even in elementary education.[156]

The political dissolution of Germany in the thirteenth century, the decadence of the monasteries, the absence of any university— Heidelberg was not founded until 1386—compromised education in Germany more than in any other country of Europe. Thomasin of Zerclaere, a didactic German poet of the thirteenth century, in his *Wälsche Gast*[157] "complains that laymen are ignorant of the seven liberal arts. Learning has become rare among the laity, whereas noble youth was formerly learned and the world was much better on that account. Princes should, therefore, pursue learning. . . . They should also honor men of learning and surround themselves with them." Thomasin must have known specifically of noble children who were unable to read, since he states explicitly that ability to read was a general accomplishment of better times now past. He constantly keeps in mind that the higher paths of learning are unfamiliar to one group of his readers, the noble laity.[153]

Notes to Chapter IV

¹ See E. Dümmler, *Geschichte des ostfränkischen Reiches*, III, 476, 477, and n. 2, where Dümmler quotes an inscription in the MS (from Schannat, *Vindemiae*, I, 223), which reads: "quod etiam venerabilis abbas Huoggi obnixis precibus a rege piissimo Arnolfo impetravit et sanctae Fuldensi ecclesiae honorabiliter restituit."

² In many of the documents of Ludwig the Child, Adalbero, who was also Ludwig's chancellor, is referred to as "noster studiosissimus nutritor"; see, e.g., *MGH. SS.*, XXI, 383, and *Monumenta Boica*, XXXIa, no. 80, 162.

³ *Libri de S. Emmerano*, I, 6 (*MGH. SS.*, IV, 551). Cf. H. Gerdes, *Geschichte des deutschen Volkes* . . . , I: 687–688.

⁴ Gerdes, *op. cit.*, I, 654 and 680, and G. Waitz, *Jahrbücher des deutschen Reichs unter Heinrich I* (3d ed.; Leipzig, 1885), 13–14.

⁵ *Vita Mathildis reginae antiq.*, chap. 2 (*MGH. SS.*, X, 576) : "Hanc eandem, ut diximus, virginem, Herevordensi, quae inerat monasterio, non inter sanctimoniales numeranda, sed ad quaeque utilia libris operibusque nutrienda." According to the later *Vita*, chaps. 2, 3 (*MGH. SS.*, IV, 284, 285) : ". . . in coenobio Herivordinense egregiam hospitare puellam nomine Mahthildam, genere nobilem, specie exoptabilem, et moribus illustrem, ut cum ava sua abbatissa disceret psalmodialem librum et industrias operum. . . . Puella mirum in modum proficiebat in cunctis, capax in studio disciplinae litteralis et operum industriis."

⁶ Widukind, *Res gestae Saxonicae*, III, 74 (*MGH. SS.*, III, 466) : "Domesticos omnes famulos et ancillas variis artibus, litteris quoque instituit; nam et ipsa litteras novit, quas post mortem regis lucide satis didicit."

⁷ Chap. 16 (*MGH. SS.*, IV, 294, 8) : "Ut ergo cognovit gloriosa regina *ex litteris*, dilectum filium suum ex hac vita migrasse, pallor in facie apparuit, et gelidus tremor per omnia membra cucurrit, et liber, quem in manibus tenebat, cadentem vultum suscepit."

⁸ *Ibid.*, 299, 9: "Nam et quo primum monasterium construxit, hanc consuetudinem semper habuit, ut ipsa scolam intraret, et singularum studia intente pernosceret." Cf. also Gerdes, *op. cit.*, I, 682.

⁹ *Res gestae Saxonicae*, II, 36 (*MGH. SS.*, III, 447) : "Ingenium ei admodum mirandum; nam post mortem Edidis reginae, cum antea nescierit, litteras in tantum didicit, ut pleniter libros legere et intelligere noverit. Praeterea Romana lingua Slavanicaque loqui scit." See also the later *Vita Mathildis*, chap. 15 (*MGH. SS.*, IV, 292) : "Post obitum Edith illustris reginae . . . sacras lectiones studiose legebat." Cf. J. Kelle, *Geschichte der deutschen Litteratur von den ältesten Zeiten bis zur Mitte des elften Jahrhunderts* (Berlin, 1892), I, 208 and 383. We may give Otto's first queen, Edith, credit for the somewhat formal education which Ludolf received. See Thietmar, *Chronicon*, II, chap. 2 ; *MGH. SS.*, III, 744.

¹⁰ Flodoard, *Annales* ad a. 948 (*MGH. SS.*, III, 396) ; cf. Wattenbach, *DGQ* (6th ed.), I, 315.

¹¹ *MGH. SS.*, II, 139: "Perlecta epistola, Otto eam patri et matri fidus inter-

pres Saxonice reponens insinuavit." The fact that Ekkehard says "patri et matri" does not mean than the translation was also for Adelheid's benefit, for at another place Ekkehard himself says that Adelheid was "litteratissima"; it must mean simply that Adelheid was present.

[12] See Widukind's remark ("praeterea Romana lingua Slavanicaque loqui scit"), cited in n. 9 above, and the *Casus S. Galli (MGH. SS.*, II, 140) : "Tandem ille terribilis egressus, cum Ottonem ducem cum eis offendisset assistentem, arridens et *bôn mân* [= bonum mane] habere romanisce dixit."

[13] *Historia Ottonis*, chap. 11 *(MGH. SS.*, III, 343) : "His auditis imperator, quia Romani eius loquelam propriam, hoc est Saxonicam, intelligere nequiebant, Liudprando Cremonensi episcopo praecepit, ut Latino sermone haec Romanis omnibus quae secuntur exprimeret."

[14] See Gerbert's letters, ed. J. Havet, nos. 6, 20, 74, 97, 128, 204, 208, 215 ; and cf. Ch. Jourdain, *Mém. de l'Inst. Nat. de France: Acad. des inscr. et belles-lettres*, XXVIII, pt. 1 (1874), 90.

[15] *Casus S. Galli (MGH. SS.*, II, 146) : "Misit tandem abbas litteras Ottonibus et reginae in Saxoniam cum muneribus, sciscitans tempus adventus eorum, necnon et Ekkehardo quaternionem, omnem seriem Sandrati tenentem; quam ille Ottoni filio cum in secretis legere daret, in tantos hyroniae cachinnos solutus est, ut mater eius superveniens, quid esset, quereret. At ille scripturam illam ipse dans, legere eam rogavit—nam litteratissima erat."

[16] See Odilo's *Epitaph on Saint Adelheid*, chap. 20 *(MGH. SS.*, IV, 644), where he describes the queen as being "wrapped up in her reading (*lectionibus intenta*)."

[17] See Thietmar, *Chronicon*, IV, 5 *(MGH. SS.*, III, 769).

[18] See *Casus S. Galli (MGH. SS.*, II, 126), and the interesting but incredible story of the gruesome prank which young Otto is supposed to have played on his uncle Bruno, which the *Annalista Saxo* tells *(MGH. SS.*, VI, 631) : in brief, the young prince placed the corpse of a boy of his own age in his bed and covered it with his own garments so that it looked as though he himself had died; and when Bruno, who had gone out to celebrate hours, returned, he naturally broke forth in loud lamentations which attracted the other members of the family; thereupon, while all were standing about the bed weeping, young Otto walked back into the room, with the explanation, "I knew of no better way to get revenge for the shame of so many beatings." Cf. Wattenbach, *DGQ* (6th ed.), I, 317, and Specht, *Geschichte des Unterrichtswesens . . .* , 209–210.

[19] See Uhlirz, *Jahrbücher des deutschen Reichs unter Otto den Grossen*, II, 2, n. 4.

[20] In Richer of Rheims, *Historiarum libri tres*, II, 67 *(MGH. SS.*, III, 621) : "vir magni ingenii, totiusque virtutis, liberalium litterarum scientia clarus, adeo ut in disputando ex arte et proponeret, et probabiliter concluderet"; and the story of the philosophical dispute, especially chap. 56 (*ibid.*, 619) : "Tulit [sc. Gerbertus] itaque ad palatium figuram eandem, et coram Ottone augusto iis qui sapientiores videbantur eam explicavit. Augustus vero cum et ipse talium studiosissimus haberetur, an Gerbertus erraverit, admirabatur." Cf. Wattenbach, *DGQ* (6th ed.), I, 318 and n. 2.

²¹ *Casus S. Galli*, chap. 144 (*MGH. SS.*, II, 147): "Illo [*sic*] autem libris optimis illectus, plures abstulit; quorum tamen aliquos, Ekkehardo rogante, postea reddidit." Cf. Gerdes, *op. cit.*, I, 656.

²² Gerdes, *op. cit.*, I, 656, and Köpke-Dümmler, *Jahrbücher des deutschen Reichs unter Otto den Grossen*, 480.

²³ Cf. Wattenbach, *DGQ* (6th ed), I, 318, and Gerdes, *op. cit.*, I, 674.

²⁴ Thus, according to Gerdes, *op. cit.*, I, 665. See also Thangmar's *Vita Bernwardi*, chaps. 2 and 51 (*MGH. SS.*, IV, 759 and 779).

²⁵ Adhemar de Chabannes, *Hist. libri tres*, III, 31 (*MGH. SS.*, IV, 129), describes Otto as one "qui philosophiae intentus." Cf. also Kleinclausz, *L'empire carolingien* . . . , 560 and n. 1.

²⁶ Gerdes, *op. cit.*, I, 656–657; see also Gerbert's letters, ed. Havet, no. 157, and App. II, 140 and 238.

²⁷ Adalbert, *Vita Heinrici II*, chap. 3 (*MGH. SS.*, IV, 792): "Hiltensheim, ubi a puero enutritus et litteras edoctus fuit." *Chronicon Tegernseense*, chap. 3 (Pez, *Thesaurus anecdotorum* . . . , III, pt. 3, 504): "erat enim in ecclesia Hildinsheim literarum studiis a puero edoctus." Thietmar, *Chron.*, V, pref. verses (*MGH. SS.*, III, 790): "Nutrit preclarum Wolfgangus presul alumnum." Cf. S. Hirsch, *Jahrbücher des deutschen Reichs unter Heinrich II*, I, 90, n. 1 and 92, n. 1, and Wattenbach, *DGQ* (6th ed.), I, 319.

²⁸ See esp. the dedication of the unknown author of the later *Vita Mathildis*, written expressly for Henry II (*MGH. SS.*, IV, 283): "Cum multis sit notum, vos scientia disciplinaque artium diversarum praeditum, plurima perlegisse volumina, sanctorum vitam patrum in se continentia, quorum exemplis," etc., also, Constantinus, *Vita Adalberonis*, chap. 16 (*ibid.*, 663): "Rex, quem fallere nemo poterat, quia erat homo litteris adprime imbutus"; Adalbert, *Vita Heinrici* II, chap. 1 (*ibid.*, 792): "erat omni litterarum studio principaliter imbutus"; Thangmar's overdrawn statement in the *Vita Bernwardi*, chap. 22 (*ibid.*, 768): "Heinricus . . . in quem Dominus cunctos thesauros divinae et humanae sapientiae contulit"; and the letter of Bebo, a deacon of Bamberg, to King Henry (Jaffé, *Bibl. rer. Germ.*, V, 484–497). Cf. esp. Hirsch, *Heinrich II*, I, 91 and n. 3.

²⁹ Giesebrecht, *Geschichte der deutschen Kaiserzeit* (5th ed.; Leipzig, 1881), I, 670, 701, 858; V. Rose, *Hermes*, VIII, 46.

³⁰ F. Leitschuh, *Führer durch die königl. Bibliothek zu Bamberg* (1889), 38 f.

³¹ See Falk, *Archiv. f. Kulturgesch.*, XV (1922), 173–174, for particulars, and compare: H. Fischer, *Zentralbl. f. Bibliothekswesen*, XXIV (1907), 364; O. Hartwig, *ibid.*, III (1886), 165 f.; Breslau, *Neues Archiv*, XXI, 141 f.; L. Traube, *Abhandl. d. k. Bayer. Akad.*, XXIV (1904), and XXVI (1912), 1 f. (ed. by E. K. Rand).

³² *Vita Meinwerki*, chaps. 186, 187: *MGH. SS.*, XI, 150.

³³ According to the editor, G. Waitz, the *Vita* was written after 1199, perhaps in the year 1200; cf. *MGH. SS.*, IV, 790.

³⁴ *Vita S. Cunegundis*, chap. 5 (cf. *ibid.*, 823): "Semper eam legere aut legentem audire videres"; chap. 7 (cf. *ibid.*, 823): "Utam ... quam a primis annis educatam, omni disciplina, secularium quoque literarum scientia instrux-

erat"; chap. 3 (cf. *ibid.*, 822): "Quanta vero elemosinarum largitate, quanta orationis instantia pro beati coniugis defuncti anima desudaverit, in subscripta pagina, quam ipsa per se—nam litterarum et artium aliarum . . . peritissima fuit—conposuit et scripsit, quicumque scire voluerit, cognoscere poterit." Cf. Wattenbach, *DGQ* (6th ed.), II, 384, and Kelle, *op. cit.*, 228 and 392.

[35] *Jahrbücher des deutschen Reichs unter Heinrich III* (Leipzig, 1881), I, 36.

[36] Adam of Bremen, *Gesta Hammaburgensis ecclesiae pontificum*, Bk. III, chap. 54 (ed. Schmeidler; Leipzig, 1917, p. 199). Gregory VII's letter is in Jaffé-Loewenfeld, *Regesta pontificum romanorum* . . . , no. 4928. It is dated January 25, 1075.

[37] *Op. cit.*, I, 680; cf. also, I, 657.

[38] *Ibid.*, I, 681.

[39] *DGQ* (6th ed.), I, 322. In support of his contention, Wattenbach cites Ruotger, *Vita Brunonis*, chaps. 5–7 (*MGH. SS.*, IV, 256–257), but the passage is not very conclusive evidence. It is mainly a panegyric in praise of Bruno, and proves only that there was enough learning and a sufficient number of erudite ecclesiastics at the court to make instruction possible.

[40] *Op. cit.*, 322, n. 3.

[41] *Jahrbücher . . . Otto den Grossen*, 545 and n. 4. Dümmler's objection to Wattenbach's thesis follows essentially the line of argument laid down in the note above.

[42] *Geschichte der deutschen Kaiserzeit*, I, 570, and *Deutsche Geschichte*, II, 230.

[43] *L'empire carolingien*, 559, n. 2.

[44] *Geschichte des Unterrichtswesens* . . . , 238.

[45] Chap. 37 (*MGH. SS.*, VIII, 643).

[46] According to the editor, G. Waitz, *ibid.*, 637.

[47] *Chronicon Eberspergense*, ed. W. Arndt (*MGH. SS.*, XX, 14): "Postquam vero Germanum regnum a Romanis recesserat, Sigipertus et Theodericus ac deinde Carolus iura dictabant, quae si quis potens ac nobilis legere nesciret, ignominiosus videbatur, sicut in me coevisque meis, qui iura didicimus, apparet. Moderni vero filios suos neglegunt iura docere; qui quandoque pro suo libitu et possibilitate mendoso iure quosque iuvant aut deprimunt et per exlegem temeritatem"; Wattenbach, *DGQ* (6th ed.), I, 321 and n. 4.

[48] See W. Arndt, *op. cit.*, 9, and esp. Hirsch, *Heinrich II*, I, 151, n.

[49] Cf. Ebert, *Gesch. d. lateinischen Literatur des Mittelalters*, III, 115, and Gerdes, *op. cit.*, 5, 681.

[50] Gumpold, *Vita Vencezlavi*, chap. 4 (*MGH. SS.*, IV, 214, 27): "Qui vero mirae claritatis ac amandae indolis, dum floridam iuventutis aetatem primum attigisset, patre adhuc vivo, ad litterarum disponi exercitia desiderans, paternumque crebro flagitamine deflectens animum, eius transmissu in civitate Bunsza litteris addiscendis est positus."

[51] *Annalista Saxo*, ad a. 1010 (*MGH. SS.*, VI, 661): "Erat hic venerabilis comes litteratus et in divino servicio valde studiosus, adeo ut ter se daret in proprium servum sancte Dei genitrice Marie tociensque se redimeret cum libris et reliquis ornamentis ecclesiasticis."

[52] Alpertus, *De diversitate temporum*, I, 11 (*MGH. SS.*, IV, 705): "si quando contigit ut a secularibus negotiis quietus esse poterat, aut iusta iudicia tractabat, aut lectioni tanto studio insistebat, ut a quibusdam insipientibus monachicam vitam illum agere derideretur." Cf. Gerdes, *op. cit.*, I, 681.

[53] *Casus S. Galli*, chap. 135 (*MGH. SS.*, II, 142).

[54] *Vita S. Leonis IX*, I, 1: Mabillon, *AA. SS. ord. S. Bened.* (Venice ed.), Saec. VI, 2, 52: "pater ejus native Teutonicus, Imperatoris Conradi consobrinus in patria lingua atque latina disertissimus."

[55] *Ibid.:* "mater quoque latina, aeque utriusque linguae perita." Cf. Jourdain, *op. cit.*, 90 and n. 2. O. Delarc, *Un pape alsacien: Léon IX et son temps* (Paris, 1876), 4–5. In discussing the education of Leo IX (Bruno), Delarc says (6–7) that Berthold, bishop of Toul (995–1018) "had founded a school in his episcopal city for the sons of the nobility which was attended at the time of Bruno's arrival by two of Bruno's cousins, both named Adalbero." But this statement is misleading, as the sequel shows clearly that the school was nothing more than the ordinary episcopal school, the chief purpose of which was the training of future leaders in the Church. Of the three boys mentioned here, one died before he reached the age of manhood, another became bishop of Metz, and Bruno became pope.

[56] Cf. K. Weinhold, *Die deutschen Frauen in dem Mittelalter* (2d ed.; Vienna, 1882), I, 128–129; also Wattenbach, *DGQ* (6th ed.), I, 320, and Gerdes, *op. cit.*, I, 681–682.

[57] *Vita Burchardi* (*MGH. SS.*, IV, 838): "Nam, tantum psalterio excepto, libros penitus ignoro."

[58] See the *Casus S. Galli* (*MGH. SS.*, II, 122–126, esp. 125).

[59] See Wipo, *Vita Chuonradi*, chap. 6 (*MGH. SS.*, XI, 262): "Quamquam enim litteras ignoraret, tamen omnem clerum cum amabiliter et liberaliter palam tum convenienti disciplina secreto prudenter instituit."

[60] *Chronicon Novaliciense*, app. 17 (*MGH. SS.*, VII, 128): "per omnia litterarum inscius atque idiota."

[61] Cf. Gerdes, *op. cit.*, II, 48, who suggests that the reason for Conrad's ignorance was that a liberal education was not customary among the lay nobility of Conrad's day. Gerdes' observation is true, but too axiomatic; more likely, Conrad was simply not interested.

[62] See Ekkehard's later interlinear explanations of the schoolboy exercises he wrote at the dictation of Notker (*MGH. SS.*, II, 58): "Kisila imperatrix operum eius [i.e., Notkeri] avidissima, psalterium ipsum et Iob sibi exemplari sollicite fecit." Cf. Wattenbach, *DGQ* (6th ed.), II, 1, n. 1, and Kelle, *op. cit.*, I, 264.

[63] See Wipo's verses in praise of Gisela, *Tetralogus, carmen legis*, vss. 158 ff. (*MGH. SS.*, XI, 250):

> "Felix sit mater memorando carmine digna
> Gisela, de Caroli procedens sanguine Magni.
> . . . .
> Haec operam dederat, quod rex [i.e., Henry III] in lege studebat;
> Illa sibi libros persuaserat esse legendos,
> Ut varios ritus diiudicet arte peritus."

[64] *Historiae Farfenses,* chap. 5 (*MGH. SS.,* XI, 559) : ". . . domnum Almericum, litteris optime eruditum et aecclesiasticis doctrinis magnifice imbutum, qui etiam eundem imperatorem [Henry III] liberales apices studuerat edocere."

[65] Cf. Steindorff, *op. cit.,* I, 11 ff. The entire tenor of Wipo's *Proverbia ad Heinricum Chuonradi imperatoris filium* shows Wipo's influence over the young prince (cf. *ibid.,* 12, n. 1). On Henry's education, see in general also Wattenbach, *DGQ* (6th ed.), II, 1–2; Gerdes, *op. cit.,* II, 53; Manitius, *Gesch. lat. Lit.,* II, 7; and Hauck, *Kirchengeschichte Deutschlands* (3d ed.), III, 619.

[66] App. 17 (*MGH. SS.,* VII, 128) : "bene pericia litterarum imbutus." See also Wipo, *Tetralogus,* vv. 150, 250, and vv. 82, 249.

[67] For example, the works of Wipo, and the lost work of Hermann the Lame of Reichenau on the deeds of Conrad II and Henry III, which was dedicated to the latter prince, according to Otto of Freising, *Chronicon,* VI, 33 (*MGH. SS.,* XX, 245) ; cf. Steindorff, *op. cit.,* I, 11 and n. 4. Henry's literary interests are also clearly brought out in his correspondence with Berno of Reichenau and, more especially, in Anselm of Besate's extraordinary work, *Rhetorimachia;* cf. Wattenbach, *DGQ* (6th ed.), II, 2–3 (who refers to E. Dümmler, *Anselm der Peripatiker, nebst andern Beiträgen zur Litteraturgeschichte Italiens* [Halle, 1872]). Williram of Ebersberg, in his versified paraphrase of the Song of Solomon, dedicated to young Henry IV, reminds that prince how his father (Henry III) has assisted him; cf. Manitius, *op. cit.,* II, 7–8.

[68] See the letter of Siegfrid, abbot of Tegernsee (from 1048 to 1068), to bishop W., perhaps—according to Hauck's suggestion (*Kirchengeschichte* [3d ed.], III, 620, n. 3)—William of Utrecht, published by Pez, *Thesaurus anecdotorum . . . ,* VI, 1, 237–238 : "Inibi non sunt adhuc perscripti libri quos postulabatis. Sedula ergo illic permutatio abbatum, nec non pro diversis scribendis voluminibus Imperatoris mandatum valde impediunt votivum vobis in ministrando desiderium eorundem fratrum."

[69] Ad a. 1041 (*MGH. SS.,* III, 125) : "Huius [Heinrici III] astipulatione et industria plurimi eo tempore in artibus, in aedificiis, in auctoribus, in omni genere doctrinae pollebant. Studium ubique famosissimum."

[70] Wipo, *Tetralogus,* v. 199 (*MGH. SS.,* XI, 251).

[71] See the dedication of the *De contemplatione* of John, abbot of Fécamp (also known as John the Poor), published by F. Richter in the *Archiv für Kunde österreichischer Geschichtsquellen* (1849), III, 369 : "Dudum quidem, domina Imperatrix, tibi petere placuit, ut ex scripturis colligerem luculentos brevesque sermones, in quibus juxta legem ordinis tui absque gravi labore discere posses normam bene vivendi"; and esp. 371 : "Hec ergo frequenter lege et tunc precipue, cum mentem tuam celesti afflatam desiderio vides."

[72] Besides the treatise mentioned in the previous note, the principal items of evidence are : (1) the lost book of the Anonymus Haserensis, *Libellus Agnetis imperatricis,* mentioned by the author himself in his *De episcopis Eichstetensibus,* chap. 36 (*MGH. SS.,* VII, 264) ; (2) Arnulf's *Delicie cleri,* dedicated to both Henry III and Agnes (see J. Heumer's edition and introductory remarks in *Romanische Forschungen* (1886), II, esp. 211–212, 216–217; (3) the fact that among Agnes' correspondents we find the names of such learned men as

Peter Damiani and Albert of Fructuaria (see Wattenbach, *DGQ* [6th ed.]), II, 3 and n. 2). By way of secondary authority, cf. also Gerdes, *op. cit.*, II, 125, and esp. Steindorff, *op. cit.*, I, 154.

⁷³ I, 6 (Jaffé, *Bibl. rer. Germ.*, V, 594, in *MGH. SS.*, XII, 826) : "Erat enim imperator litteris usque adeo imbutus, ut cartas, a quibuslibet sibi directas, per semet ipsum legere et intelligere prevaleret."

⁷⁴ *Dialogus*, III, 34 (Jaffé, *Bibl. rer. Germ.*, V, 827–828, in *MGH. SS.*, XX, 765) : "Nam adeo litteratus erat imperator, ut per se breves legeret ac faceret."

⁷⁵ Herbord's phrase "ac faceret" may be simply an arbitrary addition to his condensation of Ebbo's remarks. Cf. Jaffé's comments, *op. cit.*, 699 and n. 1; and, *per contra*, on the trustworthiness of Ebbo, *ibid.*, 580 f.

⁷⁶ Ebbo, *Vita Ottonis*, I, 6 (Jaffé, *Bibl. rer. Germ.*, V, 594) : "imperator Heinricus, fide et prudentia pii Ottonis agnita, secrecius eum compellans, an psalterium cordetenus psallere posset, inquisivit. Quo respondente: 'Etiam,' gravisus imperator eum sibi assidere precepit; et remotis aliis, psalmodie cum eo vacabat, quociens a negociis expeditus esse poterat. . . . Codex autem, in quo psalmos decantabat, manuali frequentia rugosus et admodum obfuscatus erat." There follows the charming tale of how Otto surprised the emperor by giving his book a new binding in the latter's absence. The same story is told also by Herbord (*ibid.*, 827).

⁷⁷ *Chronicon*, ad a. 1106 (*MGH. SS.*, VI, 239) : "More patris sui clericos et maxime literatos adherere sibi voluit, hosque honorifice tractans, nunc psalmis nunc lectione vel collatione, sive scripturarum ac liberalium artium inquisitione secum familiarius occupavit." Gerdes, *op. cit.*, II, 318, gives an inexcusably slipshod translation of this passage: "Deshalb hatte er in seiner Umgebung gelehrte Männer, darunter auch Laien, mit denen er gelehrte Studien trieb, die sich entweder auf theologische Schriften oder auf die verschiedenen Fächer der Wissenschaft erstreckten, oft beschäftigte er sich in seinen Mussestunden allein mit Lektüre." The chief offense is in translating the phrase "clericos et maxime literatos" with "gelehrte Männer, darunter auch Laien." As indicated in my translation, I think the word "literatos" should be regarded as an adjective referring back to "clericos."

⁷⁸ Even William of Malmesbury, in discussing the character of Henry IV, thought fit to add that he was "neither ignorant nor uneducated" (*Gesta regum Anglorum*, III, 288: *MGH. SS.*, X., 475) : "neque ineruditus neque ignavus"). Cf. also Wattenbach, *DGQ* (6th ed.), II, 3 and n. 3.

⁷⁹ Cf. Giesebrecht, *Geschichte der deutschen Kaiserzeit*, III, 984, and Gerdes, *op. cit.*, II, 370.

⁸⁰ *MGH. SS.*, VI, 9: "Habes igitur, serenissime imperator, amministrante caritate chronicum opus, excerptum non nostra set veterum chronographorum auctoritate, utinam non indignum, ne dicam oculis imperatoriis, set saltim minimis lectoribus tuae curiae."

⁸¹ Ekkehard, *Chronicon*, ad a. 1110 (*MGH. SS.*, VI, 243) : "Providerat autem rex, nulli a seculo regum in omni providentia secundus, sciens Romanam rem publicam olim non tantum armis quantum sapientia gubernari consuetam, se non solum armatis sed etiam litteratis viris necessario muniri, paratis scilicet ad rationem omni poscenti reddendam."

[82] *Ibid.*: "Inter quos claruit quidam Scotigena nomine David; quem dudum scolas Wirciburc regentem pro morum probitate omnique liberalium artium peritia rex sibi capellanum assumpsit. Hic itaque iussus a rege totam huius expeditionis seriem rerumque in illa gestarum stilo tam facili, qui pene nichil a communi loquela discrepet, tribus libris digessit, consulens in hoc etiam lectoribus laicis vel aliis minus doctis, quorum haec intellectus capere possit."

[83] It is a great misfortune that David's work has not been preserved for us. To try to reconstruct parts of it, for the purpose of determining its style, from those authors who used it—Ekkehard, William of Malmesbury, Ordericus Vitalis, and perhaps the Annalist of Paderborn—would be impossible. And yet, by an analogy which almost forces itself upon us, we may perhaps form a fairly definite opinion of the kind of Latin in which David wrote his narrative; for Ekkehard's words "in illo gestarum stilo" at once suggest a style similar to the simple and limited Latin of the anonymous *Gesta Francorum* of the First Crusade. David the Scot was bishop of Bangor.

In respect to the use of David's work by contemporary and later medieval chroniclers, I have followed the more reasonable position of Dietrich Schäfer ("Die Quellen für Heinrich V. Romzug," *Historische Aufsätze dem Andenken an Georg Waitz* [Hanover, 1886], 152–153) in preference to that of H. Guleke ("Der Bericht des David über den Römerzug Heinrich V. vom Jahre 1111," *Forschungen zur deutschen Geschichte*, XX [1880], 406 ff.), who attempts to prove that David's account was used also by Otto of Freising, and in the *Gesta Alberonis* and the *Annales S. Disibodi*. The comment of William of Malmesbury on the quality of David's work as history is very interesting and, in all probability, true (*Gesta regum Anglorum*, V, 420: *MGH. SS.*, X, 479): "Sed iter illud ad Romam, . . . David Scottus Bancornensis episcopus exposuit, magis in regis gratiam quam historicum deceret acclinis."

According to a note of Freeman's (*The Norman Conquest of England*, V, 210, n. 1), David was consecrated bishop of Bangor in 1120. But beyond this and the facts already mentioned, very little seems to be known about David; see Wattenbach, *DGQ* (6th ed.), II, 95–96, 195, and Giesebrecht, *Kaiserzeit* (5th ed.), III, 804 and 1209.

[84] *Tetralogus*, vss. 190–198 (*MGH. SS.*, XI, 251), quoted in full, above, Chap. III.

[85] Chap. 3 (*MGH. SS.*, XII, 38): "Quae dum aliquando sopori se dedisset, vidit per somnium se in quadam ecclesia cum quibusdam reverendi habitus viris officiose sibi obsequentibus, sacerdotalibus indutam vestimentis astare sacro altari, et *cum litteras penitus ignoraret*, omne officium missae diligenter percantasse...."

[86] The father's violent attitude is especially interesting; see chap. 4 (*ibid.*, 39): ". . . et cum iam [Theodericus] fere septennis esset, patre eius inscio, qui eum, quod ipse erat, fieri terrenum militem et rerum suarum disponebat heredem, mater visionis suae non immemor, primis eum litterarum dedit imbuendum elementis. . . . Sed omnium bonorum inimicus . . . patrem . . . contra uxoris suae bonum propositum inflammavit. Qui filium suum a litteris abstractum domi servari iussit, interminatus uxori gravia, si posthac eum praesumeret tradere his disciplinis."

[87] Chaps. 4–6 (*ibid.*, 39–40). Cf. Wattenbach, *DGQ* (6th ed.), II, 5, where he says: "Die Heiligenleben zeigen es zur Genüge, dass in der Regel der Entschluss, den Sohn lesen und, was identisch war, Latein lernen zu lassen, ihn zugleich zum geistlichen Stande bestimmte. Die Mütter thaten es oft heimlich, und die Väter wurden dann sehr zornig, wenn sie es erfuhren. In dieser Beziehung ist man gegen die frühere Zeit zurückgeschritten."

[88] *Chronicon Gozecense*, I, 2 (*MGH. SS.*, X, 142): "... more antiquorum tam litteris quam diversarum artium disciplinis apud Quedlinburg pulchre fuit instructa."

[89] *Ibid.*

[90] *Chron.*, I, 9 (*ibid.*, 144).

[91] I, 14 (*ibid.*, 148): "Ferunt etiam quia litterarum scientia adeo in curia Vuldensi instructus fuerit, ut epistolas transmissas per se legeret et intelligeret ac capellanos in divino officio errantes corrigeret."

[92] I, 13 (*ibid.*, 146): "Denique bibliotecam ex integro, Moralia Job, passionale unum, nonnullosque alios codices digna pecunia comparavit, quos asinis portantibus huc deferri mandavit." It is regrettable that the chronicler mentions by name the *Moralia* and the passional, and even adds the detail that the library was transported by means of asses, but fails to enlighten us concerning the contents of the rest of the library. Cf. Wattenbach, *DGQ* (6th ed.), II, 5 and n. 1.

[93] *De bello Saxonico*, chap. 13 (*MGH. SS.*, V, 333): "Ille nil moratus sigillum fregit, clericum suum, quid illae litterae vellent, exponere sibi praecepit."

[94] See Friedrich Seiler's ed. (Halle, 1882), Intro., 160 ff.

[95] *Ibid.*, vv. 223–228, p. 234:

> "Rodlieb dilecte matris cernens inopine
> Ad sese missum quendam bene suscipit illum.
> Ad quem sic dixit: 'mea mater sospes, ai, sit.'
> Respondit: 'uiuit, ualet et bene uel tibi misit
> Istas litterulas, melius quibus ac mihi credas,'
> Susceptaque dice sciolum facit hanc recitare."

[96] See *DGQ* (6th ed.), II, 4, where Wattenbach delivers himself of the following almost meaningless statement: "Vornehme Knaben wurden auch jetzt noch am Hofe erzogen, die kaiserliche Capelle vereinigte zu allen Zeiten eine anzahl ausgezeichnete Männer von gründlicher Bildung, doch tritt die Hofschule nirgends bedeutend hervor, und es war auch nicht nöthig, denn jene [Kloster- und Dom-] Schulen deren Anfänge wir im vorigen Abschnitt betrachteten hatten sich überall zu selbständigem Gedeihen entwickelt und tragen nun ihre volle Frucht."

[97] See the account, already referred to, of the training of Dedo, the brother of Frederick II of Saxony, at the court of Henry III (*Chron. Gozecense*, I, 2: *MGH. SS.*, X, 142): "... domina Agnes ... Dedonem sub rege Heinrico tercio rebus militaribus implicavit."

[98] Thus, e. g., Specht, *op. cit.*, 285–286.

[99] Not to be confused with the historian of the same name, Marianus Scotus of Mainz. Cf. Waitz's remark in the preface to his edition of the *Chronicon* of the recluse of Mainz, *MGH. SS.*, V, 484, n. 22.

[100] *Vita B. Mariani abb. Ratispon.*, II, 9: *AA. SS.* (ed. novissima), Feb., II, 367: "Eodem quoque tempore multos libellos, multaque manualia psalteria viduis indigentibus, ac Clericis pauperibus ejusdem civitatis pro remedio animae suae, sine ulla spe terrena quaestus scriptitaverat."

[101] The *Vita* cited was written by a monk of Regensburg, sometime after 1160. See Bollandus' preface, *ibid.*, 364.

[102] "Nobilium filios in suo comitatu plurimos habere solebat, quibus exempla honestatis et curialis administrationis exhibebat. Inter quos Eckenbertum ... hortatusque eum ut in discendo psalterio operam daret. Et dicebat, *literarum peritia nemini militaturo obesse*, seculum relicturo plurimum prodesse." I quote from Specht, *op cit.*, 246, n. 2. Wattenbach cites a thirteenth-century German translation in rhyme, *DGQ* (6th ed.), II, 402. Specht's citation comes from Ludewig, *Reliquiae manuscriptorum* (Frankfort, 1720), II, 79; the text of the *Historia b. Eckanberti* has been published also by H. Boos, in *Monumenta Wormatiensia* (1893), 129–142.

[103] See p. 90, above.

[104] *Chronica Polonorum*, II, 4 (*MGH. SS.*, IX, 446): "Zbignevus, a Wladislavo duce de concubina progenitus, in Cracoviensi civitate adultus iam aetate litteris datus fuit, eumque noverca sua in Saxoniam docendum monasterio monialium transmandavit." Cf. Specht, *op. cit.*, 283 and n. 2.

[105] *Chron. Polonorum*, II, 16 (*ibid.*, 450): "Zbignevus ... properando adveniens, orationem fratris, *ut litteratus* et maior aetate, *rethorice coloravit*, ac populum tumultuantem ad fidelitatem fratris et contrarietatem Zethei luculenta oratione sequenti vehementer animavit." For the complicated details of the political history involved, see the old but very useful and scholarly work of R. Roeppel, *Geschichte Polens* (Hamburg, 1840 ff.), I, 214 ff., esp. 215 and 222.

[106] This is clearly brought out in the *Chronicon Polono-Silesiacum* (*MGH. SS.*, XIX, 560): "Habuit autem iste Vladislaus filium ex concubina, qui ob odium in suam novercam in desertis educatus, dictus est Zbignewus." Cf. also Wattenbach's apt comment (*DGQ*, II, 5, n. 2): "Indem der Bastard Sbignew von seinem Vater Wladislaw von Polen in Krakau *litteris datus* wurde, war er zum geistlichen Stande bestimmt."

[107] *MGH. SS.*, IX, 456: "... super reges universos suo tempore degentes literali scientia erudito." Cf. I. A. Tessler, *Geschichte von Ungarn*, 194.

[108] For Lothar's character and person, see W. Bernhardi, *Lothar von Supplinburg* (in the *Jahrbücher* series; Leipzig, 1879), esp. 790–798.

[109] See William of Tyre, *Historia*, XVI, 21 (*Recueil des historiens des croisades, Occidentaux*, I, 740):"Quibus verbis [of the Greek guides to Iconium] Imperator, sicut *vir simplex* erat, persuasus." Gerhoh of Reichersberg (*De investigatione antichristi*, I, 71) expressly accuses the king of credulity: "Rex quidem noster credens omnia simpliciter et fideliter agi pomeria irrumpens ..." (at Damascus). I quote this passage from W. Bernhardi, *Konrad III* (Leipzig, 1883), 928, n. 45, since F. Scheilberger's edition (1875) of the works of Gerhoh is not available to me, and the excerpts from the *De invest. antichr.* published elsewhere do not include this particular chapter.

[110] See the letter of Wibald of Corvey to Manegold of Paderborn (Jaffé, *Bibl. rer. Germ.*, I, 283, *Epist.* 167): "Mirabatur dominus noster C(onradus) rex ea, quae a litteratis vafre dicebantur; et, probari non posse, hominem esse asinum, aiebat. Iocundi eramus in convivio, et plerique nobiscum non illiterati. Dicebam ei, hoc in rerum natura non posse effici; set ex concessione indeterminata, nascens a vero mendatium, falsa conclusione astringi. Cum non intelligeret, ridiculo eum sophismate adorsus sum: 'Unum,' inquam, 'habetis oculum?' Quod cum dedisset, subieci: 'Duos,' inquam, 'oculos habetis?' Quod cum absolute annuisset, 'Unus,' inquam, 'et duo tres sunt; tres igitur oculos habetis.' Captus verbi cavillatione iurabat, se tantum duos habere. Multis tamen et his similibus determinare doctus, iocundam vitam dicebat habere litteratos." One is almost tempted to add that Wibald's syllogism forthwith gave the lie direct to Conrad's contention: "probari non potest hominem esse asinum."

[111] By Rahewin, in his continuation of the *Gesta Friderici* of Otto of Freising, IV, 86 (*MGH. SS.*, XX, 490): "Scripturas et antiquorum regum gesta sedulo perquirit."

[112] *Ibid.*: "In patria lingua admodum facundus, Latinam vero melius intelligere quam pronunciare."

[113] See the *Chronicon* of Sicardus (bishop of Cremona, d. 1215; Muratori, *SS. rer. Ital.*, VII, 598 D): "fuit miles strenuus, et magnanimus, mitis, affabilis, *illiteratus*, sed morali experentia doctus." Cf. Rahewin's account of the manner in which Frederick's speech at Roncaglia, November 14, 1158, was received (*Gesta Friderici*, IV, 5: *MGH. SS.*, XX, 446): "His dictis, magnus favor omnium prosequitur admirantium et stupentium, quod *qui litteras non nosset*, quique parum adhuc supra adolescenten ageret aetatem, in oratione sua tantae prudentiae tantaeque facundiae gratiam accepisset."

[114] *Gesta Friderici*, IV, 3 (*ibid.*, 445): ". . . imperator . . . sedens in eminentiori, unde ab omnibus videri poterat et audiri, circumsedente eum corona venerandorum quos praenominavimus, heroum, *per interpretem elocutus est.*" The text of the speech is in the following chapter.

[115] The text of the speech, as recorded in Latin by Otto of Freising, in the *Gesta Friderici*, II, 30 (*ibid.*, 405).

[116] Romuald, *Annales*, ad a. 1177 (*MGH. SS.*, XIX, 453): "Postquam papa loqui desiit, imperator, deposito pallio, de suo faldestolio surgens, cepit in lingua Teotonica concionari, Christiano cancellario verba sua vulgariter exponente."

[117] *Ibid.*: "Cumque dicto evangelio papa ascendisset pulpitum, ut alloqueretur populum, imperator accedens propius, cepit verba eius attentius auscultare. Cuius devotionem papa diligenter attendens, verba, que ipse litteratorie proferebat, fecit per patriarcham Aquileie in lingua Teotonica evidenter exponi." Du Cange (under *literate*) defines *litteratorie* as being synonymous with *Latine*, and cites the foregoing passage as an example.

[118] Cf. Wattenbach, *DGQ* (6th ed.), II, 246, n. 3.

[119] Witness his *Privilegium scolasticis* of 1158 at Roncaglia (*MGH. SS.*, II, 1, 114).

[120] See his continuation of the *Chronica* of Otto of Freising, chap. 21 (*MGH. SS.*, XX, 314) : ". . . liberosque suos omnes litteris apprime erudiri faciens, . . ."

[121] See esp. Th. Toeche, *Heinrich VI* (in the *Jahrbücher* series; Leipzig, 1867), 27–28. The dedication of the *Memoria seculorum*, in *MGH. SS.*, XXII, 105. Cf. B. Schmeidler, *op. cit.*, 22.

[122] See the *Chronica* of Alberic of Troisfontaines, ad a. 1185 (*MGH. SS.*, XXIII, 858) : ". . . Heinricus, dotibus insignitus scientie litteralis et floribus eloquentie redimitus et eruditus apostolicis institutis et legibus imperatorie maiestatis."

[123] See the *Historia regum terrae sanctae* of Oliver (a *scholasticus* of Köln, later bishop of Paderborn, and finally cardinal-bishop of Sabina; d. 1227), chap. 65: "Princeps valde discretus et lingua latina competenter eruditus." I quote Oliver's remark from Toeche, *op. cit.*, 501, n. 2, since the *Historia regum terrae sanctae* has been published only by J. G. Eccard, in his *Corpus historicum medii aevi* (1st ed.; Leipzig, 1723; 2d, Frankfort, 1743), a rare old collection not available to me.

[124] *Otia imperialia* (*MGH. SS.*, XXVII, 380) : "Erat autem Henricus vir apud moderatos modestus, apud rebelles atrocissimus, hostibus invictus, contumacibus severus, proditoribus immisericors, *literatis ipse literatior.*"

[125] *Op. cit.*, 498.

[126] See his characterization in the work known as the *Continuatio Aquicinctina*, ad a. 1197 (*MGH. SS.*, VI, 434) : "Hic statura personalis non fuit, sed litteratura eius, magnanimitas, iusticia et prudentia pulchritudinem Absolonis superavit."

[127] *Annales*, ad a. 1191 (*MGH. SS.*, XVII, 385) : "Iste Heinricus audacia et largitate, iusticia et veritate, litteratura et sapientia et aliis virtutibus pollens, imperium suo brevi tempore bene rexit. . . ."

[128] In the *Pantheon, XXIV*, 10 (*MGH. SS.*, XXII, 269) : "Qui licet natura et litteratura super omnes coetaneos sapientia et sensuum subtilitate videatur pollere."

[129] Cf. E. Winkelmann, *Philipp von Schwaben und Otto IV. von Braunschweig* (in the *Jahrbücher* series; Leipzig, 1873–1878), I, 470.

[130] See the *Chronicon* of Robert of Auxerre (d. 1212), ad a. 1208 (*MGH. SS.*, XXVI, 272) : "Fuit autem Phylippus vir moderationis eximie et equitatis amator et *impensius litteris eruditus.*"

[131] Arnold of Lübeck, *Chronica Slavorum*, VII, 12 (*MGH. SS.*, XXI, 244) : "Erat enim vir mansuetus et humilis et admodum affabilis. Et quia litteratus erat, divina devotus valde frequentabat. Et cum in ecclesia inter alios lectiones vel responsoria recitaret, clericos sive scolares pauperes a se non removebat, sed quasi conscolasticos eos habebat."

[132] For the person and character of Otto IV, see Winkelmann, *op. cit.*, I, 74 ff. and II, 467.

[133] See esp. the following words (*MGH. SS.*, XXVII, 366) : "Quia ergo optimum nature fatigate remedium est amare novitates et gaudere variis, nec decet tam sacras aures spiritu mimorum fallaci ventilari, dignum duxi aliquid auribus vestris ingerere, quo humana operetur recuperacio." Gervase of Tilbury

(*ca.* 1165 = ?), though he remained a layman, was originally designed for the priesthood and was sent abroad early in life to join the *familia* of William, archbishop of Rheims, and in this household and while in training for orders he laid the foundations of the learning by which he was afterwards distinguished. On his work *Otia imperialia,* a sort of encyclopedia of wonders written for the emperor Otto IV, see Potthast, *Bibliotheca historica medii aevi* (2d ed.), I, 507, which fails to mention Liebrecht, *Des Gervasius von Tilbury Otia imperialia* (Hanover, 1656) and a good anonymous article in the *Church Quarterly Review,* II (1876), 465–490.

[134] "Heinrich der Löwe als Beförderer von Kunst und Wissenschaft," *HZ,* 127 (1922), 64.

[135] Reference to Alwin Schultz, *Höfisches Leben zur Zeit des Minnesanges* (1st ed.), I, 120; in 2d ed. (Leipzig, 1899), I, 157.

[136] *Geschichte des deutschen Volkes* . . . , III, 655–657.

[137] It is not clear to what Gerdes is referring here.

[138] The references given here to Arnold, *Chronica Slavorum,* III, 5 (*MGH. SS.,* XXI, 147), and to Albert of Stade, *MGH. SS.,* XVI, 371, 7, are discussed below.

[139] The reference given to *Dialogus miraculorum,* I, 4, is not pertinent.

[140] Cf. Specht, *op. cit.,* 241 ff.

[141] As Gerdes himself has recognized; see *op. cit.,* 655 ff. (tr. above) and 643–644.

[142] See the *Lippiflorium* of Magister Justinus (written *ca.* 1250), published by Ed. Winkelmann, in *Mittheilungen aus dem Gebiete der Geschichte Liv-, Esth-, und Kurlands,* XI (1868), 423, vv. 23 ff.

> "ponitur ad studium puer in puerilibus annis,
> ne mens ad libitum sit vaga lege carens,
> non ut grammaticae solum doceatur in arte,
> quin etiam studeat moribus ipse bonis.
>
> . . . .
> Ergo tam famae causa quam sanguinis alti
> Hildesiensis eum colligit ecclesia,
> in qua canonicus et amabilis omnibus estat."

[143] See Winkelmann's discussion, *ibid.,* 464–467.

[144] See the *Chronicon Lyvoniae* of Henry of Lithuania (*MGH. SS.,* XXIII, 277): ". . . Bernardus comes . . . a Deo castigatus . . . compunctus, religionem Cysterciensis ordinis assumpsit, et *aliquot annis religionem discens et literas,* auctoritatem a domno papa verbum Dei predicandi et in Lyvoniam proficiscendi accepit. . . ." Cf. Wattenbach, *DGQ* (6th ed.), II, 246, n. 3, who fails, however, to give his references.

[145] *Chron. Slav.,* VII, 12 (*MGH. SS.,* XXI, 243–244): "[Otto] perspexit in cedula maculam quandam exteriorem sicque concepit suspicionem, veniensque ad suum quendam familiarem: 'Aperi,' inquit, 'michi litteras, ut earum sciam tenorem.' Qui perspectis litteris expavit, dicens: 'Rogo ut Dei intuitu litteras me vobis exponere non artetis, quia nichil aliud nisi mortem michi imminere video, si eas exposuero.' Sicque acceptis litteris palatinus alteri nimis importune insistebat et ita tenorem ipsarum cognoscebat."

[146] *Annales Stederburgenses,* ad a. 1194 (*MGH. SS.,* XVI, 230): "Antiqua

scripta cronicorum colligi praecepit et conscribi et coram recitari, et in hac occupatione saepe totam noctem duxit insomnem." Two verses from a poem in honor of Henry the Lion which are found in an early thirteenth-century MS of the *Chronica Boemorum* of Cosmas, published by R. Koepke (*MGH. SS.*, IX, 29), probably refer to the same thing:

"Et vita vete-⎱ rum　　　　Nosset per scripta prio-⎱ rum."
Atque statum mise-⎰　　　　Per mores sciret eo-　⎰

[147] See esp. Philippi, *op. cit.*, 63, n. 2, and ff. Philippi believes that Henry received a liberal education in his youth, but M. Philippson, *Heinrich der Löwe, Herzog von Bayern und Sachsen: sein Leben und seine Zeit* (2d ed.; Leipzig, 1918), 383 and esp. 552, holds that Henry did not acquire any interest in higher culture until after his marriage to Mathilda, daughter of Henry II of England. Philippi's evidence is by no means convincing.

[148] See Philippi, *op. cit.*, 61 ff.

[149] "Got selbe hat den sin gegebin
deme herzogen der ez schriben liez.
sine capellane er hiez
die rede suchen an den schriften
und bat daz sie ez tichten
an rimen wolden,
wan sie ensolden
nicht schriben wan die warheit,
als ez zu latine steit.
. . . .
ez enwere an dem meister nicht bliben,
er hette ez gerimet an er solde."

I have quoted from the edition of Felix Heidlauf (Berlin, 1915), p. xii; it is given also by Philippi, *op. cit.*, 62, with minor variant readings.

To cite here another example of Henry's patronage of the vernacular literature: one of his *ministeriales*, Eilhart von Oberg, wrote up the epic story of Tristan and Isolt, in Low German verse, long before Gottfried von Strassburg wrote his version, but since Gottfried's treatment of the theme was more brilliant the version of Eilhart fell into neglect and only a few fragments of it have survived (*ibid.*, 60).

[150] *Chron. Slav.*, III, 5 (*MGH. SS.*, XXI, 147): "Scientia quoque litterali non parum profecerunt, quia nobiliores terre filios suos non solum ad clerum promovendum, verum etiam secularibus rebus instituendos Parisius mittunt. Ubi litteratura simul et idiomate lingue terre illius imbuti, non solum in artibus, sed etiam in theologia multum invaluerunt. Siquidem propter naturalem lingue celeritatem non solum in argumentis dialecticis subtiles inveniuntur, sed etiam in negotiis ecclesiasticis tractandis boni decretiste sive legiste comprobantur." Cf. Gerdes, *op. cit.*, III, 656 and n. 3.

[151] *Annales Stadenses*, ad a. 1246 (*MGH. SS.*, XVI, 371). That these boys had studied in Paris is an inference suggested by Gerdes, *op. cit.*, III, 656.

[152] *Chronica*, XI, 7 (*MGH. SS.*, XIX, 130): "vir sapiens et strenuus et laudabiliter litteratus."

[153] Thus the *Sachsenspiegel* (thirteenth century), I, 24, 3 (in the 3d ed. of C. G. Homeyer [Berlin, 1861], 183), makes mention of "the Psalter and all

books pertaining to divine service, which the women are accustomed to read." Cf., further, Wattenbach, *DGQ* (6th ed.), I, 320, n. 1; Weinhold, *Die deutschen Frauen in dem Mittelalter*, I, 129; and especially Specht, *op. cit.*, 279.

[154] See the *Annales Stadenses* on Saint Hildegard (d. 1179) (*MGH. SS.*, XVI, 330): "Haec cum quadraginta duorum esset annorum, magnae choruscationis igneum lumen aperto coelo adveniens totum cerebrum eius transfudit et totum cor et totum pectus eius, et sic eam sanctus Spiritus inflammavit, ut statim omnium katholicorum librorum seriem, tam novi quam veteris testamenti, ad integrum intelligeret, cum tamen nichil umquam didicerit, nisi solum psalterium more nobilium puellarum. . . ." Similarly, the *Chronicon* of Alberic, ad a. 1140 (*MGH. SS.*, XXIII, 834): "solum psalterium legere didicerat more nobilium puellarum a quadam inclusa in monte sancti Desibodi." Also, the thirteenth-century poem in praise of study and the clerical life, in which the following bit of advice, or, rather, base hope, is given to the young student:

> "Si vero grammaticam nequis scire plene,
> Defectu ingenui, defectu crumene,
> Horas et psalterium discas valde bene,
> Scolas si necesse est puellarum tene."

Published by R. Peiper, in *Zeitschr. f. deut. Phil.*, V (1874), 183.

[155] *Annales* or *Chronicon Boemorum*, ad a. 1153 (*MGH. SS.*, XVII, 664): ". . . litteris et Latino optime eruditam eloquio, quod maxime domizellarum nobilium exornat decorem." Cf. Wattenbach, *DGQ* (6th ed.), II, 247, n. 3.

[156] See the *Breslauer Urkundenbuch*, ed. G. Korn (Breslau, 1870), 35, no. 32: ". . . ita duximus ordinandum, scilicet ut infra muros civitatis Vratislauiensis iuxta ecclesiam sancte Marie Magdalene scole fiant, in quibus pueri parvuli doceantur et discant alphabetum cum oracione dominica et salutacionem beate Marie virginis cum symbolo psalterio et septem psalmis, discant eciam ibidem cantum, ut in ecclesiis ad honorem dei legere valeant et cantare. Audiant etiam in eisdem scolis Donatum, Cathonem, et Theodolum ac regulas pueriles." Cf. Specht, *op. cit.*, 250.

[157] H. Heske, *Thomasin von Zerclaere* (Heidelberg, 1933).

[158] Sister Mary Paul Goetz, *The Concept of Nobility in German Didactic Literature of the Thirteenth Century* (Washington, D. C., 1935), 58. On educational ideals and conditions in Germany in the thirteenth century see also R. Limmer, *Bildungszustände und Bildungsideen des dreizehnten Jahrhunderts* (Munich, 1928).

Chapter V

LAY EDUCATION IN ANGLO-SAXON ENGLAND

How widely a knowledge of Latin was diffused among the Celtic population of Roman Britain, it is impossible to determine. There is some reason to believe that Latin was familiar not only to the native aristocracy, some of whom became identified with the Roman ruling group, but also to certain lower classes of the Celtic population. Professor Lunt has summed up the evidence in these words:

In Britain the government began early to encourage the use of Latin by the natives. Literary allusions give some ground for the assumption that the aristocratic and professional classes spoke Latin. More valuable are the inscriptions scratched on tiles and pots by workmen and servants. Enough inscriptions of this sort have been found to establish a probability that in the third and fourth centuries Latin was a familiar tongue to such urban classes as artisans and servants, which were recruited mainly from the native population. They indicate a possibility, indeed, that Latin was used by the similar classes on some of the rural estates. The evidence is not sufficient, on the other hand, to preclude the possibility that Celtic remained the language of common usage among the peasants and even among the artisans of some of the towns. The evidence throws but a flickering light on the linguistic situation in Roman Britain.[1]

With the withdrawal of the Roman legions from Britain early in the fifth century, however, and the subsequent almost complete extinction of Roman institutions and culture, the Latin language sank into oblivion, at least among the laity.

We do not have to wait until the time of Alfred the Great to find traces of lay education in Anglo-Saxon Britain. Aldfrith, king of Northumbria (593–617), was a lover of literature, and the first private owner of a library in the British Isles.[2] He obtained books from Wearmouth, Canterbury, Malmesbury, and Iona. The abbot Adamnan dedicated his *De locis sanctis* to him, and, according to Bede, by Aldfrith's generosity it was passed on to inferior persons to read.[3] Bede also tells us that in the year 631, or soon after, Sigebert, king of the East Angles (631–634), "desiring to follow that goodly order which he saw practised in France, set up a school in which boys should be instructed in letters, by the help of bishop

---

Felix whom he had gotten from Kent, and who appointed them masters and teachers after the manner of the men of Kent."[4] On the basis of this passage Leach had argued that Augustine must have founded a school of grammar at Canterbury in 598 modeled upon the "Graeco-Roman institutions, in which Horace and Juvenal, Jerome and St. Augustine had learnt the scansion of hexameters and the accredited methods of speech-making and argument,"[5] and having for its purpose the dissemination of a general education, especially in the Latin language and Latin literature, "as much needed by the statesman, the lawyer, the civil servant, and the clerk as by the priest or cleric."[6] This contention, however, has recently been attacked by Mr. Putnam Fennell Jones, who asserts that "the available evidence does not point to any such secularity and semi-independence of English education in Augustine's day," as Leach would have us believe.[7] It is clear that Bede's statement proves the existence of some sort of school in Kent before the coming of Archbishop Theodore and Abbot Hadrian in 669, but since we have no other direct evidence, the exact nature of the school must remain a mystery.[8]

Some attention seems to have been paid to the education of Anglo-Saxon princes. O. M. Dalton has pointed out[9] that in the seventh century Anglo-Saxon princes and princesses were often sent to Frankish Gaul to be educated. Thus Eanfled the daughter and Wuscfrea the son of Edwin, king of Northumbria (d. 633), were sent by their mother, Queen Ethelberga, "into France to be brought up in the court of King Dagobert," who was her second cousin.[10] Others were sent to monasteries in Gaul, and though undoubtedly the education they received there was chiefly religious, it "may well have carried with it some elements of literature."[11] We know of at least one Anglo-Saxon prince in the eighth century who was able to read Latin. Bede sent the first draft of his *Historia ecclesiastica* to Ceowulf, king of Northumbria (729–764), to be read for criticism, and later sent him the final draft that the king might study it at leisure and have it transcribed.[12] In the correspondence of Saint Boniface there is a series of five little poems, at least two of which, one addressed to Aldhelm, the other to a certain Oua, were written by Aethilwald, who is often identified with Ethelbald, king of Mercia (716–757). It has been pointed out, however, by the late Montague James[13] that this identification is not correct.

Evidence derived from eighth-century charters seems to imply illiteracy, or at least inability to write, among the Anglo-Saxon laity. A distinction is often, though not always, made between the signatures of ecclesiastics, who frequently use some such formula as *Ego . . . subscripsi,* and those of lay persons, who generally use *Signum manus . . . ,* with the name in genitive form following.[14] Occasionally someone definitely indicates that he is illiterate, as does Wihtred, king of Kent (689–725), who makes his mark *pro ignorantia litterarum.* Chadwick believes that the distinction between the kinds of signatures used by the clergy and laity implies "a tradition that only the clergy were expected to be able to sign their names."[15]

A highly confused account of Alfred the Great's early training is given by his pious biographer, Asser. We are told that, through the negligence of his parents and those who had charge of him, he remained illiterate until his twelfth year or even later.[16] This state of illiteracy probably refers to his inability to read Saxon, since the chapter following contains the well-known anecdote of how Alfred learned to "read" Saxon in one day in order to get the book offered as a reward by his mother.[17] Apparently he desired to learn Latin letters in his youth, but was unable to do so on account of the lack of masters.[18] Not until about 887, when he was nearly forty years old, did he learn to read Latin and at the same time to translate Latin into English.[19] We may infer from these and other bits of information given by Asser that, while it was not unusual for the children of the nobility to study English, or at least learn to read it, the study of Latin letters was almost nonexistent in Alfred's youth and early manhood.

From Alfred himself we receive a dark picture of the cultural conditions which prevailed in his time and which he labored to improve. In his introduction to Gregory's *Pastoral Care* which he sent to the English bishops he writes thus:

So clean fallen away is learning now in the Angle race, that there are very few on this side Humber who would know how to render their service-book into English, or to read off an epistle out of Latin into English, and I ween there would not be many on the other side of Humber.[20]

The very fact that most of Alfred's own intellectual labor consisted in translating Latin works into Old English indicates the limited knowledge of Latin among the laity of his day, or even among the clergy. His interest in the education of the laity is revealed in the same introduction, where he issues instructions that the sons of the nobility are to be taught to read English in their childhood. We are also told by Asser that he established a school at his court which was attended by "almost all the noble children of the whole realm and even by many not of noble birth."[21]

In this school, books of both tongues, Latin and English, were assiduously read; and they [the students] had time to learn writing also, and became studious and ingenious in the liberal arts, before they had the strength to turn themselves to other avocations, such as hunting, and the other accomplishments in which noble youths should be conversant.[22]

Adult persons, even royal officials, were compelled by Alfred to get some education. "Almost all the ealdormen, reeves and thegns," says Asser, the king's biographer, "who had been illiterate from childhood, took to their books, preferring to study laboriously the unaccustomed learning rather than to lose their jobs." We learn also that of the five children of Alfred who survived infancy, Edward, his successor, and Aelfthryth, who later was married to Baldwin II, count of Flanders, and his youngest child, Aethelweard, a boy[23]—these three made excellent progress in their studies. Although Asser's words[24] concerning the education of Edward and Aelfthryth perhaps indicate a greater proficiency in English than in Latin, nevertheless we may assume that the royal children were trained in the rudiments of Latin.

Alfred's influence on the culture of the English laity is described in somewhat exaggerated terms, perhaps, by Sir Charles Oman:[25]

Alfred's exertions gave England for many years an educated governing class, in which laymen as well as clergy were included. How long the impulse lasted may be judged from the fact that three full generations after his death there were lay magnates capable of writing freely in Latin. His kinsman Aethelweard, the descendant in the fourth degree of his brother Aethelred, *patricius, consul, et quaestor,* as he oddly styles himself (presumably meaning that he was an aetheling and an ealdorman, and had been a king's reeve), was able to compile a chronicle, which he dedicated to his distant cousin Mathilda,[26] the great-granddaughter of Alfred, somewhere about the year 975. Its Latin is pompous and rhetorical, adorned with affected Greek words and inappropriate classical tags, but it is astonishing to find in the tenth century a high secular official of royal descent who can write a Latin book of any sort, still more so one who does it for pure love of historical research and love of family antiquities. The phenomenon is unparalleled in the lands of Continental Christendom.

Aethelweard's[27] achievement in writing the *Chronicorum libri quatuor* was indeed notable, since it is "the only Latin chronicle that bridges the gap of two centuries between Asser and Florence of Worcester."[28] It can hardly be called "unparalleled," however, for the Continent can boast of the even more remarkable work of two lay historians, Nithard, in the ninth century, and the anonymous author of a *History of the First Crusade* written in the eleventh century. The level of lay culture in tenth-century England was almost certainly not so high as Oman would have us believe. King Edgar (959–975) ordered Aethelwald, the bishop of Winchester, to translate the Rule of St. Benedict into English, "for secular men who turned to the monastic life and knew no Latin."[29] The movement for monastic reform under King Edgar is itself a proof that culture was at a very low ebb, even within the Church. "The cessation of religious instruction had been so complete that even a knowledge of ecclesiastical Latin was rare, and a translation was necessary if the monks were to know what was the code under which they were living."[30] The most favorable conclusion we can draw is that Latin was not entirely forsaken by laymen and was at least cultivated by some of the Anglo-Saxon kings in this period. Even this conclusion rests only on the evidence of a twelfth-century writer citing an "old" authority whose reliability cannot be established. In his account of King Aethelstan (924–940), William of Malmesbury writes:

Concerning this king a strong persuasion is prevalent among the English, that one more just or learned never governed the kingdom. That he was versed in literature, I discovered a few days since, in a certain old volume, wherein the writer struggles with the difficulty of the task, unable to express his meaning as he wished. Indeed, I would subjoin his words for brevity's sake, were they not extravagant beyond belief in the praise of the king, and just in that style of writing which Cicero, the prince of Roman eloquence, in his book of Rhetoric denominates "bombast." The custom of the time excuses the diction, and the affection for Athelstan, who was yet living, gave countenance to the excess of praise.[31]

A last rare example of English lay interest in books before 1066 is found in Lambeth MS 149, which is written in a hand very similar to that of the famous *Exeter Book*,[32] and which bears an inscription recording its presentation in 1018 to an unknown monastery by *Aetheluvardus dux,* who married a granddaughter of his namesake, probably the chronicler Aethelweard mentioned above.

Notes to Chapter V

[1] W. E. Lunt, *History of England* (New York and London, 1928), 29. Cf. F. Haverfield, *The Romanization of Roman Britain* (Oxford, Clarendon Press, 1915), 30 f.

[2] A. S. Cook, "The Possible Begetter of Old English Beowulf and Widsith," *Connecticut Academy of Arts and Sciences*, 1922, 25.

[3] *Historia ecclesiastica*, V, 15, trans. by J. E. King ("The Loeb Classical Library"), II, 285.

[4] *Ibid.*, III, 18 (King, I, 413).

[5] A. F. Leach, *The Schools of Medieval England* (New York, 1915), 13, and see 2–3; cf. also his *Educational Charters and Documents, 598 to 1909* (Cambridge, 1911), p. xi.

[6] Leach, *Schools of Medieval England*, 7.

[7] "The Gregorian Mission and English Education," *Speculum* (1928), III, 335 ff.

[8] Cf. *ibid.*, 335, n. 1.

[9] Introduction to tr., *History of the Franks*, I, 189, 412–413.

[10] Bede, *Hist. eccl.*, II, 20 (King, 1, 319).

[11] Dalton, tr., *History of the Franks*, I, 413.

[12] See Bede's letter to Ceowulf (in King's edition), I, 2: "Historiam Gentis Anglorum Ecclesiasticam quam nuper edideram, libentissime tibi desideranti, rex, et prius ad legendum ac probandum transmisi, et nunc ad transscribendum ac plenius ex tempore meditandum retransmitto." Cf. K. J. Holzknecht, *Literary Patronage in the Middle Ages* (Philadelphia, 1923), 90.

[13] In the *Cambridge History of English Literature*, I, 86. Cf. also in confirmation the *Dictionary of National Biography* (under "Ethelbald"), which mentions Stubbs as authority (but gives no reference).

[14] See H. M. Chadwick, *The Growth of Literature* (Cambridge, 1932), 1, 479.

[15] *Loc. cit.*

[16] *De rebus gestis Aelfredi* (ed. W. Stevenson; Oxford, Clarendon Press, 1904), chap. 22, 20.

[17] *Ibid.*, chap. 23, 20.

[18] *Ibid.*, chap. 25, 21.

[19] *Ibid.*, chap. 86, 73: "divino instinctu legere et interpretari simul uno eodemque die primitus inchoavit."

[20] As translated by C. Oman, *England before the Norman Conquest* (3d ed.; London, 1913), 476.

[21] *De rebus gestis Aelfredi*, chap. 75, and cf. Stevenson's note, 300.

[22] Oman, *op. cit.*, 477–478.

[23] Of the other two children, Aethelflaed, the eldest, who was married to the ealdorman Aethelred, may perhaps have reached maturity before the court school was established; Aethelgifu, a younger daughter, later became abbess of Shaftesbury, and therefore does not concern us, even though she undoubtedly received at least as good an education as her brothers and her other remaining sister.

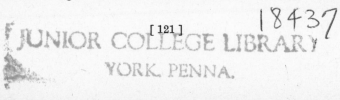

[24] *Op. cit.*, 59: "et psalmos et Saxonicos libros et maxime Saxonica carmina studiose didicere, et *frequentissime libris utuntur.*"

[25] *Op. cit.*, 478.

[26] According to W. Hunt, in the *Dictionary of National Biography* (under "Ethelwerd"), this Matilda was the great-great-granddaughter of Alfred, and the daughter of Liudolf of Swabia, the son of Otto I and Edith, and not the daughter of Edith herself, as Oman has it (*op. cit.*, 478, n. 2). But since the one (the daughter of Edith and Otto) was abbess of Quedlinburg and the other (the daughter of Liudolf and Ida) was abbess of Essen, neither was a lay-woman. It is therefore useless for our purposes to try to determine the identity of the one to whom Aethelweard dedicated his chronicle. Cf. the genealogical tables in Stokvis, *Manuel d'histoire de généalogie* (Leyden, 1888–1891), III, 218 and 251.

[27] Aethelweard the ealdorman is mentioned also by Miss Rose Graham, "The Intellectual Influence of English Monasticism between the Tenth and the Twelfth Centuries," *Transactions of the Royal Historical Society*, XVII (1903), 39.

[28] C. Gross, *Sources and Literature of English History*, no. 1366.

[29] Graham, *op. cit.*, 25.

[30] Mary Bateson, "Rules for Monks and Secular Canons after the Revival under King Edgar," *English Historical Review*, IX (1894), 692.

[31] *Gesta regum Anglorum*, II, 132 (ed. Stubbs, I, 144): "De hoc rege non invalida apud Anglos fama seritur, quod nemo legalius vel litteratius rem-publicam administraverit. Quanquam litteras illum scisse, pauci admodum dies sunt quod didicerim in quodam sane volumine vestuto, in quo scriptor cum difficultate materiae luctabatur, judicium animi sui non valens pro voto pro-ferre. Cujus hic verba pro compendio subjicerem, nisi quia ultra opinionem in laudibus principis vagatur, eo dicendi genere quod suffultum rex facundiae Romanae Tullius in rhetoricis appellat. Eloquium excusat consuetudo illius temporis, laudum nimietatem adornat favor Ethelstani adhuc viventis." The translation is that given by Holzknecht, *Literary Patronage in the Middle Ages*, 83–84. Malmesbury goes on to quote a poem in honor of Aethelstan, evidently taken from the same old volume to which he has just referred, which has a few lines concerning Aethelstan's education.

> "Ad patris edictum datus in documenta scholarum,
> Extimuit rigidos ferula crepitante magistros;
> Et potans avidis doctrinae mella medullis,
> Decurrit teneros sed non pueriliter annos."

The date of this anonymous writer cannot be determined, as no other fragment of his work seems to have been preserved; cf. Stubbs's trans., I, 145, n. 2.

[32] *The Exeter Book of Old English Poetry*. With introductory chapters by R. W. Chambers, Max Forster, and Robin Flower. Printed and published for the Dean and Chapter of Exeter Cathedral (London, Humphries, 1933).

Chapter VI

FRANCE AND FLANDERS
(From *ca.* 900 to *ca.* 1300)

AFTER THE BRIEF PERIOD of intellectual brilliance at the court of Charles the Bald had come to an end (877), there followed a long period of darkness in the history of lay learning, especially in northern France. Except in two areas, Aquitaine and Anjou, where the nobility still kept alive a tradition of culture and learning, it was rare indeed to find a layman who possessed a knowledge of Latin. The Vulgar Latin which had long been spoken by a large part of the population of Gaul had now become so changed from Classical Latin that it was no longer regarded as Latin but rather as a different tongue, the *lingua romana* or Old French. Latin maintained itself as the language of learning, but it was no longer used as the vehicle of ordinary speech. Thus Richer tells us that at a meeting between Charles the Simple and Henry I of Saxony, the French and German youths present, "as they are wont, began with much animosity to flay each other with curses, each in his own particular tongue."[1] The Carolingian princes at Laon still spoke their ancestral Frankish, but the dukes of Paris spoke French long before the end of the tenth century.[2]

Conditions in lay society were not favorable to study, and few laymen found either time or opportunity to acquire a knowledge of letters. This fact is reflected in a document of 889, according to which Hucbald, a learned monk of Saint-Amand, was sent to Saint-Omer "in order to instruct the lord abbot Rudolf, our superior"; thus the lay abbot was trying to obtain some measure of the education which he now needed in his new rôle, but had not hitherto acquired.[3] A striking exception to the general rule of illiteracy among laymen is Gerald, count of Aurillac and founder of the monastery of that name. Odo of Cluny's account of the youth and early training of Gerald shows clearly that this noble had received an education which was extraordinary for a man of the world. Imbued with a genuine love of learning, he acquired an excellent command of Latin, and in his knowledge of the Scriptures he surpassed many of the clerics and scholars of his day. Odo's narrative, however, shows that ordinarily the sons of the nobility who were intended for secular life only "skimmed the Psalter" by way of education. It also shows that Gerald's intensive studies were due to sickness in his youth which made it seem probable that he would pursue an ecclesiastical career.[4] The low estate to which culture in general had fallen is revealed in the story of the founding of Aurillac. Gerald wished to obtain for his monastery only monks of the highest type, and in order to realize this ideal he was finally forced to send some noble youths to be trained at the monastery of Vabres. His efforts were fruitless, however; the boys on their return to Aurillac speedily relaxed into undisciplined ways because there were no teachers at the new monastery.[5]

The attitude that letters were the special province of the clergy is reflected also in the *Vita S. Odonis,* written by Odo's disciple, John. Odo was originally intended for a career in the Church, and was therefore as a young lad placed in charge of a priest to be taught the elements of grammar.[6] But as the boy grew older his father began to wean him away from the idea of an ecclesiastical career and finally sent him to the court of Duke William of Aquitaine, where Odo spent his time in hunting and hawking.[7] True to the behavior pattern of saints, however, Odo fell ill, and his father made haste to redeem his original vow, dedicating Odo to Saint Martin. Odo, now aged nineteen, went off to Tours, took the tonsure, and resumed his studies, devoting himself especially to sacred letters.[8]

From our point of view, Abbo, the father of Odo of Cluny, is more interesting than Odo himself. According to John of Salerno, Abbo was described by his son as a man who "seemed to be different in manner and deed from the men of the present generation. For he knew by heart the histories of the ancients and the *Novella* of Justinian."[9] This statement can hardly be accepted literally, but it is safe to assume that Abbo had some knowledge of history and law which distinguished him from the ordinary layman.[10] It would be interesting to know if Abbo could write Latin as well as read it.[11] At any rate, it is clear that Abbo, a favorite of William the Pious of Aquitaine, himself a literate prince, was a layman of unusual culture for his time. It is even possible that he owned a goodly library. We know that when Odo set out in 909 for the monastery of Baume in Burgundy, he carried with him a library of one hundred volumes.[12] Although some of these books had probably been acquired in his years of study at Tours and in Paris, it seems reasonable to suppose that the nucleus of the collection had been inherited from his father. It was no easy matter in those days to collect a large library in a short space of time.

William the Pious of Aquitaine (d. 918) probably had a very good knowledge of Latin letters. He was able to write, at least to sign his own name. His autograph appears in the subscription to the deed of 910 by which he established the monastery of Cluny.[13] From the same subscription it appears that his wife, Gelberata, was unable to write. Although the presence of the *signum* instead of the personal signature does not necessarily mean inability to write, in this document it probably indicates illiteracy, since the personal signatures of William and of several ecclesiastics seem to imply the desirability of such signatures.[14]

Léon Maître would have us believe that the ability to write was not so uncommon in this century as it is generally thought to be. He says that Rudolf of Burgundy, king of France from 923 to 936, could at least write his own name, and cites in support of his contention the following verses, which precede the subscription to a document of Rudolf in 925 in favor of the monastery of Saint-Amand:

Utque hoc preceptum firmum per secula duret
Et credant homines cuncti per tempora mundi,
Subsignante manu propria firmatio paret,
Atque anulus nostrum pinxit suppresus agalma.[15]

As far as I know, no facsimile of this document has been published, but we may safely assume, even without paleographical confirmation, that the personal signature of the king consisted of nothing more than his mark, since the actual subscription reads "Signum Radulphi Regis gloriosissimi," a fact which Maître overlooked.[16]

As a matter of fact, all the French kings of this period, down to and including Hugh Capet, were probably illiterate. Thus Louis IV, d'Outre-mer (936–954), was not even able to understand Latin. At a synod held in Ingelheim in 948, the papal letters had to be translated into German for the benefit of the two kings present, Louis and Otto I.[17] Unlike the emperor, however, Louis never seems to have made any attempt to acquire a knowledge of letters. There is a well-known tale, of somewhat doubtful veracity, to the effect that Louis once came to Tours on the eve of the summer feast of

St. Martin, and there found Fulk II, the Good (942–960), among the canons of the church, dressed in clerical garb and chanting his devotions with fervor. To Louis and his followers this seemed a ludicrous sight. "He sings like a priest!" was their comment. But Fulk could himself use satire on occasion. When he heard of the manner in which he had been ridiculed, he sent Louis a brief note: "To the king of the Franks, the count of Anjou: greetings. Know, my lord, that an unlettered king is a crowned ass!"[18] Even if we regard the story as legendary, we may still believe that the conditions implied in it were actual,[19] and that it thus reflects, in contrast to the illiteracy of the French king and his nobility, the learning and culture of Fulk the Good of Anjou. Fulk is even said to have composed an excellent sequence of twelve responses in honor of Saint Martin.[20] The wife of Louis d'Outre-mer, Gerberga, the sister of Otto I, may have had a better education than her husband, for Adso, the famous teacher at the episcopal school of Toul, wrote his *Libellus de Antichristo* at her request.[21]

An interesting item in the anonymous eleventh-century *Life of Saint Gerard of Brogne* (d. ca. 959) tells how Gerard, a soldier of renown and trusted councilor of Count Bérenger of Namur, having decided to forsake the world, entered a monastery and, although he was a bearded man, eagerly set about learning his letters from the monks.[22] This bit of evidence, although it cannot be accepted without reservation, seems to confirm the belief that in the tenth century the average layman in northern France and the Low Countries was illiterate.[23]

Southern France presents a different picture. Folcuin in his *Gesta abbatum Lobiensium* tells an incident in the life of Rather of Verona which is valuable for its implications. While Rather, temporarily ousted from his bishopric, was staying in Provence, he undertook upon request to instruct in letters the son of a very rich man, and for this lad he composed a book on grammar which he called *Sparadorsum* or *The Back-sparer* because by using it a boy could save himself from beatings.[24] There is nothing in the passage to indicate that the rich man's son was destined for the Church; hence we may reasonably infer that this is an instance of interest in learning on the part of the upper classes in southern France.

The founder of the Capetian line knew no Latin. Richer relates that at a meeting held in 981 between Otto II and Hugh Capet,

Otto spoke Latin and a bishop translated his words for Hugh's benefit.[25] It seems clear, therefore, that Hugh did not understand German and that his vernacular speech had so far departed from Latin that he needed an interpreter in order to understand the emperor. The synods held during this period likewise reflect the general ignorance of Latin. The vernacular seems to have been used at most of them.[26] Although this might be interpreted as revealing a lack of familiarity with Latin on the part of the clergy, it is more reasonable to assume that the vernacular was used for the sake of the lay magnates present.

The first Capetian king to whom we can definitely attribute a knowledge of Latin is Robert II, the Pious (996–1031), who studied under Gerbert, the greatest scholar of his day, at the cathedral school of Rheims.[27] Among his fellow students were such men as Fulbert of Chartres, Gerard of Crépy-en-Valois, and the converted Jew, Herbert, afterward abbot of Lagny.[28] Richer, who knew Robert as a fellow student, says that he was "well versed in divine and canon law, and applied himself to the liberal arts."[29] Raoul Glaber also bears witness to his learning.[30] Robert's interest in books is shown in a letter which Amblardus, abbot of Solignac, wrote to Herveus, custodian of St. Martin of Tours; Amblardus tells Herveus that he has sent the requested copy of the *Vita Eligii* and urges Herveus to show the book to King Robert, who had expressed a desire to see it.[31] Hariulf depicts Robert as a king who never failed to derive solace from books, and even carried them about with him on his travels.[32] Certain documents of this period are dated "regnante rege philosopho," thus showing that his contemporaries esteemed Robert not only as a pious but also as a learned king.[33] His learning and culture have been compared with the like acquirements of Henry II of Germany and William V, the Great, of Aquitaine.[34]

We have already referred to the relatively high cultural level which prevailed at the court of the dukes of Aquitaine; and we may even infer that it was in large part owing to his Aquitanian mother, Adelaide, daughter of William III (Tête d'Etoupe), that Robert received such a good education.[35]

The most recent historian of the dukes of Aquitaine considers at some length the literacy of William IV.[36] He argues speciously that the peculiar autograph *signa* or marks of the duke which appear in the documents of which he was either author or witness are "indicative of a taste for drawing or at least writing," especially since such *signa* were usually left to be made by the scribe. Such evidence, however, is not conclusive, and William's literacy remains purely conjectural.

The literacy of William V, the Great (993–1030), has an entirely different status. He was the most interesting literate noble in France in his generation. Undoubtedly, the province of the Limousin was the most cultured territory in France in the first part of the eleventh century.

The indications of literary activity in Aquitania under William the Great... are concentrated. They group around Limoges most significantly and they prove that artistic composition in both Latin and Provençal was cultivated in that town during the eleventh century, if not during the last half of the tenth. Limoges was undoubtedly a point of contact between the two literatures and a meeting-place. There we may pardonably conjecture a collaboration between the cloister and the market.[37]

In a letter of Fulbert of Chartres to Hildegair, treasurer of the church of St. Hilary in Poitiers, relating that he is sending him copies of Priscian and Donatus, the bishop adds that he is also enclosing one of two books which the duke had asked to have transcribed at Chartres for him. "I thought that I had sent one of these before," he writes.[38]

Adhemar of Chabannes tells us that this famous duke learned his letters in his youth, had a good knowledge of the Scriptures, and kept a library in his palace. When free from affairs of state, he would spend his time reading, and would even pass the long winter nights by lamplight among his books until sleep conquered him. This picture reminds the chronicler of Louis the Pious and Charlemagne, and of those early emperors of old, Theodosius and Augustus, who occupied themselves not only with reading but with writing, besides.[39] On the basis of this passage from Adhemar, the authors of the *Histoire littéraire de la France*,[40] as well as a more recent authority,[41] credit William V with the ability to wield the pen as well as the sword.[42] Such an interpretation is certainly open to question, however, and it seems more probable that Adhemar was referring only to reading when he used the word *elucubrans*.[43] But the puzzle with respect to Duke William's reading ability is not yet resolved. For we do not know whether the books which he read in bed when he could not sleep were written in Latin or in the vernacular. The fact that his letters are written in Latin does not prove conclusively that he could read Latin, so it may have been that his reading knowledge was limited to works in the popular tongue. And yet the six letters of the duke which have survived are so personal in tone that we are forced to believe that they were dictated by the duke, if not actually written by him *manu propria*.[44] Duke William seems to have had a special interest in building up his library;[45] and one of his prize acquisitions was a MS written in letters of gold, a gift, curiously enough, from the unlettered Norse king, Canute the Great.[46] The tradition of culture at the Aquitanian court must have been maintained throughout the eleventh century; otherwise, it would be almost impossible to account for the extraordinary achievements of William IX, the Troubadour (1086–1126), the grandson of William the Great. The Latin teacher of William IX was Radulf Arden, archdeacon of Poitiers, a cleric of unusual learning, who added some acquaintance with Greek and Hebrew to his knowledge of Latin; it was he who in 1101 accompanied William on his notorious pilgrimage to the Holy Land.[47] The fact that the duke of Aquitaine was the first of the troubadours to apply the formal rules of poetry to his songs proves that he had received a sound literary training in Latin.[48] The rise of a vernacular literature was, of course, to make it possible for a layman to receive a literary education without training in Latin letters.[49]

The court of the counts of Anjou was probably not far behind that of the dukes of Aquitaine and counts of Poitou. Fulk IV, le Rechin (1067–1109), must have possessed an excellent knowledge of Latin for a layman; he was not only a patron of literature, but also even wrote a short Latin history of the house of Anjou.[50] The women of these courts were probably as well educated as the men. Agnes, the wife first of William V of Aquitaine and later of Geoffrey Martel of Anjou (1040–1060), at the time of her divorce from the Angevin count, paid an enormous price for a copy of a collection of the sermons of Haimo of Halberstadt.[51] Another cultured woman of the time was Ermengard, the daughter of Fulk le Rechin and wife of Alanus, duke of Brittany. The panegyric poem which Marbodus, bishop of Rennes, addressed to her, indicates that she was well versed in Latin.[52] We even possess evidence of the ability to write on the part of one woman, Almode, countess of Toulouse.

A deed of confirmation made out to the Abbey of Cluny in 1066 contains two words which were written by her own hand.[53]

Concerning the French kings of this period, it is not clear whether Henry I (1031–1060) was literate or not. At least he took care that his son, Philip I (1060–1108), received a good education. Philip learned his letters under Master Engelran, who appears in several royal documents as *pedagogus regis*.[54] He must have been a precocious child, for in 1059 at the age of seven he publicly read his own coronation oath in Latin.[55] From Suger[56] we learn that Louis VI spent part of his boyhood at Saint-Denis,[57] but it is doubtful whether he received more education than the customary instruction in the Psalter. At least there is no evidence to prove that Louis VI had a knowledge of Latin, and the same thing is true of Louis VII,[58] although we know that the latter was sent to school at Notre-Dame de Paris.[59] Even Philip II, Augustus (1180–1223), seems to have been ignorant of Latin although he was a patron of letters as well as of the arts in general.[60] Innocent III complained that much mischief was done by those who translated the papal letters to the king.[61] Philip Augustus, however, provided for the education of his son, Louis VIII.[62] The chief instructor of Louis seems to have been Stephen of Tournai. In a letter addressed to the young prince, Stephen exhorts and admonishes his pupil to apply himself to his studies because a knowledge of letters will be useful and necessary to him when he ascends the throne, both in the affairs of war and in those of peace.[63] Amalric of Chartres also had a part in the education of Louis VIII.[64] According to Giraldus Cambrensis, writing about 1200, the only prince in Europe to whom it might be worth while for an author to present his works was Louis VIII, who had been imbued from his youth with liberal studies and who was also notably generous.[65]

The most cultured of the kings of medieval France was undoubtedly Louis IX, Saint Louis. The Psalter in which Blanche of Castile taught her son to read is still a cherished manuscript.[66] He was the first king of France to realize the value and importance of a library for scholars and churchmen, and, inspired by Arabic practice, he set about creating one by having manuscripts copied and brought together in a central place.[67] His own genuine love of study proves that he was no mere collector of books.[68] If any illiterate members of the court happened to be present while he was studying, he would translate the material he was reading from Latin into French for their benefit.[69] He was even able to write with his own hand, but in French, not in Latin.[70] This illustrates the tendency in lay education in the thirteenth century. Delisle rightly asserts that lay education in France in the later thirteenth century was on a high level,[71] but it was not generally in Latin. The trend of the times was toward the vernacular. Saint Louis himself had a very good knowledge of Latin, but he was exceptional rather than typical; and even he turned to the vernacular in writing his own letters and documents. After him, there were probably few laymen who knew more than the smattering of Latin which was desirable for following church services. The education of Louis' children supplies an apt illustration. It is evident that he had them learn some Latin, but only of the churchly kind.[72] The rest of their education was probably in French. According to William of Nangis,[73] Philip III was illiterate (*illiteratus*). On the basis of this passage and the added testimony of an anonymous fragment which is plainly nothing more than a later elaboration of William's *Gesta*, Sismondi concluded that Philip could not even read.[74] The most recent biographer of Philip III, however, believes that Sismondi's judgment is too severe, especially in view of what the narrative sources on the life of Saint Louis have to say about the education of his son, and the fact that Vincent of Beauvais wrote his *De eruditione filiorum regalium* with young Philip in mind.[75] It seems probable that William of Nangis meant either that Philip III was not able to read Latin or that he was unable to write. It is difficult to believe that he could not read French. We know that Philip III requested his Dominican confessor, Lawrence, to write in French a sort of breviary, *Somme des Vertus et des Vices,* which was widely popular.[76]

There is abundant evidence to show that Philip IV, the Fair (1285–1314), received a good education.[77] He learned his letters under William of Ercuis, the author of a manual entitled *Liber rationis.*[78] Perhaps Aegidius of Rome, who wrote his manual *De regimine principum* at Philip's request (before October, 1285), also had some influence on the young prince's education.[79] The problem of greatest interest to us is how much Latin, if any, Philip knew. Wenck says:

We may take for granted that Philip had a knowledge of Latin, not because Aegidius dedicated his *De regimine principum* to him in Latin, for we might assume that Aegidius, an Italian by birth, was either unable or unwilling to write in French, even though he had lived in France since childhood; there are other facts which prove that Philip knew Latin...."[80]

He continues by emphasizing Philip's rôle as patron of letters, and cites an imposing list of writers who enjoyed the king's patronage, including such distinguished men as Guiart, Henry de Mondeville, Jean de Meun, Raymund of Béziers, Raymund Lull, Pierre Dubois, the Genoese physician Galvanus de Levanto, Laurence of Aquileia, William of Nangis, and the authors of the *Grandes Chroniques de Saint-Denis.*[81] It is true that some of these men addressed to Philip works in Latin, but this does not necessarily prove Philip's acquaintance with the language. The direct evidence concerning Philip's ability to read Latin is limited and not entirely conclusive. In his *De regimine principum,* Aegidius admonishes the prince diligently to study Latin, the language of learning,[82] but whether Philip followed this advice or not is another matter. Aegidius apparently had no illusions about the amount of Latin known in royal circles. He suggested that his book be read at court in a French translation, and thereupon Philip ordered such a translation to be made.[83] Similarly, in the dedication to his translation of the *De consolatione philosophiae,* Jean de Meun says that although the king understands Latin well, nevertheless he has translated Boethius' work into French to make it more easily understood. Do Jean de Meun's words actually mean that Philip could read Latin, or are they, as Paulin Paris suggests,[84] merely the flattering words of a courtier to a patron who could read Latin not at all or at best with difficulty? Finally, in 1298 Raymund Lull presented to King Philip the Latin version of his philosophical and moralizing treatise, *Arbor philosophiae amoris,* and at the same time gave Queen Jeanne the same work in French. Wenck interprets this fact to mean that Philip read Latin while Jeanne could read only French.[85] On the basis of the evidence presented it seems reasonable to infer that Philip IV had some slight knowledge of Latin, but that he preferred to read French.

Jeanne de Navarre probably had less knowledge of Latin than her husband. When her confessor, Durand de Champagne, wrote his manual of Christian ethics for women, *Speculum dominarum,* in Latin, the queen had it translated into French.[86] A difficulty arises in the fact that Jeanne requested Raymund of Béziers to translate the Spanish version of *Kalilah and Dimnah* (*The Fables of Bidpai*), recently translated from Arabic, into Latin. It is possible, however, that she merely wanted a Latin version which might serve as a basis for a future French translation.[87] We have already noted that Raymund Lull gave her his *Arbor philosophiae amoris* in a French translation.

Thus, by the end of the thirteenth century in France, it would seem—at least from a study of the cultural accomplishments of the French kings—that a layman might be "lettered" without necessarily being trained in Latin. The growing ascendancy of the vernacular language had resulted in frequent translations of literary works from Latin into French. If a book intended for lay consumption was originally written in Latin, it was at once translated into French. For example, when Yves of Saint-Denis presented his history of Saint-Denis to Philip V, a French translation accompanied the original text.[88]

We shall now consider cultural conditions among the French laity in general, meaning by this term, of course, the upper classes of society. Occasionally some curious and valuable bit of information about the training and education of the nobility is revealed in hagiographical literature. Although saints' lives in general are suspect as historical sources, being composed for purposes of edification, and usually long after the decease of the saints written about, nevertheless they frequently throw light on contemporary conditions and culture. When such information agrees with other independent evidence on the same subject, it undoubtedly possesses at least corroborative value. Now the *Vita S. Pauli Virodunensis* (who died *ca.* 649), which was written in the tenth or perhaps the eleventh century,[89] says that as a boy Paul was sent to school to learn letters, "as *was* once the custom among the nobility";[90] whereas the *Vita S. Walrici* (who died *ca.* 622), written in the eleventh century, and undoubtedly several generations later than the former,[91] says that its hero went to school, "as *is* customary for the children of nobles."[92] These passages, with their use of different tenses, serve to confirm a belief which is supported by other evidence, that although there was little if any instruction in letters among the French nobility of the tenth century, by the eleventh century it had become at least somewhat more common for the sons of the nobility to receive some training in letters.

Pfister rejects as vague and valueless the remarks of Hariulf (writing in the twelfth century) concerning the importance of Saint-Riquier as an educational center for the laity in the ninth century.[83] On the other hand, in speaking of the cathedral schools of the late tenth and eleventh centuries, Pfister seeks to show that frequently they were centers for the education of the lay nobility as well as of the clergy. In proof of his statements, however, he offers no really conclusive evidence.[94] For example, he refers to Wibert's *Life of Leo IX,* which says in connection with the school of Toul, "adhaerebant nobilia examina puerorum."[95] Undoubtedly, most of the boys at Toul were of noble birth, but there is nothing to show that many or any of them intended to remain laymen. We know by name three of the young students then in attendance at the school of Toul: of these, one died before reaching manhood; another, Adalbero, became bishop of Metz (1047–1072); and the third, Bruno, became Pope Leo IX.[96] Again, with reference to the school of Rheims, Pfister quotes Gerbert as saying: "J'offre aux plus nobles des jeunes gens la nourriture des arts libéraux." But Pfister's translation of Gerbert's words is inaccurate and misleading. Gerbert actually wrote: ". . . interdum nobilissimis *scholasticis* disciplinarum liberalium suaves fructus ad vescendum offero." Gerbert is writing to Bernard, a monk of Aurillac, one of his former pupils and now engaged in teaching. His mind is reminiscent of his former students who have become "eminent teachers." He is thinking not of the eminence of birth of his pupils, but of the eminence of their achievement as teachers.[97]

One evidence of the movement toward a higher level of lay culture in eleventh-century France is the gradual emergence of a class of professionally educated laymen like those to be found in Italy. Although knowledge of Latin in this group is somewhat different from such knowledge among the nonprofessional laity, being the result of necessity rather than of cultural inclination, nevertheless the appearance of the professionally educated implies growing opportunities for the education of the laity as a whole. We possess the record of a professional layman which dates back as far as the last decade of the tenth century. Heribrand, the clerk of Chartres under whom Richer studied Hippocrates, Galen, and Soranus, was very clearly a layman, and probably a physician.[98] This early period, however, has also a darker side. When William, abbot of

Saint-Bénigne, crossed the Alps from Italy into France toward the
end of the tenth century to begin his work of reform, he found that
the parish priests of almost the entire country were unable to read
or to chant the Psalms. Thereupon he set about founding schools
where they might be trained.[99]

Toward the end of the eleventh century, however, educational
opportunities began to improve in France. Evidences of public instruction in letters became more and more numerous, especially in
Paris.[100] It is true that most of the teachers who can be identified
were or eventually became ecclesiastics, but many of them seem
never to have taken orders. The existence of such lay teachers undoubtedly increased the chances for education among the children
of the nobility. One of the most famous of these teachers is known
to history simply as Magister Manegold.[101] Born about 1030 in Alsace, he began his career as a teacher in Germany, where he established his reputation. He won even greater renown in France,
whither he transferred his activities about 1070. After the death of
his wife, Manegold in his old age entered a monastery. His wife
and two daughters were women of culture. The latter even followed in their father's footsteps, receiving for instruction pupils
of their own.[102]

With the rise of these wandering scholars and teachers, some of
whom were laymen, we note also a gradual increase in the number
of laymen who were interested in letters for their own sake, without
any utilitarian purpose. Abélard (born 1079), according to his own
account in the *Historia calamitatum,* owed his early education to
the zeal of a fond father, who had been instructed in letters in his
youth before he took up arms, and had later acquired such a love of
learning that he resolved that his sons also should learn their letters before being instructed in arms.[103] Men like Abélard's father,
however, were not numerous in the eleventh century. The cultural
level of the laity, as reflected in the *Autobiography* of Guibert de
Nogent, was not very high; few laymen seem to have possessed a
knowledge of Latin. We hear of a certain Clement of Bucy-le-Long,
near Soissons, the leader of a local sect, who, when charged by the
bishop with heresy, replied: "Have ye not read, masters, where it
is written in the Gospel: *'Beati eritis'*? For [Guibert comments]
being illiterate he thought *eritis* meant *heretics.* He believed also
that they were called *heretics* as being without doubt *heritors* of

God."[104] Guibert's mother, a woman of great piety, was illiterate,[105] although she, and another woman and her daughter, could recite the Litany with accuracy.[106] Even the clergy of the period were none too well versed in the language of learning. Hardly any of the priests of Laon knew even the rudiments of Latin.[107] Helinandus, bishop of Laon from 1052 to 1098, is described by Guibert as a man whose knowledge of letters was exceedingly thin.[108] And when Guibert speaks in praise of a certain monk named Robert, he adds, "moreover, he had a good knowledge of grammar," as if this fact were something unusual.[109] Concerning the opportunities for acquiring a knowledge of Latin letters, Guibert complains that "there was a little before that time [i.e., *ca.* 1050], and in a measure there is still in my time [i.e., *ca.* 1115] such a scarcity of grammarians that in the towns hardly any, and in the cities very few, could be found; and those who by good luck could be discovered had but slight knowledge and could not be compared with the itinerant clerks of these days."[110] It was precisely these unattached and wandering clerks who contributed most heavily to the increase in literacy among the laity, and apparently the beginning of their appearance in France in noticeably large numbers coincides with the time of Guibert's life (1053–1124). Guibert mentions specifically a certain clerk living at Rheims, "a fair scholar and with some skill in painting," who, in a fit of remorse over the laxity of his past life, went to Châlons to become a canon of the Church of All Saints.[111] He tells also of a boy of Jewish birth who was rescued from a massacre of Jews at Rouen about the time of the First Crusade by the son of the countess of Eu. The boy was baptized and, when he was a little older, forsook the study of Hebrew letters, in which he had made a beginning, for the study of Latin, probably with the intention of becoming a grammarian. In the end, however, to escape the pressure of the relatives who sought to bring him back to his original faith, he entered the monastery of Ely and became a monk.[112] Guibert's narrative also reveals the growing importance of French as the language of cultured laymen. A certain monk of Barizis, near Laon, undertook to teach French to two German boys who knew only their mother tongue.[113]

Under the influence of romanticism, the true character of the leaders of the First Crusade has been much distorted not only in the realm of war and conquest, but also in that of culture. Sir

Francis Palgrave[114] made statements concerning the literary education of the crusading knights which are now regarded as exag-
gerations. Godfrey of Bouillon, for example, is supposed to have
received an advanced literary training under the influence of his
mother, Ida, and at one period of his life to have contemplated
entering the priesthood. It is true that Godfrey's mother was an
educated woman,[115] but there is no direct evidence that she influ-
enced her son to study letters, or that he was once intended for the
Church.[116] Again, we know that Ponce of Baladun (or Balazun)
rightfully deserves the honor of being regarded as co-author of the
Historia Francorum together with Raymond of Agiles, canon of
Puy, but this fact is in itself no proof that Ponce was trained in
Latin. Neither can the Latin letters which the crusaders sent back
to France be regarded as proof of their knowledge of the language.
Of all the leaders of the First Crusade none has more often been
represented as a man of culture than Stephen of Blois. He was, it
is true, a man of unusual attainments,[117] but the degree of his knowledge of Latin is open to question. At least one of his letters was
written by his chaplain, Alexander,[118] and it seems reasonable to
suppose that others were composed in the same fashion.[119]

But, as in France and England, so also in the French kingdom
established by the crusaders in the Holy Land, laymen were soon
to begin to take a more active interest in letters. It seems probable
that the first of the kings of Jerusalem to have a good knowledge of
Latin was Fulk of Anjou (1131–1143), the son of the learned Fulk
le Rechin, though this conjecture cannot be supported by direct
evidence. The learning of the succeeding three rulers of the kingdom is expressly attested by William of Tyre.

Baldwin III (1143–1162) and his brother and successor Amalric
I (1162–1173) were both fairly good scholars, though the former
was the better of the two. As Bishop Stubbs has expressed it:
"Baldwin was the better professor, Amalric the better examiner;
Baldwin the more serious and orthodox, Amalric the more superficial; but both were students of history, and given to reading and
discussion—discussion which threatened now and then to go beyond
the bounds of orthodoxy."[120] It was at the request of Amalric that
William of Tyre wrote his *Gesta orientalium principum,* which is
now lost.[121] Amalric's son, Baldwin IV (1173–1183), received a more
thorough training in the liberal arts than his father or uncle. He

was instructed by William of Tyre, who tells us that the boy made good progress in his studies and acquired his father's fondness for history. The noble boys who accompanied him probably also acquired some acquaintance with Latin letters, though we are not expressly told so.[122]

By the year 1200 " . . . in the high places of feudalism men showed a taste for intellectual pleasures, appreciated books and those who made them, and set themselves to write in prose and verse. The counts of Flanders—Philip of Alsace, Baldwin VIII and Baldwin IX, the first Latin Emperor—formed a dynasty of well-lettered men. . . . In Auvergne the dauphin Robert I collected books which constituted a library entirely composed of writings relating to the heretical sects, which caused doubt about his orthodoxy."[123] In no other period of medieval France do we find record of so many well-educated men and women.

If we were to accept literally, however, the words of Peter the Venerable, abbot of Cluny (1122–1156), we should have to modify our judgment. In a famous letter written to Héloïse telling her of the death of Abélard (1142), he decries the general neglect into which liberal studies have fallen on all sides. But Peter's lament is obviously exaggerated and intended probably to serve as a foil for his praises of Héloïse's own accomplishments.[124] The very fact that Canon Fulbert had taken such care to have his niece well educated although she was not definitely intended for religious life, is highly significant. Héloïse had first learned her letters at the convent of Argenteuil, and then continued her studies at her uncle's home in Paris under Abélard, who was himself not yet a churchman.[125] She was undoubtedly educated far beyond the ordinary women of her class in that period, but she was not unique, as Peter the Venerable would make her appear to be. Adelaide of Lorraine (d. 1139), the wife of Duke Simon and mother of Matthew, was sufficiently well instructed in letters to understand spoken Latin.[126] The same is true of another Adelaide, the niece of an archdeacon of Poitiers, whose learning is praised by Peter of Blois in one of his letters.[127] Another educated woman of twelfth-century France was Marguerite, niece of Pope Calixtus II and wife of Guy, dauphin of Viennois. Her contemporary biographer relates that she had studied Latin and acquired a creditable knowledge of the language.[128] Beatrice of Burgundy, the second wife of Frederick Barbarossa, also belongs to this class of literate women.[129] She is said to have studied poetry and even to have written her own epitaph in eight Latin verses.[130]

Even the lesser feudality were to some degree affected by the broadening opportunities for education and learning in the early twelfth century. Thus Hébrard of Breteuil, a brother of the notorious robber baron Hugh de Puiset, whose depredations were suppressed by Louis VI,[131] was accustomed to carry with him a little book (*libellulum*) in which to record verses or anything which he might learn from others who were better educated than himself.[132] The sire de Loudun, who founded the later celebrated abbey of Chaise-Dieu, had received at least the elements of an education, and Herloy, a brother of the chatelain of Noyon, "had studied in his youth."[133] Peter of Chavanon, later canonized, who founded a college of canons regular in Auvergne, in the first half of the twelfth century, is said by his biographer to have been "cura educatus ac liberalibus studiis ... ab infantia mancipatus."[134] It is added that "a special disposition of Providence" had foreordained this—a phrase which shows that instruction was still exceptional among sons of the feudality.

There are numerous records of educated men among the greater feudality of France in the twelfth century. Geoffrey, count of Anjou, the progenitor of the Plantagenet kings, is described as "exceedingly well lettered, and eloquent with both the clergy and the laity."[135] He was so devoted to letters that he would not even go to war without a scholar at his side.[136] His ability to turn his learning to practical account must have astonished his contemporaries. At the siege of Montreuil-Bellay we find him consulting Vegetius' treatise on the art of war (*De re militari*).[137] William of Conches, one of the tutors of Henry II, dedicated to Geoffrey of Anjou, to whom he also had been tutor, his *Dragmaticon philosophiae* or *Dialogus de substantiis physicis,* and paid him the further compliment of making him his interlocutor in this work.[138] In his dedication, William praises Geoffrey for having instructed his children from their early years in the study of letters and not in the pursuit of idle games.[139]

An exceedingly valuable source of evidence for the culture of the lay nobility of the twelfth century is a letter written by Philip of Harvengt, abbot of Bonne-Espérance, a Premonstratensian abbey near Mons in Hainaut, to Count Philip of Flanders (1168–1191).

In substance it is a kind of *Speculum principis,* a brief essay on the Good Prince. Among other things the abbot writes thus:

If, by good chance, a prince has learned letters,—for there are many laymen who know letters, and such knowledge is not for clerics only,—he ought occasionally, when freed from the business and tumult of war, to take up a book and therein as in a mirror see his own self.

For there are many essays and letters and treatises of pagan as well as of Christian writers which offer lessons of no little value to men of noble birth. They praise excellence, they treat of warfare, they strengthen youth, they build up morals, they sharpen the wits, they induce to virtue, they denounce sloth, they arouse zeal, they delineate justice, they temper anger, they command mercy, they advise for gentleness. The prince who is of noble mind does not disdain to read or hear these and similar things, nor does he ever completely forget them in the press of business. He would, at least in an hour of quiet seclusion, rather attend to a book than unworthily give his ear to idle tales or his hand to rattling dice. I have, as I remember, always seen Count Charles reading the Psalms, both reverently and well, when attending divine service. In fact, a book in time of peace became this prince as well as his bright sword in time of war. I have, moreover, known Count Ayulf—a man of noble family, of a distinguished figure, of fine character, who often expressed a deep gratitude toward his parents because they had made him a lettered person from his youth—have known him, in talking with me, to show himself so accomplished a Latinist that one would think him nothing if not a clerk, and yet, withal, so much the knight that shortly thereafter he died in the service of his country fighting the infidel. For knighthood, or the profession of arms, does not preclude a sound knowledge of letters; indeed, in a prince, the union of both these things is as useful as it is becoming, and—as the aforesaid Ayulf was wont to assert—a prince who is not ennobled by a knowledge of letters might well be likened to a base rustic and a common brute.

Therefore, because it has been given to you to have known letters from your youth through your parents' care, and by the grace of heaven to have the power to accomplish what letters teach and recommend, continue what you are doing, and continuing bring to an end what you have begun, loving in purity Him from Whom you have received both will and power.[140]

This letter deserves some comment. The identity of Count Ayulf has long been a puzzle to scholars.[141] All we can say is that he was probably a Flemish noble who lost his life on the Second Crusade. He was certainly an extraordinarily well educated layman, able to speak as well as to read the language of learning. The Count Charles referred to is undoubtedly Charles the Good, count of Flanders from 1119 to 1127.[142] Whether or not Charles's successor, Thierry of Alsace (1128–1168), was also a lettered prince cannot be determined, but his son, Count Philip, was an educated man and

a patron of letters. He gave Chrétien de Troyes "a book of the
tales of the Grail" from which the poet drew the material for
his famous poem in the vernacular called *Perceval*.[143] He also befriended Gautier d'Epinal and the anonymous author of *Li prov-
erbe au vilain,* and collected many MSS which he placed at the
disposal of the poets who frequented his court.[144]

The tradition of learning at the court of Flanders goes back at
least as far as Count Robert I, Frisian (1072–1092). There is a
letter of Pope Gregory VII, probably of the year 1083, addressed
to the bishops of Cambrai, Noyon, and Amiens requesting them to
urge the count to abandon his support of Lambert, the heretical
bishop of Térouanne. After quoting the texts of Scripture which
the bishops are to use in their remonstrance to Count Robert, the
pope adds: "Haec omnia et horum similia sibi quia virum litteratum
eum audivimus, dicite."[145] In 1091, Robert received a letter from
Pope Urban II in which the pope took him to task for his high-
handed treatment of the clergy, and called upon him to mend his
ways and be mindful of his high station and the gifts which God
had given him. Among these gifts the pope mentions "a knowledge
of letters, a thing most rare among secular princes."[146] Nor did the
liberal tradition cease with Count Philip, mentioned above. The
princes who followed were men of culture, but their interests were
in the new vernacular literature rather than in Latin. Nicholas of
Senlis translated the *Chronicle of Turpin* into French from a Latin
MS given to him by Baldwin VIII of Flanders (d. 1195) and dedicated his translation to Yolande, the countess of Saint-Pol, Baldwin's sister.[147] Baldwin IX (d. 1205) is said to have encouraged the
translation of historical works into the vernacular, and both he
and his wife, Marie II of Champagne, were enthusiastic patrons of
the courtly poetry. It is possible that Baldwin was himself the
author of several Provençal *sirventes*.[148] We might also mention
here Roger, lord of the Château Lille, under whose patronage a
cleric assembled the *Livre des histoires,* a universal history beginning with Creation, compiled and translated from various Latin
chronicles.[149]

The counts of Flanders, however, were by no means unique in
their learning. One of their vassals, Baldwin II of Guines (d. 1205),
was as much interested in culture as his suzerain. In spite of the
fact that he could not read Latin, and probably not even French,—

though he spoke it,—he was a man of some learning and one of the most noted bibliophiles of his day. He acquired his knowledge of Latin works by having them translated into French and read to him. Having a prodigious memory, he retained almost everything he heard and gradually accumulated such a stock of erudition that he was able to argue successfully with learned clerks and clever theologians. Those who listened to him marveled, and could only say, What a man! Such, at least, is the account of Baldwin's intellectual prowess given to us by Lambert of Ardres, which is doubtless somewhat exaggerated but certainly founded on fact. Lambert tells us specifically of a number of scholars who translated Latin works into French for the count. Thus Landri of Waben translated the *Canticles,* a certain Alfred translated parts of the *Gospels* and the *Life of Saint Anthony,* a Master Godfrey translated the larger part of a work on physics, and the famous Simon of Boulogne rendered into French the *De naturis rerum.* The count's library included Saint Augustine, for theology; Dionysius the Areopagite, for philosophy; and the *Milesian Tales* and other pagan stories, for humor. All these books were read aloud to Baldwin by Hasard of Aldehem, his librarian, a layman who had been especially trained and educated for the post. Finally, to complete his intellectual labors by creative activity, Baldwin collaborated with a Master Walter Silens in the composition of a work of unknown character, curiously entitled, after its chief author, *Silentius* or the *Romance of Silence.*[150]

Renaud of Dammartin, the fourth husband of Ida of Boulogne, a neighbor and contemporary of Baldwin of Guines, was also interested in vernacular literature, particularly in history. The popular *Chronicle of Turpin* was translated into French for him by one of his clerics.[151] This intense interest in sponsoring translations from the Latin, as well as in vernacular literature in general, does not, of course, prove that the laymen concerned possessed any education in Latin letters. The tendency marks the beginning of a new epoch in lay culture, the period when Latin was no longer essential to education and culture.

Another learned layman of the twelfth century whose training in Latin letters is beyond question, was Henry I, the Liberal, count of Champagne (1152–1181). His scholarly interests are attested in letters addressed to him by John of Salisbury[152] and the monk

Nicholas of Clairvaux,[153] both of whom praise his liberality and munificence to scholars.[154] Nicholas, who was Henry's secretary, as he had been Saint Bernard's, did much to encourage his patron's pursuit of learning. "It is an old proverb," he wrote to Henry, "and one celebrated by the ancients, that as much as men are removed from the beasts, so are educated men removed from the illiterate."[155] The count was familiar with Vergil, Horace, Ovid, and Apuleius, and especially fond of reading Jerome. He owned a copy of Vegetius' *On the Art of War* which had apparently been given to him by John of Salisbury; and a beautiful MS of Valerius Maximus, copied for him by the monks of Provins, is still preserved at the Bibliothèque Nationale.[156]

Henry the Liberal, like his contemporary, Philip of Flanders, was honored with a long letter from Philip of Harvengt, abbot of Bonne-Espérance. The tenor of this letter, *On True Nobility,* is that a prince who is noble by virtue of lineage, rank, and wealth is made more truly noble by the cultivation of the liberal arts. The ancients rightly used the term "liberal arts" because a knowledge of letters frees and liberates a man from the common things of life. The true prince, therefore, should both know letters himself and encourage others who pursue learning. The abbot reminds Henry how his father, Thibault II, le Grand (1125–1152), had taken great care to give his son more than he himself had received, namely, an education. Henry had consequently been subjected for several years to the discipline of study, and had acquired such a knowledge of letters that he excelled many a cleric. He became, therefore, both knight and cleric, knight by practice of arms and cleric by love of learning. Prince and scholar, his field was letters as well as arms, and in his reading he found the ideal prince mirrored in the writers of old, pagan and Christian alike. For the reading of such literature with wisdom and understanding does not detract from the nobility of a prince, but rather revivifies him with the "liberal waters of the ancients." There are, the abbot warns Henry, different ways of reading, and different kinds of readers. The greater number are like the ass who eats thistles not from preference but from laziness; they read in indolence. But there are a few rare souls who read from zeal and genuine love of learning, and whose devotion to letters never ends. For this latter group, and for Henry in particular, the abbot adds a few words of encouragement. Do not think that it is an idle waste of time to pursue Latin learning. On the contrary, to know and use that language which God has given to His Church and in which He is revealed to us, must be pleasing to Him. It is true that God gave many languages to the peoples of the earth, and that the prophets and apostles of old spoke in Hebrew and Greek, but these languages are now dead, and Latin is the language of God. And therefore it is fit and proper that every noble man should know Latin, a noble and divine tongue, and that Henry should continue his pursuit of learning and, moreover, foster and honor those who do likewise.[157]

The court of Henry of Champagne was marked not only by Latin learning,[158] but also by an interest in the new vernacular literature. Marie, the wife of Henry, and a daughter of Louis VII of France, who ruled Champagne from 1181 to 1186 and from 1190 to 1198, was patroness of a group of courtly poets of whom Chrétien de Troyes was the outstanding figure.[159] Perhaps more than any other individual, Chrétien represents the transition from Latin to vernacular literature. Out of a Latin tale (*conte*) he constructs a French romance (*roman*). In a curious passage in *Cligès*, the scholastic source of which M. Gilson believes he has identified, Chrétien writes:

> Le livre est très ancien,
> ce qui atteste la verité de cette histoire....
> Par les livres que nous avons
> nous connaissons les hauts faits des anciens
> et la vie du temps passé.
> Or ce livre vous enseignera
> Que la Grèce fut, en chevalerie
> et en science, la plus renommée;
> puis la chevalerie passa à Rome,
> et avec elle la science
> qui sont maintenant venues en France.[160]

His patroness, Marie de France, probably had only a very meager knowledge of Latin, if any. A French translation of Genesis, made at her order, is still preserved at the Bibliothèque Nationale.[161] Blanche of Navarre, wife of Thibaut III of Champagne (d. 1201) and mother of Thibaut IV (le Chansonier), may have known a little Latin, but apparently not much. Adam of Perseigne, in sending her a number of sermons for which she had asked, expressed a fear that she would not be able to understand these Latin writings, but at the same time warned her against a translation which might alter their contents.[162]

Though it is true that Latin eventually became almost entirely unfamiliar to the laity, it is important to note that the process was a very gradual one. Latin continued to be studied by the more cultured of the laity, but to a steadily diminishing extent. This fact is indicated in another letter of Adam of Perseigne, written about the year 1200 to the countess of Chartres.

> My letter [he writes], which may already have wearied you in its prolixity, now comes to a close. If you find anything in it hard to understand, your reverend chaplain G— has both the learning and the ability to explain such difficulties to you. I should have written to you in the vernacular if I had not learned that you have acquired something of a knowledge of Latin.[163]

It is significant to observe Adam's way of referring to the vernacular; to him it is merely the layman's tongue (*sermo laicus*). The decline in the use of Latin among the French laity in the twelfth and early thirteenth centuries does not indicate, however, a retrogression in lay culture viewed as a whole, but rather the contrary. What took place was a gradual secularization of culture, and in the field of literary activity this process took the form of a transition from Latin to the vernacular. Latin literature may have held its own even up through the second quarter of the twelfth century, but after 1150 it was overshadowed by the growing vernacular literature.[164]

We must remember that the second half of the twelfth century was a period of intense productivity in the field of Old French romances. The material of these poems, when not derived from Celtic themes, was in large part drawn from Classical sources: the romances were popular stories put into entertaining vernacular literary form for the benefit of laymen unable to understand Latin.

Another indication of the high level which lay culture had attained in the thirteenth century is the fact that in France, as in Italy, the Church now ceased to be the sole guardian of history.[165] There is a certain difference, however, between France and Italy in this matter. In Italy the lay historians, the two Morenas, for example, were professionally trained men who still wrote in Latin, whereas in France the lay historians were men without extensive training in letters who wrote in the vernacular. Both of these countries far excelled Germany in historiography. Some of the best history written in France in the thirteenth century was composed by laymen. The Fourth Crusade brought forth three historical works of lay authorship, the immortal *Memoirs* of Villehardouin and the accounts of Henry of Valenciennes and Robert of Clary. We know that Villehardouin dictated his *Memoirs,* and the same may be true of the other two writers. All wrote in the vernacular.[166]

Notwithstanding the relatively high cultural level of the French laity in the thirteenth century, there were still noblemen who could not read or write. Thus, Jean de Nanteuil, lord chamberlain to Louis IX, was unable personally to subscribe to a document, "because he had no knowledge of letters."[167] Jean de Nanteuil was probably an exception, however, for it would seem that the art of writing was fairly general among the French laity in the thirteenth century.[168] Jean, sire de Joinville, the biographer of Saint Louis, was able both to read and to write. There is extant the original of a document of 1294 which contains a subscription of two lines written in Joinville's own hand.[169] Since Joinville regularly used the vernacular, the extent of his knowledge of Latin cannot be determined. It was probably not great, for he seems not to have been a very bookish sort of person.[170] On the other hand, Isabelle, the sister of Saint Louis, may have been well versed in Latin letters. Her biographer, Agnes of Harcourt, tells us that the princess herself corrected the Latin of the letters which her chaplains wrote for her.[171]

There are other indications as well that French noblewomen of the time of Saint Louis received some education. The confessor of Queen Margaret relates how the poor widows of knights who had perished in the Holy Land came seeking aid of the king, and how the king asked each woman whether any of her daughters had a knowledge of letters, and finally promised that he would have those who had been instructed in letters received at the abbey of Pontoise.[172] An interesting bit of evidence is contained in a story related by Thomas de Chantimpré (d. 1270) in his *Bonum universale.* A peasant girl who was eager to learn the Psalter, but too poor to acquire one, appealed to the Mother of God. The Virgin appeared to the girl in a dream and told her to frequent the place where the young ladies of the parish were being taught to read by their mistress, with the result that the rich young women finally banded together and bought a Psalter for her.[173] Unfortunately these anecdotes do not reveal to what extent Latin was included in the instruction received by the young noblewomen. If any Latin was taught them, it was probably only enough to enable them to follow the services of the Church and understand the most frequently used psalms. In the face of the rising tide of vernacular literature it is impossible to believe that the ordinary young noblewoman paid much attention to the language of learning.

It is by no means true, however, that Latin now fell completely into neglect among the laity. An early fourteenth-century catalogue of a layman's library, that of the Château de la Ferté in Ponthieu, lists forty-six volumes of which at least five or six were in Latin. The rest were written in the vernacular, works of edification and romance for the most part.[174] Two items in this catalogue are of especial interest. One of them informs us that a certain Mesire Jean de Pequigni had borrowed a "livre du Trésor" (probably Brunetto Latini's work, as Beaurepaire conjectures) from the library, and had died without returning it. The other tells us that Midemisele de la Ferté had borrowed a French *Life of Saint Martin* and the *Secretum secretorum,* a pseudo-Aristotelian treatise on medicine. The latter work is cited by its Latin title, and may have been either in Latin or in a French translation which retained the Latin title. We know that this work was exceedingly popular and had been translated into French before 1300.[175] This catalogue is valuable in showing that the lay interest in Latin, meager as it may have been, at least persisted. It also reveals a high type of lay culture.[176]

Notes to Chapter VI

[1] *Historiarum libri quatuor*, I, 20 (*MGH. SS.*, III, 575) : " ... Germanorum Gallorumque juvenes linguarum idiomate offensi, ut eorum mos est cum multaanimositate maledictis sese lacessire coeperunt." (The date was 920.) Cf. Freeman, *The Norman Conquest of England* (3d ed.), I, 618.

[2] See Freeman, *op. cit.*, 158 and App. V, 617–620. Cf. F. Lot, *Les derniers Carolingiens* (Paris, 1891), 308–311.

[3] See Folcuin's *Gesta abbatum Sithiensium* (*MGH. SS.*, XIII, 623, n. 3) and cf. Dümmler, *Ostfr. Reich.*, III, 651, n. 3.

[4] It seems worth while to give this highly interesting passage in full. *Vita S. Geraldi*, I, 4–5 (Migne, *PL*, 133, 645) : "Qui [Geraldus] divina providente gratia studiis litterarum applicatus est, ea tantum parentum voluntate, ut decurso psalterio, mox saecularibus exercitiis, sicut nobilibus pueris mos est, erudiretur. Scilicet et Molossos ageret, arcista fieret, cappos et accipitres competenti jactu emittere consuesceret. Sed ne inani studio deditus, tempus ad discendum litteras congruum in vacuo transiret, divino nutu dispositum est, ut diutius aegrotaret. Tali equidem infirmitatis languore, ut a saeculari exercitio retraheretur, sed ad discendi studium non impediretur. Siquidem minutis jugiter pustulis ita replebatur, ut per longum tempus protractae, jam non putarentur posse sanari. Qua de causa genitor ejus cum matre decernit, ut litterarum studiis arctius applicaretur. Quo videlicet, si usibus saeculi minus esset aptus, ad ecclesiasticum officium redderetur accommodus. Hac igitur occasione factum est, ut non modo cantum disceret, quin etiam et grammaticam praelibaret. Quod ei postea multum profuit, cum acies ingenii per illud exercitium elimata, ad omne quod vellet, acutior redderetur. Inerat autem illi vivax mentis sagacitas, et ad discendum quae vellet satis prompta.

"Transmissa pueritia cum jam adolesceret membrorum robur novicum corporis consumpsit humorem. Tam velox autem factus est, ut equorum terga facili saltu transvolaret. Et quia viribus corporis fortiter agiliscebat, armatam militiam assuescere quaerebatur. Sed jam dulce scripturarum adolescentis animum subarraverat, ad cujus studium affectuosius anhelabat. Ob hoc licet militaribus emineret officiis, delectatione tamen litterarum illectus; in illis voluntaria pigritia lentulus, in hujus sedulitate erat assuetus. Credo jam sentiscebat quia, juxta Scripturae testimonium, *melior est sapientia quam vires* [*Sap.* vi, 1], et nihil est locupletius illa. Et quoniam facile videtur ab his qui diligunt eam, mentem ejusdem adolescentis praeoccupabat, ut ei se prior ostenderet, ut esset dulcis allocutio cogitationis ejus. Nullo igitur impedimento Geraldus poterat occupari, quin ad amorem discendi recurreret. Unde factum est, ut propemodum pleniter Scripturarum seriem disceret, atque multos clericorum quantumlibet sciolos in ejus cognitione praeiret." By way of secondary literature, see esp. Poncelet, "La plus ancienne vie de S. Géraud d'Aurillac," *Analecta Bollandiana*, XIV (1895), 89 ff.; E. Sackur, *Die Cluniacenser* ... (Halle), II (1894), 33; Molinier, *Les sources* ..., II, 116, no. 1524; and A. Ebert, *Histoire générale de la littérature du moyen âge en Occident* (trans. by J. Aymeric and J. Condamin; Paris, 1883–1889), III, 210–211.

⁵ *Vita S. Geraldi,* II, 6 (Migne, *PL,* 133, 674): "Dum vero domus [i. e., monasterii] fabricam continuaret, animo semper volvebat qualiter posset reperire monachos qui bene morati essent, et locum sub regulari proposito incolere potuissent. Sed cum reperiendi raritas difficultatem intulisset, anxiabatur ille, et quidnam faceret nesciebat. Tum vero nobiles quosdam pueros ad Vabrense coenobium direxit. Nam tunc regularis observantiae fervor incalescebat, ut scilicet apud fraternitatem illam sub norma regulari iidem pueri imbuerentur. ... Porro cum iidem pueri reverti juberentur, *quia magistri defuerunt,* mox puellari mollitia resoluti, rigorem disciplinae neglexerunt. Et ita contigit, ut res ad effectum non veniret."

⁶ *Vita S. Odonis,* I, 5–7 (Migne, *PL,* 133, 45–46).

⁷ I, 8 (*ibid.,* col. 47): "coepitque pater meus per incrementa temporum me ab ecclesiastico subtrahere ordine, et militaribus exercitiis applicare; qua de re intra domum Guillelmi me tradidit serviturum comiti. Relictis tandem litterarum studiis, venatorum aucupumque coepi deservire officiis."

⁸ I, 9–13 (*ibid.,* 47–49). Odo was now a monk, and although it is, therefore, not strictly pertinent to lay culture, it is interesting to note that later we find him at Paris studying the *"Dialectics* of Saint Augustine sent to his son Deodatus," and Martianus Capella on the seven liberal arts, as well as music, under the direction of Remigius of Auxerre; cf. I, 3 and 19 (*ibid.,* 45 and 52).

⁹ I, 5 (*ibid.,* 46): "... alterius moris esse videbatur et actibus, quam nunc homines praesentis temporis esse videntur. Veterum namque historias, Justiniani Novellam memoriter retinebat."

¹⁰ Cf. esp. Sackur, *op. cit.,* I, 44–45; Manitius, *Gesch. der latein. Lit. des Mittelalters,* II, 20 and 133; and Ebert, *op. cit.,* III, 171, who somewhat carelessly neglects to mention Abbo's knowledge of history and, on the other hand, credits him with actually having memorized the *Novella.*

¹¹ Sackur (*op. cit.,* I, 44, n. 4) has conjectured that Odo's father is to be identified with the *Abbo legislator* whose *signum* appears in a document of Tours, dated September 29, 898. This document is published by E. Mabille, in his introduction to the *Chroniques des comtes d'Anjou* (ed. Marchegay and Salmon; Paris, 1856–1871), p. xcii. But even if this suggestion is correct, it does not necessarily prove that Abbo was unable to write.

¹² *Vita S. Odonis,* I, 23 (Migne, *PL,* 133, 54).

¹³ A facsimile has been published by F. L. Bruel, *Cluni: album historique et archéologique* (1910), which I have not been able to consult. My information comes from Redlich, *Urkundenlehre ...,* 40 and n. 3, who reports that the subscription runs thus: "X *Wilelmus* [so far in William's hand; what follows is in the hand of the scribe]: ego hanc auctoritatem fieri firmare rogavi ac manu propria roboravi."

¹⁴ After William's subscription, there follows immediately that of Gelberata: "Signum Gelberate ... uxoris eius," in the hand of the scribe; next, the signatures of several ecclesiastics, in their own hands; and finally, the *signa* of the other witnesses, in the hand of the scribe (*ibid.*).

¹⁵ *Les écoles épiscopales et monastiques de l'Occident* (2d ed.; Paris, 1924), 172 and n. 3.

[16] See the text of the document, in Bouquet, *HF*, IX, 566 D.

[17] Flodoard, *Annales* ad a. 948 (*MGH. SS.*, III, 396) ; cf. Ph. Lauer, *Le règne de Louis IV d'Outre-mer* (Paris, 1900), 235, n. 3. See also Freeman, *op. cit.*, I, 618, where he remarks: "Lewis therefore spoke German no less than Otto. Otto, however, could speak French on occasion, which makes the employment of German still more important."

[18] I have followed the twelfth-century *Historia comitum Andegavensium* of Thomas of Loches in *Chroniques des comtes d'Anjou*, ed. Marchegay and Salmon, 321. For a later redaction of the same story, see *ibid.*, 71. Since the king of France is not mentioned by name, it is possible that the story refers to Lothair (954–986), Louis' son and successor; but the consensus among scholars is that, if the story is valid in the first place, it applies to Louis d'Outre-mer; cf. Ph. Lauer, *op. cit.*, 235, n. 4, and Carl von Kalckstein, *Gesch. des französischen Königthums unter den ersten Capetingern* (Leipzig, 1877), I, 220 n.

[19] See L. Halphen's critical statement to this effect, *La comté d'Anjou au XIe siècle* (Paris, 1906), 1, n. 1.

[20] This, too, according to Thomas of Loches, in *Chroniques des comtes d'Anjou*, 321: "Composuit idem reverendae memoriae consul historiam duodecim responsoriorum, cantu et melodia luculentam, in honore beati Martini."

[21] In Migne, *PL*, 101, 1289; cf. Kalckstein, *op. cit.*, I, 219 and n. 3, Ebert, *op. cit.*, III, 479, and Gerdes, *op. cit.*, I, 682.

[22] *Vita Gerardi abbatis Bronensis*, chap. 9 (*MGH. SS.*, XV, 659): " ... suppliciter coepit exposcere, ut sibi liceret litteras addiscere. Super quo fratribus admodum admirantibus, quod vir iam dudum barbatus applicari vellet ulterius studiis litterarum puerilibus, dum id diatim expeteret importunius, uni eorum traditur erudiendus." Cf. Specht, *op. cit.*, 235 and n. 3.

[23] The *Vita* was written in the first half of the eleventh century, according to Molinier (*Les sources ...* , II, 175, no. 1808) and therefore probably reflects conditions of that time as well.

[24] *Gesta abbatum Lobiensium*, chap. 20 (*MGH. SS.*, IV, 64): "Postea cum in ea parte Burgundiae, quae Provincia dicitur, mansitaret, filium cuiusdam viri ditissimi, nomine Rocstagnum, ad imbuendum litteris postulatus recepit, ad quem librum de arte grammatica conscripsit, quem librum gentilicio loquendi more Sparadorsum vocavit, pro eo quod qui illum in scholis assuesceret puerulus, dorsum a flagris servare posset." The work seems no longer to be extant; see Pertz, *ibid.*, n. 46, and the comments of the brothers Ballerini to their edition of the *Opera* of Rather, pp. xiv, lvi (in Migne, *PL*, 136, 20 and 50).

[25] *Historiarum libri quatuor*, III, 85 (*MGH. SS.*, III, 625): "dux etiam solus cum solo episcopo introduceretur, ut rege latiariter [*for* latiniter] loquente, episcopus latinitatis interpres, duci quicquid diceretur indicaret."

[26] See Richer, *Historiarum libri quatuor*, IV, 100 (*MGH. SS.*, III, 654), for the synod held at Mouzon in 995, and Gerbert's report (*ibid.*, 658) on the synod at Verzy (diocese of Rheims) in 991. Cf. F. Lot, *Etudes sur le règne de Hugues Capet* (Paris, 1903), 33, n. 1.

[27] Helgaud (or, Helgaldus), *Vita Rothberti regis* (Bouquet, *Recueil des historiens* ... , X, 99 C) : "Fuit idem Rex sapientissimus literarum, cujus prudentissimo cordi erant insita a Deo data perfectae scientiae dona. Nam a piissima matre Scolae Remensi traditus, domno Girberto ad erudiendum est datus, qui eum sufficenter liberalibus instrueret disciplinis, ut in omnibus Deo omnipotenti complaceret virtutibus almis. Factumque est."

[28] See the *Historia inventionis Sancti Wolfranni,* chap. vii (d'Achery, *Spicilegium* [nov. ed.; Paris, 1723], II, 286), and cf. F. Lot, *Hugues Capet,* 107 and 121, n. 5.

[29] *Hist. libri quatuor,* IV, 13 (*MGH. SS.,* III, 634) : "et divinis ac canonicis institutis clarissimus haberetur; liberalibus studiis incumberet."

[30] *Hist. libri quinque,* II, 1 (ed. M. Prou, 26) : "Habebat [sc. Hugo] enim filium, admodum prudentem, nomine Rotbertum, artium etiam litterarum studiis plurimun eruditum."

[31] Bouquet, *HF,* X, 492 B: "Vitam beatissimi Eligii Confessoris atque Episcopi, quam dudum a nobis poposcitis, expressimus ut potuimus, ac Deo volente, vestrae praesentiae destinavimus. Precamur itaque vos, reverentissime pater, ut cum avide eam sumpseritis, ac bene memoriae commendatam habueritis, etiam Rotberto Regi ostendatis; ut ex ea cognoscat, quanta familiaritate ac benignitate circa locum nostrum sollicitudinem habere debeat. Cum enim ego apud vos habitarem, ac cum illo frequenter locutus fuissem, ipse mihi rogavit, ut ego ei eam habere facerem."

[32] See the account of Robert's journey to Rome (whether that of 1010 or that of 1016 is meant, is not clear) in company with Abbot Angelrannus of Saint-Riquier, in the *Chronicon Centulense,* IV, 2 (ed. F. Lot, 181) : "Verum quod in ipso itinere relatum est gestum fuisse, dignum videtur inseri historiae; si quidem multimoda assertione insinuatus est ita per omnem viam [sc. Angelrannum] Deo regique in divino servito militasse, ut librorum nunquam indiguerit juvari solamine; quod an fieri potuerit, non inertes judicent, sed studiosi examinent." The passage is somewhat obscure. The words "ut librorum nunquam indiguerit juvari solamine," which I have applied to the king, may perhaps have been meant to refer to the abbot. But in either interpretation Robert is here seriously interested in books.

[33] See Ch. Pfister, *Etudes sur le règne de Robert le Pieux (996–1031)* (Paris, 1885), 34 and n. 3. Cf. also *ibid.,* 16 and 34–36, from which most of the references here given have been culled, and where the education and learning of Robert II are discussed in great detail.

[34] W. M. Newman, *The Kings, the Court, and the Royal Power in France in the Eleventh Century* (Toulouse diss., 1929), 10.

[35] Luchaire, *Inst. mon.,* I, 17. Pfister, *op. cit.,* 389, however, thinks Adelaide was of Italian origin.

[36] A. Richard, *Histoire des comtes de Poitou* (Paris, 1903), I, 138.

[37] F. M. Warren, *Proceedings of the Modern Language Association,* XXIV (1909), p. lxix.

[38] Hilda Johnstone, "Fulbert, Bishop of Chartres," *Church Quarterly Review,* CII (1929), 51. Cf. below, note 45.

[39] *Chronicon*, III, 54 (ed. J. Chavanon, 176–177): "Fuit dux iste a puericia doctus litteris, et satis noticiam scripturarum habuit. Librorum copiam in palatio suo servavit, et si forte a tumultu vacaret, lectioni per se ipsum operam dabat, longioribus noctibus elucubrans in libris, donec somno vinceretur. Hoc Hludovicus imperator, hoc pater ejus Magnus Karolus assuescebant. Theodosius quoque victor augustus in aula palatii, non modo legendo, verum et scribendo creberrime exercitabatur. Nam Octavianus Cesar Augustus post lectionem propria manu praelia sua et gesta Romanorum et alia quaeque non segnis scribebat."

[40] VII, 284 and 288.

[41] Richard, *op. cit.*, I, 209–210.

[42] Richard even goes so far as to say, "Il eut une bibliothèque dans son palais, et pour l'acroître, il se livra lui-même à la transcription des manuscrits." But I know of no facts which would justify this statement, and Richard cites none.

[43] The *crux interpretationis* of the passage is the phrase, "longioribus noctibus elucubrans in libris." In the classical authors *elucubrare* is usually used in reference to an act of composition or writing performed by lamplight; but the idea of writing is incidental, and is not implicit in the verb; its primary meaning is to do something by lamplight. That Adhemar was here as yet thinking only of reading when he wrote *elucubrans*, seems to me to be indicated by the manner in which he introduces Theodosius, who sought diversion "not only in reading, but also in writing."

[44] In Migne, *PL*, 141, 827–832. Cf. *Hist. litt. de la France*, VII, 284 and 288.

[45] See the letter of Fulbert of Chartres to H[ildegarius] (Migne, *PL*, 141, 271): "Mitto vobis unum ex duobus libellis quos amicus noster comes G. rogavit transcribi." Cf. above, note 38.

[46] See Labbé, *Concilia*, IX, 882; and cf. Richard, *op. cit.*, I, 194, 210, and L. M. Larson, *Canute the Great* (London, 1912), 264–265, 298.

[47] See Richard, *op. cit.*, I, 433, n. 2, and M. Grabmann, *Die Geschichte der scholastischen Methode* (Freiburg-in-Breisgau and St. Louis, Mo., 1909–1911), I, 246–247.

[48] Cf. Richard, *op. cit.*, I, 502–503.

[49] In Old French the verb signifying 'to read' meant *to read Latin*, the language of all public instruments, and all medieval literature except Anglo-Saxon until the rise of vernacular literature in the twelfth century, So

"Li reis Marsilies fut escolez de lire"

in *Chanson de Roland*, line 485. Cf. *Modern Philology*, XXI (1923), 108. The historical works of the early Middle Ages were written in Latin, by clerks for clerks. Down to the twelfth century, laymen unable to understand Latin depended for their knowledge of history almost wholly on the *chansons de geste*. "Les chansons de geste ne sont, en principe, que des récits historiques mis a la portée des illettrés," says Paul Meyer.

[50] See Molinier, *Les sources* ... , II, 48–49; F. M. Powicke, *The Loss of Normandy* (Manchester, 1913), 36; and esp. Halphen, *op. cit.*, pp. vi and 191, n. 2, and his "Etude sur l'authenticité du fragment de chronique attribué à Foulque le Rechin," *Bibliothèque de la Faculté des lettres de Paris*, XIII (1901),

7–48. The latest and best edition of the chronicle written by Fulk is in *Chroniques des comtes d'Anjou* (ed. Halphen and Poupardin), 232 ff.

[51] See the letter of *frater R.* to his abbot, published by Mabillon in his *AA. SS. ord. S. Bened.*, LXI, n. vi (Lucca ed., IV, 528; Paris ed., IV, 574) : "Pater carissimo, scire vos volumus, quod codicem, de quo audivistis, pretio magno a Martino qui est modo praesul, comitissia emit. Una vice libri causa centum oves illi dedit; altera vice causa ipsius libri unum modium frumenti, et alterum figalis, et tertium de milio. Iterum hac eadem causa centum oves: altera vice quasdam pelles martirinas. Cumque separavit se a comite, quator libratas, ovium emendi causa, ab illa accepit. Postquam autem requisivit denarios, ille conqueri coepit de libro. Illa statim dimisit illi, quod sibi debebat." Cf. Ch. Jourdain, *Mém. de l'Inst. Nat. de France: Acad. des inscr. et belles-lettres*, XXVIII, pt. 1, 90 and n. 3, and the *Hist. litt. de la France*, VII, 3, which erroneously identifies the countess referred to with Grace, the second wife of Geoffrey Martel.

[52] The poem is in Migne, *PL*, 171, 1659. Cf. Ch. Jourdain, *op. cit.*, 92 and n. 3.

[53] In 1855 L. Delisle reported in his article, "De l'instruction littéraire de la noblesse française au moyen âge, à propos d'un autograph du sire de Joinville," *Le Correspondant*, XXXVI (1855), 450, that the original document was still preserved in the Bibliothèque Impériale, where he had examined it. (Delisle's article was published first in the *Journal générale de l'instruction publique*, XXIV [1855], 322 ff., and later also in the *Journal de Rennes*, feuilleton de 30 juin 1855).

[54] M. Prou, *Recueil des actes de Philippe I*ᵉʳ, *roi de France (1059–1108)* (Paris, 1908), Intro., p. clii and n. 8, and 7, 12, 94, nos. 2, 3, 30. Cf. Newman, *op. cit.*, 25, n. 101, and 40–41.

[55] *Coronatio Philippi I* (Bouquet, *HF*, XI, 32 B) : ". . . domnus Archiepiscopus vertit se ad eum, et exposuit ei fidem Catholicam; sciscitans ab eo utrum hanc crederet, et defendere vellet. Quo annuente, delata est ejus professio: quam accipiens, ipse legit, dum adhuc septennis esset; eique subscripsit." The subscription probably consisted only in making the *signum;* see Prou, *Recueil des actes . . .* , p. cxviii.

[56] *Vie de Louis le Gros* (ed. A. Molinier; Paris, 1887) and *De rebus in administratione sua gestis* (ed. Lecoy de la Marche; Paris, 1867), 200.

[57] Cf. A. Luchaire, *Louis VI le Gros: annales de sa vie et de son règne* (Paris, 1890), 4, no. 3.

[58] Cf. R. Hirsch, *Studien zur Geschichte König Ludwigs VII. von Frankreich (1119–1160)* (Leipzig, 1892), 2.

[59] See the document given by A. Luchaire, *Etudes sur les actes de Louis VII* (Paris, 1885), no. 391.

[60] Cf. Luchaire, *in* Lavisse, *Histoire de France*, III, pt. 1, 283.

[61] *Ibid.*, 283.

[62] See the opening verses of the fifth book of the *Carolinus* or *De rebus gestis Caroli Magni carmen hexametrum*, written for the instruction and edification of young Louis, by Giles of Paris (Bouquet, *HF*, XVII, 289 E). Cf. Ch. Petit-Dutaillis, *Etude sur la vie et le règne de Louis VIII* (Paris, 1894), 4–5.

[63] Migne, *PL*, 211, 499: "Domine mi charissime, rogamus, monemus, consulimus in fide quam debemus vobis, ut per omnia post dilectionem Dei et domini regis vestri patris, intendatis litteris discendis, quia vobis et regno vestro utiles erunt et necessariae in consiliis palatii, et negotiis regni, et concordia pacis et in victoria belli."

[64] See the *Chronicon* of the anonymous canon of Laon, ad a. 1212 (Bouquet, *HF*, XVIII, 714 E): "Item sciendum est quod iste magister Almaricus fuit cum domino Ludovico primogenito Regis Francorum, quia credebatur vir esse bonae conversationis et opinionis illaesae."

[65] See the preface to Gerald's *De principis instructione* (*Opera*, VIII, 6–7), dedicated to Posterity: "quoniam opuscula nostra quae juveniles olim anni ambitu pleni laboriose produxerant, alia principibus edita fuerant, alia praelatis, et infructuose ... hos aliosque conatus nostros." Gerald therefore decided to abandon the attempt to arouse interest (and liberality) for his work among princes, with the possible exception of Louis VIII: "Caeterum si cuipiam modernorum principum opuscula nostra, quae provectior aetas elaboraverit, praesentanda fuerint, unum elegimus, cui prae caeteris digne magis praesentari posse videntur, Ludowicum scilicet Philippi Francorum regis filium primaevum: tum quia litteris et liberalibus studiis affatim est a teneris annis imbutus (quae virtus quidem, quanto in principibus est hodie rarior, tanto, ubi affuerit, longe pretiosior et praeclarior), tum etiam quia liberalitate conspicuus."

[66] Lecoy de la Marche, *Saint Louis* (Paris, 1893), 194.

[67] See esp. Geoffroi de Beaulieu, *Vita S. Ludovici*, xiii (Bouquet, *HF*, XX, 15 A): "Audivit fidelis Rex, dum adhuc esset ultra mare, de quodam magno Sarracenorum soldano, quod omnia librorum genera, quae necessaria esse poterant philosophis Sarracenis, diligenter faciebat inquiri, et sumptibus suis scribi, et in armario suo recondi; ut litterati eorum librorum copiam possent habere, quoties indigerent. Considerans igitur pius Rex, quod filii tenebrarum prudentiores esse videntur filiis lucis, et erroris sui amplius zelatores quam sint filii ecclesiae verae fidei christianae; concepit, quod revertens in Franciam, omnes libros sacrae Scripturae, quos utiles et authenticos in diversis armariis abbatiarum invenire valeret, transcribi sumptibus suis faceret, ut tam ipse quam viri litterati ac religiosi familiares sui in ipsis studere possent, ad utilitatem ipsorum et aedificationem proximorum. Sicut cogitavit, ita et reversus perfecit, et locum aptum et fortem ad hoc aedificari fecit, scilicet Parisiis in capellae suae thesauro, ubi plurima originalia tam Augustini, Ambrosii, Hieronymi, atque Gregorii, necnon et aliorum orthodoxorum doctorum libros sedule congregavit: in quibus, quando sibi vacabat, valde libenter studebat, et aliis ad studendum libenter concedebat. ... Potius autem volebat de novo facere libros scribi, quam emere jam conscriptos, dicens, quod hoc modo sacrorum librorum numerus et utilitas copiosius augebatur."

[68] *Ibid.*, 15 D: "Non libenter legebat in scriptis magistralibus, sed in sanctorum libris authenticis et probatis."

[69] *Ibid.*, 15 C: "Maxime autem dum sibi vacare poterat ad studendum propter dormitationem diurnam, antequam prodiret in publicum, sive ad loquendum cum adventantibus, sive ad vesperas audiendum, [operam impendebat]...."

Quando studebat in libris, et aliqui de familiaribus suis erant praesentes, qui litteras ignorabant, quod intelligebat legendo, proprie et optime noverat coram illis transferre in gallicum de latino." Cf. also the remarks of the *Gesta* written by the anonymous monk of Saint-Denis, *ibid.*, 47 A, and the description of Saint Louis at his studies, given by William of Saint-Pathus, the confessor of Queen Marguerite, in his *Vie de Saint Louis* (ed. Delaborde, 1899), 52–54.

⁷⁰ See esp. chap. 14 of Geoffroi's *Vita* (Bouquet, *HF*, XX, 7–8) where mention is made of Louis's final instructions to his son, and of a letter to his daughter Isabelle, both written *manu sua*. Of the parting instructions, Geoffroi says expressly: "ante suam infirmitatem extremam scripsit *in Gallico* manu sua salutaria documenta..." and further, "Horum documentorum manu sua scriptorum post mortem ipsius ego copiam habui et sicut melius et brevius potui *transtuli de Gallico in Latinum*, quae documenta sunt haec." Cf. the *Gesta* of the anonymous monk of Saint-Denis, *ibid.*, 47 E.

⁷¹ *Op. cit.*, 447. Cf. C. V. Langlois, *Saint Louis* (Paris, 1886), 9, and Lecoy de la Marche, *op. cit.*, 195.

⁷² Geoffroi's *Vita, HF*, XX, 7 D: "Volebat siquidem, quod pueri jam adultae aetati propinqui quotidie non solum Missam, sed et Matutinas, et Horas canonicas cum cantu audirent, et quod ad audiendum sermones secum adessent, et quod singuli litteras addiscerent, et Horas beatae Virginis dicerent." *Ibid.*, 8 A: "... ut illic sacris institutis et litteris instruerentur."

⁷³ *Gesta Philippi* (Bouquet, *HF*, XX, 466 B).

⁷⁴ *Histoire des Français* (Paris, 1821–1844), VIII, 203–204.

⁷⁵ Ch. Langlois, *Le règne de Philippe III le Hardi* (Paris, 1887), 3–4.

⁷⁶ *Ibid.*, 5 and n. 5.

⁷⁷ Yves of Saint-Denis says of him (Bouquet, *HF*, XXI, 205 H): "Fuit et sufficienter litteris eruditus."

⁷⁸ In documents of the years 1298 and 1303, the king refers to his former teacher thus: "dilecti et familiaris clerici nostri magistri Guillelmi de Erqueto, canonici Laudunensis, qui ... notitiam litterarum in nostre juventutis primordio nobis dedit ..." and in 1314 William refers to the king as "rex Philippus, quem litterarum scientiam edocuit et instruxit"; these passages are cited by Karl Wenck in his admirable study, *Philip der Schöne von Frankreich, seine Persönlichkeit und das Urteil der Zeitgenossen* (Programmschrift der Universität Marburg, 15. Oktober, 1905), 4 and n. 1. Wenck has gone into the subject with the fullest detail, and gives chapter and verse for every item of evidence. The material which is here presented is based entirely on his researches.

⁷⁹ Wenck, *op. cit.*, 5 and n. 2.   ⁸³ *Ibid.*, 7 and n. 2.

⁸⁰ *Ibid.*, 9.   ⁸⁴ In the *Hist. litt. de la France*, XXVIII, 409.

⁸¹ *Ibid.*, 10 ff.   ⁸⁵ Wenck, *op. cit.*, 11.

⁸² *Ibid.*, 9.   ⁸⁶ *Ibid.*, 19.

⁸⁷ Raymund says that he was commissioned to translate the work from Spanish into Latin "que lingua communior est et intelligibilior ceteris"; see Wenck, 18.

⁸⁸ *Ibid.*, 20.

⁸⁹ Cf. Molinier, *Les sources ...*, I, 135, no. 471.

[90] Mabillon, *AA. SS. ord. S. Bened.* (Venice ed.), II, 258: "...liberalium studiis litterarum (sicut olim moris erat nobilibus) traditur imbuendus." Cf. Wattenbach, *DGQ* (6th ed.), I, 321, n. 4.

[91] Molinier, *Les sources*..., I, 151, no. 511.

[92] Mabillon, *AA. SS. ord. S. Bened.*, II, 71: "...audivit in locis vicinorum propinquis qualiter nobilium parvulorum mos est doctoribus instruere scholas."

[93] Pfister, *Etudes sur le règne de Robert le Pieux*, 5, n. 1. Hariulf's statement (*Chronicon Centulense*, III, 10, ed. Lot, 118): "Nec enim unquam aliquis de nobilibus loquens aliud nobilius quaesivit, si sancti Richarii monachorum nobilitas ei nuntiata fuit. In hoc enim coenobio duces, comites, filii ducum, filii etiam regum educabantur. Omnis sublimior dignitas, quaquaversum per regnum Francorum posita, in Sancti Richarii monasterio se parentem habere gaudebat."

[94] *Op. cit.*, 13–14 and notes.

[95] Mabillon, *AA. SS. ord. S. Bened.* (Venice ed.), Saec. VI, 2, 53.

[96] See Wibert's *Vita*, I, 3, *in* Mabillon, *AA. SS. ord. S. Bened.* (Venice ed.), and cf. O. Delarc, *Un pape alsacien: Léon IX et son temps*, 6–7, whose interpretation of the facts, it must be added, is just as loose as Pfister's.

[97] *Lettres de Gerbert* (ed. Havet), no. 92. The word *scholasticus* does not mean pupil, but teacher. "'Scholares aeque ac Magistros a scriptoribus ea aetate Scholasticos fuisse appellatos notandum est' (Bouquet,X,p.206,note a). *scholasticus* signifie écolâtre, chef d'école."—Havet, *Lettres de Gerbert*, 5, n. 7.

[98] Richer describes him simply as "domnus Herbrandus magnae liberalitatis atque scientiae vir" (*Historiarum libri quatuor*, IV, 50 [*MGH. SS.*, III, 643]). Cf. L. Maître, *Les écoles épiscopales et monastiques*..., 165, 171.

[99] See the *Vita* of the saint, written by Raoul Glaber, in Migne, *PL*, 142, 709–710: "Interea cernens vigilantissimus Pater quoniam non solum illo in loco [i.e., Fécamp], sed etiam per totam provinciam illam, nec non per totam Galliam, in plebeiis maxime scientiam psallendi ac legendi deficere et annullari clericis, instituit scholas sacri ministerii, quibus pro Dei amore assidui instarent fratres hujus officii docti, ubi siquidem gratis largiretur cunctis doctrinae beneficium ad coenobia sibi commissa confluentibus, nullusque qui ad haec vellet accedere, prohiberetur: quin potius tam servis quam liberis, divitibus cum egenis, uniforme charitatis impenderetur documentum. Plures etiam ex ipsis, ex coenobiis, utpote rerum tenues, accipiebant victum. Ex quibus quoque nonnulli in sanctae conversationis monachorum devenere habitum. Cujus denique institutionis labor nimium optabilem diversis ecclesiis contulit fructum." I have quoted this passage at length because it is cited by Ch. Pfister (*Etudes sur le règne de Robert le Pieux*, 6 and n. 4), in my opinion without valid grounds, in connection with the general subject of monastic schools, more particularly monastic schools for externs. Pfister's statement, to which he appends the passage quoted above, reads as follows: "Il y avait à cette époque deux sortes d'écoles dans les abbayes: les unes intérieures pour les oblats, voués souvent dès leur naissance à la vie monastique; les autres extérieures pour les jeunes gens du dehors qui, libres ou serfs, riches ou pauvres, y recevaient en général gratis, les premiers éléments de l'instruction. Quelques-uns même, trop

pauvres pour subvenir à leurs besoins, étaient nourris par les religieux." But I fail to see where our source says anything of schools "pour les jeunes gens du dehors"—by which phrase Pfister evidently meant laymen. The schools which William of Saint-Bénigne organized were for the training of priests ("scholas sacri ministerii"). It would seem that Pfister understood the word "plebeiis" as being the equivalent of "laicis," and as standing thus in contrast to "clericis." But, in the first place, it may be questioned whether any contrast was intended, for "plebeiis" can be an adjective modifying "clericis"; or, if a contrast was intended, then it was undoubtedly one between the lower and the upper clergy. The word *plebeii* must here mean, as it often does, parish priests, the plebeian clergy. It cannot refer to the laity, for the very term at once excludes any thought of the nobility, and surely William of Bénigne did not expect the common people—the peasantry, if you please—to be able to read Latin!

[100] See the list of teachers who were active in Paris before the founding of the university there, given by Valet de Viriville, *Histoire de l'instruction publique en Europe* (Paris, 1849), 382. Rashdall erred seriously in writing (I, 95) : "In northern France all intellectual life was confined to the cloister or to schools which were merely dependencies of the cloister, because the governing class itself was composed of but two great orders—the military and the clerical—in the latter of which alone was there any demand for learning."

[101] He was, for long, identified with Manegold of Lautenbach, the famous publicist and bitter antagonist of the emperor Henry IV. But Giesebrecht ("Manegold von Lautenbach," *Akademie der Wissenschaften, München*, Sitzungsberichte, 2, 1868, 297 ff.) proved conclusively that this identity is false.

[102] See the *Chronicon* of Richard of Cluny (Muratori, *Antiquitates* . . . , IV, 1085) : "His temporibus florere coepit in Theutonica terra Menegaldus Philosophus, divinis et saecularibus literis ultra coaetaneos suos eruditus. Uxor quoque et filii ejus religione florentes, multam in Scripturis habuere notitiam, et discipulos proprios filiae ejus praedictae docebant." For the other details given above, see Giesebrecht, *op. cit.*, esp. 305–312.

[103] *Opera* (ed. Cousin; 1849), I, 3: "Patrem autem habebam litteris aliquantulum imbutum antequam militari cingulo insigniretur. Unde postmodum tanto litteras amore complexus est, ut quoscunque filios haberet, litteris antequam armis instrui disponeret. Sicque profecto actum est."

[104] Guibert de Nogent, *De vita sua* (ed. G. Bourgin; Paris, 1907), III, 17. Upon this heretical movement see Luchaire *in* Lavisse, *Histoire de France*, II, pt. 2, 359. B. Monod, *Le moine Guibert et son temps (1053–1124)* (Paris, 1905), 209, thinks that they were an offshoot of the Waldensians. In general it may be said that the leaders among these heretical groups were ignorant of Latin, even the Catharists. In an account of an inquisition at Toulouse in 1178 we read: "Cumque unus illorum articulos illos conscriptos exponere et Latine loqui vellet, vix duo verba conjungere potuit, utpote qui linguam Latinam penitus ignovit."—Benedict of Peterborough, *Chronica*, I, 201 (ed. Stubbs). Compare the official report of Cardinal Peter of St. Chrysogenus, chairman of the inquisitorial commission, on p. 203.

[105] *De vita sua*, I, 14, 19.   [106] *Ibid.*, III, 18.   [107] *Ibid.*, III, 4.

[108] "... litteratura pertenuis," *ibid.*, II, 2.

[109] *Ibid.*, I, 23.

[110] *Ibid.*, I, 4. The second date given above is that of the time in which the *Autobiography* was written; cf. Molinier, *Les sources ...*, II, 186, no. 1856.

[111] *De vita sua*, II, 6.

[112] *Ibid.*, II, 5.

[113] *Ibid.*, III, 5.

[114] *The History of Normandy and of England* (London, 1857–1878), IV, 563–566.

[115] See her *Vita* written within a generation of her death (1113) by an anonymous monk of Saint-Vaast, in *AA. SS.*, April 11, 142: "litteris imbuta est, usque ad aetatem congruam in annis suis puerilibus."

[116] See Kurt Breysig's thorough study, "Gottfried von Bouillon vor dem Kreuzzuge," *Westdeutsche Zeitschrift für Geschichte und Kunst*, XVII (1898), 169–201.

[117] Baudri of Dol, *Historia Jerosolimitana*, III, 12 (*Recueil des historiens des croisades, Occidentaux*, IV, 71), calls him "homo facundus et singularis scientiae."

[118] *Ibid.*, III, 890: "Dum vero capellanus meus Alexander sequenti die Paschae cum summa festinatione has litteras scriberet...."

[119] P. Riant, *Inventaire critique des lettres historiques des croisades* (Paris, 1880), 150, n. 2, points out that the panegyrical poem of Hildebert of Mans (Migne, *PL*, 171, 297) supposedly addressed to Stephen of Blois, was in reality addressed to an archdeacon of Nantes or Saintes.

[120] *Lectures in European History* (London, 1904), 136–137. See William of Tyre, *Historia*, XVI, 2 (*Recueil des historiens des croisades, Occidentaux*, I, 705–706): "erat autem [sc. Baldwin III] et commode litteratus, et fratre suo domino Amalrico, qui ei successit, multo amplius: cum vero quid otii ex occupationibus publicis decerpere poterat, libenter incumbebat lectioni; historiarum precipue auditor, antiquorum regum et optimorum principum gesta moresque diligenter investigabat: litteratorum maxime, sed et prudentum laicorum confabulationibus plurimum recreabatur." *Hist.*, XIX, 2 (*ibid.*, 884–885): "Modice litteratus erat [sc. Amalric], et fratre multo minus,... legendi studio, cum aliquid otii regni occupationes indulgebant, juxta id quod regibus solet contigere, satis commode erat instructus. In quaestionibus argutior, in earum solutionibus plurimum recreabatur. Historiarum, prae caeteris lectionibus, erat avidus auditor, memor perpetuo, promptus et fidelissimus recitator."

[121] See the *Historia*, XIX, 21 (*ibid.*, I, 917).

[122] William of Tyre, *Hist.*, XXI, 1 (*ibid.*, I, 1004–1005): "Hunc puerum adhuc, annorum circiter novem, dum nos archidiaconatum administraremus Tyrensem, pater multum pro ejus eruditione sollicitus, multis precibus et sub obtentu gratiae suae, nobis erudiendum tradidit et liberalibus studiis imbuendum.... Proficiebat tamen in studio litterarum, singulisque diebus magis et magis bonae spei et amplectandae indolis succrescebat.... historiarum more patris avidus auditor."

[123] Luchaire, *La société française au temps de Philippe-Auguste* (2d ed., tr. by Krehbiel; Paris, 1909), 377.

[124] The letter is in Migne, *PL*, 189, 347. Peter is harking back to the days of Héloïse's youth: "Audiebam tunc temporis, mulierem [i.e., Héloïse], licet necdum saeculi nexibus expeditam, litteratoriae scientiae, quod perrarum est, et studio, licet saecularis, sapientiae summam operam dare, nec mundi voluntatibus, nugis, vel deliciis ab hoc utili discendarum artium proposito retrahi posse. Cumque ab his exercitiis detestanda desidia totus pene torpeat mundus, et ubi subsistere possit pes sapientiae, non dicam apud sexum femineum, a quo ex toto explosus est, sed vix apud ipsos viriles animos invenire valeat, tu illo efferendo studio tuo, et mulieres omnes evicisti, et pene viros universos superasti."

[125] Cf. especially Ch. Jourdain, *op. cit.*, 92–95.

[126] See *S. Bernardi vita tertia, auctore Gaufrido*, 3 (Migne, *PL*, 185, 527): "Ducissa Lotharingiae . . . cum adhuc corporis voluptatibus supra modum dedita esset, contigit venerabilem Virum [i.e., Bernard] pro pace quadam rogare Ducem pariter, atque ipsam. Dumque loquens extenderet manum, casu factum est, ut Ducissae chlamydem tangeret. Cui unus de astantibus arridens: 'Super religiosam, inquit, mulierem extendisti manum, pater.' At ille: 'Nondum venit hora ejus.' Audiens Ducissa (siquidem litteras noverat) compuncta est vehementer. . . ."

[127] See the letters addressed to the girl's uncle, *Epist.*, 54 (Migne, *PL*, 207, 166): "Quia tamen plurimum litterata est, ego ipsam adhuc et litteris, et viva voce aggrediar, volens in ea experiri quid in talibus post gratiam Dei possit humana facundia."

[128] See the *Hist. litt. de la France*, IX, 132. Unfortunately, the *Vita Margaritae* written by William of Grenoble about 1163 (published by Martène, *Amplissima collectio*, VI, 1201–1214) is not now available to me.

[129] See *Acerbi Morenae continuatio, MGH. SS.*, XVIII, 640: "Beatrix vero . . . litterata, et Dei cultrix."

[130] See the *Hist. litt. de la France*, IX, 131; the poem, according to the Benedictine authors, was published by Kaspar Brusch (or Bruschius) in an old sixteenth-century collection of miscellanea which I have not been able to consult.

[131] See Luchaire, *Louis VI le Gros . . .*, nos. 108, 110, 114, 119, 128.

[132] Bouquet, *HF*, XII, 236.

[133] *Vita S. Gerardi* (a brother of Saint Bernard, d. 1138), *AA. SS.*, June 13, II, 701.

[134] D'Achery, *Spicilegium* (nov. ed.; Paris, 1723), II, 155.

[135] *Gesta consulum Andegavorum*, in *Chroniques des comtes d'Anjou*, ed. Halphen and Poupardin, 71: "optime litteratus, inter clericos et laicos facundissimus." Cf. the story told by Jean de Marmoutier (*Historia Gaufredi, ibid.*, 178), in which Geoffrey, as a mere boy, converses very learnedly and eloquently with Henry I of England.

[136] *Historia Gaufredi, ibid.*, 212: "Quibus sane studiis in hanc virtutum eminentiam vir illustris excreverit, clarum ei est qui diligentius pensaverit vitam ejus. Cum enim ab ineunte etate scientiam litterarum degustasset, tanto ardore

in his versabatur, ut nec inter arma pateretur dehabere litterarum doctorem."
Cf. Kate Norgate, *England under the Angevin Kings* (London and New York,
1887), I, 262.

[137] *Historia Gaufredi, ibid.*, 218: "Consulit super hoc litteratus consul legendo
Vegecium Renatum, qui de re dixit militari." Boutaric (*Revue des questions
historiques*, XVII [1875], 19) incorrectly refers this story to Fulk le Rechin.

[138] See R. L. Poole, *Illustrations of the History of Medieval Thought* (2d rev.
ed.; London, 1920), 299; J. Chartrou, *L'Anjou de 1109 à 1151* (Paris, 1928),
221; Hauréau, *Histoire de la philosophie scolastique*, I, pt. 1, p. 441.

[139] "In te tamen et in filiis tuis aliquid spei consistit; quos non, ut alii, ludo
alearum sed studio literarum, tenera aetate imbuisti." Quoted from Chartrou,
op. cit., 221, n. 1. As far as I know, the only edition of this treatise is that of
G. Gratarolo, a Basel physician, published at Strassburg, 1567, which I have
not been able to consult. For Geoffrey's reputation as a man of culture, see also
the panegyric poem of Stephen of Rouen (fl. *ca.* 1170) published by R. Howlett
in his edition of the *Chronicles of the Reign of Stephen*, II, 772–773 (Rolls
Series) :   "Justiciae cultor, sincerus pacis amator,
            Juris sectator, legum firmissimus ultor,
            Sola salus patriae, speculum lux atque sophiae,
            Artibus imbutus septenis, sensus acutus,
            Precluis orator, logicae nec segnis amator,
            Rhetoricos flores edoctus sive colores,
            Cautus et a puero falsum discernere vero,
            Multimoda specie perfusus phylosphiae.
            In prosa Cicero, versu Maro cederet illi,
            In logica Socrates, armis equandus Achilli."

[140] *Epist.*, 16 (Migne, *PL*, 203, 148–149) : "Qui si forte litteras didicit, quorum scientia non est tantummodo clericorum, multi enim noverunt litteras in
gradu sive ordine laicorum: nonnunquam feriatus a tumultu vel negotio militari, assumpto sibi codice debet tanquam in speculo se mirari.

"Sunt quidem tam aethnicorum quam orthodoxorum tractatus expoliti vel
epistolae vel commenta, quae viris nobilibus non parvae utilitatis offerunt
documenta: dignitatem ornant, militiam ordinant, roborant juventutem; mores aedificant, animos acuunt, promovent ad virtutem; torporem arguunt,
zelum suscitant, describunt aequitatem, iram temperant, commendant clemen-
tiam, suggerunt lenitatem. Haec et horum similia legere vel audire princeps
mente nobilis non fastidit, eorumque memoriam ad curas temporalium penitus
non allidit: indignum ducens aurem fabulis, aleis revocantibus manum dare,
et non magis codicellum, saltem furtim hora sibi congrua praesentare. Vidi, ut
recolo, cum comes Carolus divinis altaribus assistebat, reverenter et decenter
legendis psalmulis insistebat, et ut limatus mucro cum sumendae tempus aderat ultionis, sic decebat devotum principem libellus tempore lectionis. Vidi et
comitem Ayulfum, nobilem genere, egregium forma, moribus informatum, qui,
magnas parentibus gratias referens quod eum a puero fecerunt litteratum, sic
mihi colloquens se Latinum exhibuit, ut non nisi clericus videretur, sic se red-
dens et militem, ut paulo post ad paganos pugnans pro patria moreretur. Non
enim scientiae fortis militia vel militiae praejudicat honesta scientia litterarum, imo in principe copula tam utilis, tam conveniens est duarum ut, sicut

praedictus Ayulfus asserebat, princeps quem non nobilitat scientia litteralis, non parum degenerans sit quasi rusticanus et quodammodo bestialis.

"Porro quia tibi et parentum cura litteras a pueritia dedit nosse, et quod litterae praedicant et commendant, superna gratia dedit posse: fac quod facis, imo profice et proficiens perfice quod coepisti; eum pure diligens a quo ut hoc velis et valeas, accepisti."

The letter was probably written shortly after 1168, the year in which Philip succeeded his father as count. For the life and writings of Philip of Harvengt, see *Hist. litt. de la France*, XIV, 268–295. Cf. also Maître, *op. cit.*, 171.

[141] See the *Hist. litt. de la France*, XIV, 280.

[142] Cf. *ibid.*, 280. See *Histoire du meurtre de Charles le Bon, Comte de Flandre (1127–1128) par Galbert de Bruges* (ed. H. Pirenne; Paris, 1891).

[143] I do not know upon what ground Luchaire (*La société française* ..., 401) calls the book which Philip gave Chrétien "un poème anglo-normand." See Chrétien's dedication to Philip, lines 1–68, in the edition of Alfons Hilka, *Der Percevalroman* (Halle, 1932; Vol. V of *Sämmtliche erhaltene Werke des Christian von Troyes*, ed. by W. Foerster), 1–4; and cf. Hilka's comments, pp. xxiv and 617.

[144] Pirenne, *Histoire de Belgique* (1st ed.), I, 321.

[145] *Register* IX, 35 (ed. Caspar, p. 622).

[146] See the letter, quoted by Lambert in his *Genealogiae comitum Flandriae* (*MGH. SS.*, IX, 310): "Memento, karissime fili, quantum omnipotenti Deo debeas, qui te contra voluntatem parentum tuorum de parvo magnum, de paupere divitem, de humili gloriosum principem fecit, et quod maximum est inter seculi principes rarum, dote litterarum, scientiae atque religionis donavit." Cf. Pirenne, *Histoire de Belgique*, I, 145, n. 2.

[147] *Ibid.*, I, 323.

[148] *Ibid.*, 321–323.

[149] *Ibid.*, 323. For the material presented in this paragraph, cf. Luchaire, *La société française* ..., 402, and esp. G. Paris, *La littérature française au moyen âge* (2d ed.; Paris, 1890), pp. 137–138, nos. 94–95.

[150] See the *Historia comitum Ghisnensium* or *Chronicon Ghisnense et Ardense* of Lambert of Ardres, chaps. 80–81, in the edition of J. Heller (1879), *MGH. SS.*, XXIV, 598; in the edition of Godefroy-Ménilglaise (1855), 171–175. Cf. esp. the latter's notes, *ibid.*, 434–435, and Luchaire, *La société française* ..., 403–404. On Lambert of Ardres, see Heller's introduction, *op. cit.*, 550 ff., and the article of F. L. Ganshoff, "A propos de la Chronique de Lambert d'Ardres," in *Mélanges d'histoire du moyen âge offerts à M. Ferdinand Lot* (Paris, 1925), 205–234.

[151] H. Malo, *Renaud de Dammartin* (Paris, 1898), 115 f., 119; cf. Maître, *op. cit.*, 174, and the *Hist. litt. de la France*, XVII, 373, 732.

[152] In Bouquet, *HF*, XVI, 515.

[153] *Ibid.*, 700.

[154] On the widespread nature of public education in Champagne, see d'Arbois de Jubainville, *Histoire des ducs et des comtes de Champagne* ... (Paris, 1859–1869), III, 184 f.

[155] Bouquet, *HF*, XVI, 700: "Vetus etenim proverbium est, et ore veterum celebrata sententia: Quantum a belluis homines, tantum distant a laicis litterati." It is interesting to note Nicolas' use of the words *laici* and *litterati* here; to his mind, *laici* is synonymous with *illitterati*. This striking proof of the general ignorance of letters among the laity is also revealed in Goliardic poetry. See the *Carmina Burana*, ed. Schmeller, 1894, 179, no. 101:

"Litteratos convocat
decus virginale,
laicorum execrat
pectus bestiale:"

and 198, no. 124:

"Ergo litteris
cetus hic imbutus
signa Veneris
'militet' secutus,
estimetur autem laicus 'ut' brutus,
nam ad artem surdus est et mutus."

[156] See esp. d'Arbois de Jubainville, *op. cit.*, III, 189 ff., and cf. Maître, *op. cit.*, 171–172.

[157] *Epist.* 17 (Migne, *PL*, 203, 152–154): "Porro tuus ille pater quem mira in pauperes liberalitas insignivit, cujus non animum avaritia, non manum tenacitas irretivit: te, quem suum haeredem disponebat, honesta scientia praemunivit, dum provida sollicitudine studiis a puero liberalibus erudivit. Et recte. Quem enim reddit nobilem sanguis ingenuus, series parentelae, quem divitem possessio, dominum servitus vel obsequium clientelae; dignum fuit ut a vulgarium ignorantia, et brutorum hominum stolida caecitate, scientia litteralis educeret, et clara praeditum redderet libertate. Unde et litterarum scientiam recte vocant aethnici liberalem, quia eum qui labore et studio sortitur gratiam litteralem, a confuso vulgi consortio et a multitudine liberat publicana, ne pressus et oppressus teneatur compede et hebetudine rusticana. Multum ergo debes patri tuo cujus tibi cura et diligentia sic providit, qui non solum quae sua erant, sed et quae obtinere non meruerat, filio non invidit, ut cum te multis populis disponeret comitatus excellentia principari, vellet quoque super caeteros comites litterarum scientia sublimari. ... scholarem disciplinam per annos aliquot prosecutus sub magistrali ferula, liberalem es scientiam assecutus; et juxta modum temporis et personae, tantis, ut aiunt, litteris es imbutus, ut quamplures clericos transcendas in eorum nequaquam numero constitutus. Quamvis enim appositus litteris te fore clericum non praescires, sed accingendum gladiali balteo et implicandum negotiis militaribus praesentires: adversus tamen litteras non odio, non fastidio torpuisti, sed labore cum gratia earum commendabilem tibi scientiam acquisisti. Ad hoc autem additur, quod cum in litteris adeptus sis intelligendi gratiam et profectum, erga eas applicas quamdam animi diligentiam et affectum, et miles nobilis, princepsque militum, sic amas et honoras milites loricatos, ut clericali more diligas litteras, benigne colligas litteratos. Aliquando enim militare negotium causas decertantium, strepitus forensium intermittis, teque tibi vindicans, ad clericale otium te remittis: at assumpto codice gaudes lectionis serie revoluta, in qua tanquam in speculo tua tibi lucet facies absoluta. Nam sive aethnicorum sive Catholi-

corum scripta relegas, codices perscruteris, si pretiosum a vili prudens lector separare juxta prophetae consilium non graveris. . . .

"Haec et similia horum cum legis et frequenter relegis in Scriptura, cum prudenter intelligis et discernere diligis a quibusque noxiis profutura: non recedis a principe, nec a rectore nobili populorum, nec ignavus degeneras, sed teipsum quasi regeneras aquis liberalibus antiquorum. . . .

"Sunt quidem innumeri qui surdo litteras transeunt intellectu, sunt plures qui intelligunt, sed amplecti negligunt ex affectu: sciunt neque sentiunt languentes fastidio non amore, ut asinus comedens carduos non succo trahitur, non sapore. Sunt alii inter multa praedictorum agmina satis rari, agiles intellectu, studii patientes, scientiae non ignari, qui cum invenerint litteras, in earum amore adeo sunt avari, ut quantumvis aut opibus aut genere, aut dignitatis excellentia sint praeclari: eas tamen contemptu prodigo elabi non sufferant, sed unca manu teneant et conservent, et, ut plus dicam, solliciti frequentius eas vel oculo vel auditu patulo coacervent. Qui etsi curis exterioribus occupantur, litterarum tamen amorem et sollicitudinem non deponunt, nunquam dicunt: Sufficit, nullam in scientia metam ponunt; sed cum tempus et cura patitur, revisunt litteras et frequentant, et subtracti negotii, litterali otio se praesentant. Nec ignavum est otium, sed utile negotium litteris inservire, et quid rite vel delectat vel expediat, in eis frequentius invenire, quas ad hoc in Ecclesia Deus, ut arbitror, voluit frequentari, ut earum frequentia ipse quem praedicant possit cognitus plus amari. Cum enim pluribus et dissimilibus linguis Deus uti velit diversas hominum nationes, et vel ab invicem discerni vario, vel eodem confoederari labio plurimas regiones: eam linguam, nisi fallor, quodam reverentiae et amoris privilegio vult praeferri, quam versari inter sacra ecclesiastica et ad posteros litteris vult transferri. Unde etsi Hebraea et Graeca eo date sunt ordine patribus ab antiquo, tamen quia non usu, sed fama sola ad nos quasi veniunt de longinquo, eisdem valefacto, ad Latinam praesentem noster utcunque se applicat intellectus, et, nisi forte duri sumus et reprobi, intelligentiam sequitur et affectus. Eam quippe linguam debet quisque affectuosa reverentia venerari, per quam sibi Deum verum audit expressius praedicari: per quam nostra redemptio, cunctorum resurrectio, sanctorum glorificatio, verius innotescit, et, ut concludam breviter, ipsa Dei et eorum quae sunt Dei cognitio legentibus et non negligentibus dilucescit. Recte ergo viro nobili litterarum placet nobilis officina, cujus exercitio cuditur salutaris morum, scientiae, fidei disciplina, ita ut si cuilibet vulgares linguae praesto sint caeterae, non Latina, ipsius pace dixerim, hebetudo eum teneat asinina. Quod tu recte considerans, Latinam linguam litteralemque scientiam non ignoras, et eos quos percipis apprime litteratos, diligis et honoras: majores quosque reverentia, minores plerosque munerans donativis, eosque indigentes de necessitatibus eruens oppressivis." Also published in Bouquet, *HF*, XVI, 703–706.

[158] Some monks of Provins copied a Valerius Maximus for Count Henry of Champagne. L. Maître, *Les écoles de Chartres*, p. 171. Cf. above, note 156.

[159] John R. William, "William of the White Hands and Men of Letters," in *Anniversary Essays in Medieval History presented to Charles Homer Haskins* (Boston, 1929), 365–366; d'Arbois de Jubainville, *op. cit.*, III, chap. 5.

[160] Cited by Gustave Cohen, "Un grand romancier au XII⁰ siècle: Chrestien de Troies," *Revue des cours et des conférences*, XXVIII (1926–27) pt. 1, 459.

[161] D'Arbois de Jubainville, *op. cit.*, IV, 640.

[162] See the abbot's letter, in Migne, *PL*, 211, 691–692: "Instanter, filia, tuae dilectionis devotio postulavit, quatenus sermunculos meos tibi transcriptos dirigerem, et hoc quippe ex multo desiderio deposcere videbaris. Digna plane et laudanda petitio, si quae Latine dicta sunt per te posses intelligere, aut si eo modo dicta essent, quo ex eis tibi posset aedificationis beneficium provenire. Ad hoc enim, ut arbitror, sermones ipsos expostulas, ut ex eorum lectione aedificata, proficias, dummodo tibi interdum forte vacanti ab aliquo exponantur. Scito, filia, quod sententia cujuslibet dicti, si de lingua in linguam translata fuerit, vix in peregrino idiomate, sua ei sapiditas vel compositio remanebit." Cf. d'Arbois de Jubainville, *op. cit.*, IV, 197.

[163] Migne, *PL*, 211, 686: "Sed jam in Mariae laudibus finem suum sortiatur epistola: quam forsitan tibi facit sui ipsius prolixitas onerosam. Si quid in ea durum vel difficile intellectui tuo occurrerit, habes penes te G. venerabilem capellanum, qui tibi possit et sciat singulas difficultates explanare. Laico sermone tibi scripsisse debueram, nisi quia te comperi Latini sermonis aliquantulam intelligentiam percepisse." The countess concerned is not mentioned by name. She may have been either Alice, daughter of Louis VII of France and widow of Thibaut of Chartres (d. 1191, at the siege of Acre), or Catherine, daughter of Radulf, count of Clermont-en-Beauvoisis; cf. *ibid.*, the note of the editor, Dom Martène. For Adam of Perseigne, see *Hist. litt. de la France*, XVI, 437–447.

[164] Cf. F. M. Warren, "Features of Style in Early French Narrative Poetry," *Modern Philology*, III (1905–06), 185–187.

[165] Cf. Wattenbach's fine statement, *DGQ* (6th ed.), II, 251.

[166] See Molinier, *Les sources* ..., nos. 2348–2350, and his Intro., nos. 180–181, III, 40–42, and V, pp. cxxv–cxxvii.

[167] The subscription reads: "Ego Petrus, canonicus de Roscha, de mandato domini Johannis de Nantolio qui rogatus huic interfuit testamento et sigillum suum apposuit, testamento huic subscripsi pro eo, CUM IPSE NON HABERET NOTICIAM LITTERARUM." Cited from the description of the document (Archiv. Nat., Trésor des Chartes, J 406, no. 6, Musée des Archives, no. 270) given by L. Gautier, in his article "L'enfance d'un baron," *Revue des questions historiques*, XXXII (1882), 430, n. 1.

[168] Cf. Prou, *Manuel de paléographie*, 200.

[169] "Et comman à touz mes serjanz que il les paiet à dès san délai. Ce fu escrit de ma mein." See the description in Delisle's article, "De l'instruction littéraire de la noblesse française," *Le Correspondant* (1855), XXXVI, 444.

[170] See Molinier, *Les sources* ..., III, 105, no. 2537.

[171] I have been forced to use the Latin translation of the *Vita* published by the Bollandists, *AA. SS.*, August, VI, 800, since the original French version, published by Du Cange in his edition of Joinville (1668), is not available. Cf. Ch. Jourdain, *op. cit.*, 102, and Molinier, *Les sources* ..., III, 120, no. 2552.

[172] Bouquet, *HF*, XX, 94–95 (in the edition of Delaborde, 89). Cf. Jourdain, *op. cit.*, 101.

[173] I cite this story from Delisle, *op. cit.*, 449–450, since Colveneere's edition (published at Douai, first in 1597 and again in 1605 and 1627) of the *Bonum universale* is not available to me. According to Delisle, the story is found in Book I, chap. 23 (edition of 1627), p. 93.

[174] The catalogue has been published, with a brief introduction, by Ch. de Beaurepaire, in *Bibliothèque de l'Ecole des Chartes*, 3d ser., III (1852), 559–562.

[175] By Geoffrey of Waterford, a Dominican from Ireland. See L. Thorndike, *A History of Magic and Experimental Science* (New York, 1923), II, 276. According to Valentine Rose, *De Aristotelis librorum ordine et auctoritate* (Berlin, 1854), 184, Old French MSS of the *Secretum secretorum* are very numerous.

[176] Cf. Delisle, *op. cit.*, 450.

Chapter VII

NORMANDY AND NORMAN-ANGEVIN ENGLAND[1]

THE LIMITED EVIDENCE which we possess concerning the culture of the Norman nobility does not lead to the conclusion that the immediate descendants of Rollo and his companions were interested in Latin learning. A statement of Adhemar of Chabannes which might at first glance induce us to believe that the Normans soon adopted the Latin tongue, can hardly be accepted literally.[2] According to Dudo of Saint-Quentin, the earliest historian of Normandy, both William Longsword (927–943) and his son, Richard I (943–996), were "educated" by a certain Count Botho, one of Rollo's companions. This training, however, probably had nothing to do with letters.[3] Dudo's history, it is true, is itself proof that these early Normans had some appreciation of the value of a written record, at least of their own past, for it was written at the request of Richard I, and was based chiefly on the oral testimony of Count Raoul of Ivry, Richard's brother, and was finally completed at the instance of Richard II (996–1027).[4] This fact does not mean, however, that the dukes mentioned had any knowledge of Latin. Normandy seems to have been a culturally backward country until well into the eleventh century. In the words of Ordericus Vitalis, "Under the first six dukes of Normandy, scarcely a single Norman applied himself to liberal studies; nor was there any teacher found, until God, the provider of all, brought Lanfranc to the Norman shores."[5] Orderic's picture may be somewhat overdrawn,[6] but it is undoubtedly true that the average Norman noble was unlettered. Herluin, the noble who founded Bec (1034), was illiterate until he retired from the world to build his monastery; at the age of forty he began to learn to read.[7] At most, the Norman layman may have learned the Psalms,[8] like his English contemporaries.[9] Some Norman monks seem to have been none too well grounded in Latin,[10] and even churchmen in high places were sometimes illiterate.[11]

Freeman has written: "We must remember that, in every country of Western Europe, the sound of one language beside the ver-

---

nacular must have been perfectly familiar. Everybody in England was used to the sound of Latin as well as to the sound of English. Everybody in Normandy was used to the sound of Latin as well as to the sound of French."[12] This statement is undoubtedly true, but it is not easy to determine to what degree familiarity with the sound of Latin entailed an intelligent understanding of the language. It seems highly probably that there was no real comprehension of Latin except among those who had been formally instructed in it in their youth or in later life.

Whether or not William the Conqueror was able to understand Latin, cannot be determined definitely.[13] Probably he and many another medieval nobleman possessed a kind of half-understanding of Latin that was spoken or read aloud; that is, they could comprehend common and recurrent biblical and liturgical phrases, and simple sentences. Certainly William had not had any literary instruction. The guardians of his youth, including Turold or Turchetil, who is known to us as William's *pedagogus,* were men of war rather than men of learning.[14] The "good education" which the authors of the *Histoire littéraire de la France*[15] claim for William, consisted of nothing more than the customary training in arms and the usual knightly virtues.[16] To suppose that William could write is sheer fantasy.[17]

Of William's wife, Mathilda, the daughter of Baldwin V of Flanders, Palgrave has written without reservation that "the Latin language was familiar to her. Yet let it be observed that we do not reckon this acquirement as anything very extraordinary. What French afterwards became, the Latin continued to be in the eleventh century, the token of education constituting the distinction between the higher and the lower classes of society."[18] This gross exaggeration—not to say misrepresentation—is unwarranted by the evidence. If such an educational test had been applied to the English nobility of the eleventh century, most of the nobles would have been reduced to the status of the peasantry. There is no doubt, however, that Mathilda was far ahead of her husband, and of most of her lay contemporaries, in the matter of learning. According to Ordericus Vitalis, she had a "knowledge of letters"; in other words, she was able to read Latin.[19]

It may have been Mathilda's influence which prompted the Conqueror to give his sons what he had not received, an education.

Robert Curthose, the eldest son, was entrusted at an early age to tutors or "counselors" whose names have come down to us in charters of the day. Chief of these were Hilger, "pedagogus Roberti filii comitis," "Raherius consiliarius infantis," and "Tetboldus grammaticus."[20] But how far Robert profited from the instruction of his tutors is a matter of doubt. He received no flattering title like the *Beauclerc* of his brother Henry I, and there is no direct evidence that he knew Latin.[21] To judge from a speech put by Ordericus in the mouth of Robert, who is quarreling with his father, the young prince regarded grammarians with some distaste.[22] If, however, as has been supposed, Robert was actually the author of an extant poem in the Welsh language, "it may perhaps be allowed that in his youth he had acquired at least a taste and capacity for things literary."[23]

Concerning the education of William Rufus, little can be said. William of Malmesbury relates that he was "reared" by Lanfranc, but it is doubtful whether any training in letters was included. Freeman states in one of his letters that William was illiterate (*illiteratus*), giving, however, no explicit authority for such a conclusion.[24] Cecilia, the eldest daughter of William and Mathilda, received an unusually good education, doubtless partly because she was destined to become a nun. She eventually became abbess of her mother's foundation, La Trinité, at Caen.[25]

Of all the children of the Conqueror, Adela and Henry I take the honors in learning. Adela, the wife of Stephen of Blois, was justly celebrated in her day as a woman of great culture. She received letters and laudatory poems from some of the most learned men of the time, and we have ample evidence that she was able to read the works which were addressed to her. Her ability to read is revealed in the letters of Hildebert of Lavardin, bishop of Le Mans.[26] Baudri of Dol praises her love of poetry and delight in books.[27] Hugh, a learned monk of Fleury, dedicated his *Historia ecclesiastica* to her rather than to "illiterate princes who scorn the art of literature."[28] Ives of Chartres was also among Adela's correspondents.[29]

Henry I has come down to us as Henry Beauclerc or Henry the Scholar. In a recent study of Henry's claim to such a title, however, Professor Charles W. David has attempted to show that his "great fame as a learned king is the product of a later age, not of the age in which he lived."[30] It is also stated that "there are no works in either Latin, English, or French, which can be attributed to Henry I, and [that] his claim to authorship must definitely be abandoned."[31] Professor David argues further that the assertion of Freeman that Henry I "spoke English familiarly" rests on documents which are forgeries.[32] Just when the name Beauclerc was first applied to the king cannot be determined definitely; the earliest statement that he was popularly known as a scholar was made more than a century after Henry's death.[33]

Our evidence concerning Henry's education and learning is limited to the statements of Ordericus Vitalis and William of Malmesbury, both of whom wrote about the year 1140. William tells us that Henry learned his letters as a child, and that he acquired a love of books which neither the tumult of war nor the stress of affairs could destroy, although he never read much in public nor sang except in a quiet way. And although he had to read hastily and at odd moments, nevertheless this reading stood him in good stead as a ruler, for, as Plato has said, "Happy would be the state if philosophers would reign, or kings be philosophers." Learning, therefore, made him a wise and just king. As a boy, and even in his father's presence, he used to quote the proverb: "Illiterate king, crowned ass."[34] To this last item of William of Malmesbury's account, Professor David has objected that, since William the Conqueror certainly was not literate, "it is surely safe to deny that Henry was accustomed to tell his father that an illiterate monarch was a crowned ass."[35] Professor David objects that "William of Malmesbury gives as the chief reason for Henry's having received an extraordinary education, the fact that he alone among the Conqueror's sons was royally born and designed from the beginning for the kingship; [that] this argument, whether appearing in William of Malmesbury or elsewhere, was almost certainly devised and projected into the past after Henry had actually attained the kingship, [and that] there is no good reason to suppose that any special importance was attached to the royal birth of Henry by his parents or by any one else during the period when his education was being acquired."[36] It should be pointed out, however, that this contention, even if true, invalidates only the reason which William of Malmesbury gives for Henry's training, and not the assertion that Henry received an unusually good education. The opinion that the young prince did not receive an extraordinary education is based, in last analysis, upon a faulty reading of the passage referred to. William of Malmesbury does not say, as Professor David asserts, "that Henry's education was scrappily acquired." The passage, somewhat obscure in meaning, seems to imply only that after Henry became king he did not have much time for letters, and could taste their pleasures only in a cursory fashion. And the author adds that, even though acquired under these conditions, the king's learning stood him in good stead.[37] Nor can we agree with Professor David that William of Malmesbury acknowledges that Henry's "mastery of letters was not such that he could read aloud, or in the presence of others, without difficulty and embarrassment." William merely says that Henry did not read much in public, and makes no mention of any difficulty or embarrassment. Professor David has probably been led astray in his assertions by Le Prévost, who first misinterpreted the passage.[38]

Ordericus Vitalis mentions Henry I's learning in three distinct passages. In the first one, he tells us that Henry acquired his knowledge of letters in his youthful years.[39] In the second, he says almost the same thing, adding that Henry was thus "nobly imbued with knowledge both by nature and by training."[40] In the third passage, Ordericus describes how the English king, being literate, read a letter coming from the court of Philip I of France.[41]

In summary, it seems probable that Henry I was a better scholar, and more entitled to his title of Beauclerc, than Professor David would permit us to believe. Even if the name is the product of a later day, the fact remains that Henry's contemporaries, Ordericus and William of Malmesbury, regarded his learning as unusual. Certainly his learning was extraordinary for a layman and even for a king of his time. Louis VI of France was probably wholly illiterate; and, though Henry V of Germany could probably understand Latin, the literacy of his two successors, Lothar of Supplinburg and Conrad III, is at best a matter of doubt.

Both Mathilda, the wife of Henry I, and her mother, Saint Margaret, the wife of Malcolm III of Scotland, were women of unusual culture. Both were famous for their learning, secular and religious.[42] Margaret's intellectual activities have been described without stint of praise by her biographer, who was either Turgot, her confessor, later archbishop of St. Andrews, or Theodoric, an ob-

scure monk but also a contemporary.[43] He tells us that amid all her
duties as a queen, Margaret found time to devote herself to the
sacred writings and to discuss even the most subtle questions with
the learned men of her circle, in a way which often fatigued her
biographer. The virtues which she acquired in her reading she imparted to others, and especially to her husband. So great was Malcolm's love for his queen that everything dear to her was also dear
to him. Thus he would often take up one of her books, turn its pages
and look at them even though he could not read a word; and he
would even fondle lovingly her favorite books. Once he ordered a
certain manuscript to be adorned with gold and jewels, and gave it
to the queen as a token of his devotion.[44] It may be mentioned incidentally that Malcolm, though ignorant of Latin, knew English as
well as he did his native Scotch.[45]

The prologue to the *Life of Margaret* which was written at the
request of Queen Mathilda shows clearly that the latter was able
to read the account of her mother's life.[46] Mathilda was educated
under the supervision of her aunt, Christina, abbess first at Wilton
and later at Romsey, though she was not intended for the veil.[47]
Although letters from a medieval lord or lady are themselves no
proof of literacy on the part of the sender, some of Mathilda's letters seem to bear the unmistakable stamp of personal composition,
especially those to Anselm.[48] They show also that she was well read
in some of the best pagan and Christian Latin writers. Among her
other correspondents were Hildebert of Lavardin, bishop of Le
Mans, and Pope Pascal II.[49]

Adeliza of Louvain, Henry I's second wife, was greatly interested in the vernacular literary movement of her day, and took
under her patronage Geoffrey Gaimar and the Anglo-Norman poets
Philip du Than and David the Trouvère.[50] She, too, was among the
correspondents of the learned Hildebert of Le Mans, but his letters
to her offer no conclusive evidence concerning her ability to read
them personally.[51] Whether or not she knew any Latin, therefore,
must be left an open question.

Of the children of Henry I, at least one deserves the reputation
of being both a student and a patron of letters,—his natural son,
Robert, earl of Gloucester. In the words of Miss Norgate, he was
"renowned as a scholar no less than as a warrior and statesman."[52]
He was the patron and apparently the close friend of William of

Malmesbury, who dedicated to Robert his chief historical works, the *Deeds of the English Kings* and the *Modern History*, the latter having been composed at the earl's express request. The prefatory epistles of these books reveal Robert's enlightened patronage of learning,[53] but even more significant is the description of Robert given in the epilogue to the *Deeds*. Here William tells us that his patron is as learned as he is noble, knightly, just, and munificent. The earl is so fond of literature that even when he is weighed down by a mass of business, he manages to snatch a few hours for reading or hearing others read. He regulates his affairs so wisely that he does not neglect his knightly duties for letters, nor letters for knightly duties, as some others do. His love of books is an indication of how deeply he has drunk of the fountain of learning, for no one loves philosophy who has not drawn deeply from its source. William owes a debt of gratitude to Robert's father, who took care to give his son such a thorough education.[54] In his *Abbreviatio Amalarii*, William of Malmesbury gives us a charming picture of a young man named Robert sitting in the library at Malmesbury, eagerly inspecting its treasures and suggesting plans of work to the willing friend (William) at his side.[55] This Robert may have been the earl of Gloucester, but it seems more probable that he was a young monk.[56] The learning of Robert is also vouched for by other contemporary writers. Walter Map describes him as "a man of great cleverness and much learning."[57] Geoffrey of Monmouth in the dedicatory epistle of his *Historia regum Britanniae* addresses his patron thus:

> Unto this little work of mine, therefore, do thou, Robert, Earl of Gloucester, show favour, so that, being corrected by thy instruction and advice, it may be rated to have sprung not from the poor little fountain of Geoffrey of Monmouth, but, seasoned by the salt of thy wit, may be said to be the work of one whom Henry, illustrious king of the English, begot, whom philosophy nurtured in the liberal arts, and whom an innate competence made superior to warriors in the art of war,—wherefore the island of Britain now, in these days, rejoices in thee with heartfelt affection, as if possessed of another Henry.[58]

The panegyrical tone of this passage does not invalidate the fact of Robert's knowledge of letters.

Geoffrey of Monmouth had another noble patron as well. It has recently been shown that his *Historia* was originally issued with a double dedication, to Gloucester and to Waleran de Beaumont, count of Meulan (or Mellent). To Waleran the dedication reads as follows:

> And do thou also, Waleran, Count of Mellent, thou other pillar of our realm, give thy aid, that, through the common patronage of both, when presented to the world, this work may shine forth the more resplendently. For Mother Philosophy has taken thee, a scion of that most illustrious king Charles, to her bosom, and has trained thee in the exact knowledge of her sciences.[59]

The evidence of this flowery passage is supported by other sources concerning the education of both Waleran and his twin brother, Robert (the Hunchback), earl of Leicester. If the education of these noblemen is at all typical, it would seem that the sons of the nobility in twelfth-century England received far more instruction in letters than is generally supposed. After the death of their father in 1118, the two boys went to the court of Henry I, who had them educated out of gratitude for the services of the elder Beaumont. There they probably remained until they were of age, receiving the same training as that given the king's sons.[60] In 1119, when Pope Calixtus II visited Henry at Gisors, the Beaumont brothers were called upon to furnish diversion by debating on dialectics with the cardinals of the pope's retinue. The clever sophisms of the youths were too much for the cardinals, who freely confessed their surprise at finding such a flourishing state of letters in the western provinces.[61] Even admitting the benevolence of the cardinals in this affair, it is evident that the brothers had made fair progress in learning, since the disputation must have been carried on in Latin. The Latin education of both boys is also attested by other evidence.

Concerning Waleran, there is the testimony of Geoffrey of Monmouth mentioned above. In addition we have a document of his from the year 1142 which bears the following subscription: "Ego Gualerannus comes Mellenti relegi et subscripsi." This form was not, so far as I know, in common use at that time, and seems to prove Waleran's ability to read.[62] Stephen of Rouen (fl. 1170), a contemporary of Waleran, is the author of an elegiac poem in which the count is celebrated as a Quintilian in lawsuits, a Cicero in eloquence, and a Vergil in versification.[63] The exaggeration of such a description is patent, but even a panegyrist would hardly have sung such praises of an illiterate noble.

There is less evidence concerning Waleran's brother, Robert, earl of Leicester, but sufficient to prove our contention. According to the nineteenth-century editors of Dugdale's *Monasticon Angli-canum,* "in one of the MSS now in the British Museum, formerly Dr. Charles Burney's (Num. 357), are, 'Versus Sygerii Lucani in Sanctorum laudem Monachorum,' at the end of which is written in another hand: 'Rob. comes Lecestriae solebat hos versus memoriter recitare.' The verses and the remark are in a hand certainly not later than the twelfth or thirteenth century."[64] Richard Fitznigel in his *Dialogue on the Exchequer* calls the earl "virum discretum, litteris eruditum, et in negotiis forensibus exercitatum."[65]

King Stephen probably had some knowledge of Latin, since he, like the Beaumont brothers, was educated at the court of Henry I.[66] We cannot, however, be sure of the precise nature of Stephen's education. If we can trust Geoffrey of Monmouth, Stephen was "nurtured by philosophy in the liberal arts."[67] This phrase is contained in a later edition of the *Historia,* where there is a double dedication to King Stephen and Robert of Gloucester in which Geoffrey uses almost the same words as in the earlier dedication to Robert and Waleran of Meulan, substituting Stephen's name for Robert, and Robert's for Waleran. Geoffrey's description of Stephen, therefore, cannot be accepted literally, but his very inclusion of Stephen in the same category with Robert and Waleran, both men of recognized learning, seems to indicate some acquaintance with letters on Stephen's part.

Whether or not the empress Maud was trained in Latin letters, cannot be determined. As the daughter of Henry I and mother of Henry II, it is hard to believe that she was wholly illiterate. Still, if she had been well versed in letters, we might suppose that this would have been noted by Stephen of Rouen in his panegyric of the empress in the *Draco Normannicus.*[68] She probably missed the opportunity of an education in Latin when sent to Germany in 1110 at the age of eight to become the wife of the emperor, Henry V. We know that she was taught German, but there is no indication that Latin was included in her instruction.[69]

Henry II learned his letters at an early age. His first instructor, according to an anonymous chronicle of uncertain value, was a certain Master Peter of Saintes, famous in his time for a knowledge of poetry.[70] A later teacher was a certain Master Matthew, future chancellor of Henry, who had charge of his instruction "in letters and manners" during the young prince's sojourn at Bristol with his uncle, Robert of Gloucester.[71] Here he may also have studied the exact sciences under Adelard of Bath, for it was in this period that Adelard dedicated to Henry his treatise on the astrolabe.[72] It was probably after his stay in Bristol that Henry enjoyed the teaching of the most famous Norman scholar of the time, William of Conches, who prepared for his use a choice selection of philosophical maxims entitled *De honesto et utili.*[73] Walter Map would have us believe that Henry II had received such an extensive education that he "was skilled in letters as far as was fitting and useful, and had a knowledge of all the tongues from the French Sea to the Jordan," but he qualifies this extravagant statement by adding that Henry "used only Latin and French.'"[74] What Walter means by "used" is not clear; it seems to imply ability to speak both French and Latin.

After ascending the throne Henry probably had little time for reading and study. Giraldus Cambrensis complains that the king and his son Richard, to each of whom he had dedicated one of his works, were "too much concerned with business, and not enough with letters," and had not rewarded him for his labors.[75] That the author does not mean to imply, however, that Henry II and Richard were not capable of appreciating Latin literature, is evident from the fact that elsewhere he describes Henry as a man "learned in letters, a remarkable thing in these times.'"[76] We are told by another contemporary, Robert of Cricklade, that Henry devoted his leisure to studious pursuits.[77] Peter of Blois in one of his letters gives us an interesting picture of Henry's literary activities and abilities. Writing to Walter, archbishop of Palermo, he acknowledges that the Sicilian king, William II, is a good scholar, but insists that his own king, Henry, is a far better one.

When not busy with hunting or affairs of state, he is with his books. As often as he can relax from his cares, he occupies himself with reading in private, or seeks to work out some problem or other with his clerks. At the court of the English king there is school every day, constant conversation of the best scholars, and discussion of questions.[78]

The oft-repeated statement that the king used to while away the time at Mass by *scribbling* seems to be based on nothing more than the imagination of Bishop Stubbs.[79] Still, it is probably safe to conjecture that Henry II could write, at least after a fashion, notwithstanding the lack of evidence on this subject. But the contemporary accounts do not include scribbling among the king's diversions at Mass.[80]

As a patron of letters and learning Henry II was without rival in his time. He was hailed as another Maecenas. His rôle as a patron has been described by Professor Haskins, who says that the list of works dedicated to the king is "significant both for its length and its subjects. Little theology, some science and miscellany, vernacular poetry, probably some sport, much recent history, both in Latin and French, and two distinctive works on the administration of justice and finance—the whole represents not unfairly the tendencies of the king's mind."[81] The value to the kingdom of having a scholar king is noted in a letter to Henry II by Rotrou, archbishop of Rouen, who says that he has learned by personal experience how much the realm has profited from Henry's having studied the liberal arts in his youth.[82]

In his account of Henry II's arbitration of the long-standing dispute between Alphonso of Castile and Sancho of Navarre, the author of the *Gesta regis Henrici secundi,* now attributed to Richard Fitznigel, relates that Henry ordered the Spanish envoys to submit a written statement of their claims and arguments, because the English barons who had been summoned to hear the case had difficulty in understanding the speeches of the Spaniards.[83] This seems to imply that few of the barons could understand spoken Latin. Even if they did possess some knowledge of Latin, their difficulties of comprehension were doubtless increased by the peculiar Latin pronunciation of the Spanish envoys. Following in the main the account of the *Gesta,* but drawing also on his own historical imagination, Mr. Hubert Hall has given us a vivid picture of this incident which doubtless approximates closely the actual conditions:[84]

At the announcement of the King that the case was open to both parties to dispute in turn upon their respective allegations . . . the Bishop of Palenza rose and claimed the favour of the King and his Council on behalf of a native advocate of great repute, who was prepared to argue the cause of his master, Alphonso of Castile.

The King having signified his assent, the advocate referred to came forward and addressed the council with great fluency in choice Castilian Latin, interspersed with quotations from legal authorities. This discourse, which embraced a statement of the lineage of the kings of Castile and Navarre, and a narrative of the historical events connected with the violent usurpation of the territories now claimed by King Alphonso, was illustrated by references to numerous original charters and other documents, which, being handed in from time to time by the Bishop of Palenza, were read aloud by the Vice-chancellor, after which they were closely inspected by Henry himself.

When the Castilian advocate had concluded his argument, an advocate on the side of the King of Navarre replied at length in similar style, denying the allegations of his adversary, and advancing a counter claim to other territories ... supporting also his contention by reference to documentary evidence. In the course of both arguments, the King frequently interrupted, demanding an explanation in clerical Latin of certain passages. The councillors also seemed to exhibit marked signs of impatience from time to time, and at length, almost before the Navarrese had well concluded his speech, Richard de Luci addressed the King to the effect that, without any disrespect to the representatives of the powerful and virtuous princes here present, it was plain that the bishops and barons whom the King had summoned to assist in the decisions of this cause were unable to comprehend the allegations of either side any more than if they were spoken in a barbarous tongue, and, therefore, it seemed to him desirable that the advocates should be required to use the Norman tongue, which, he added, was held in most high esteem in the courts of divers Christian kingdoms. To this proposition the Bishop of London offered as an amendment that clerical Latin should be admitted; but this was negatived by a murmur of dissent amongst the lay nobility present, and a lively interchange of views followed on both sides. The King, however, put a stop to the discussion in a peremptory manner, and gave his decision in favour of admitting clerical Latin, but only in written allegations, with which each party was to furnish the Council within three days, in order that when these documents had been clearly explained and discussed by the Council, judgment might be given without further parley. . . .

After the meeting had been adjourned the clerical party . . . began to argue the points of procedure that had arisen during the recent hearing, and especially the pretensions of the baronage that only the French tongue should be admitted. Concerning this subject, the Treasurer (Richard Fitznigel) . . . had much to say, advancing many reasons on either side, but himself leaning somewhat to that of the barons, on the ground that the record of every plea should be made in the vulgar tongue, as being a proclamation more solemn than any deposition in writing; though now, he added, matters were somewhat altered, except in the ancient franchises.

There is no evidence to show that Eleanor of Aquitaine, Henry II's queen, had any knowledge of Latin. Stubbs observed that she was no doubt well educated for her time, but that her reputation for learning rests largely on a confusion of Aquitanian with Provençal culture.[85] All her extant letters seem to have been composed and written by secretaries.[86]

It seems highly probable that all the children of Henry II and Eleanor were instructed in at least the elements of Latin, but it is impossible to determine exactly what each one learned. "Of the king's daughters we know little more than that they were all married to princes who took a conspicuous place among the pioneers of medieval culture."[87] Mathilda, the eldest, was the wife of Henry the Lion of Saxony; Eleanor, the second, married Alfonso of Castile, the founder of the University of Palencia; and Joan, the youngest, who was brought up at the abbey of Fontevraud, was the wife, first, of William II of Sicily, a patron of letters and himself a man of learning, and then of Raymond VI of Toulouse.[88] Concerning the king's sons the evidence is fuller.

The education of the eldest son, Henry, was entrusted to Thomas Becket. At that period of his career Becket was better qualified to instruct the boy in arms than in letters; he seems only to have supervised the knightly training and to have left the prince's literary training to tutors or *magistri*,[89] whose fees are recorded in the Pipe Rolls.[90] That the liberal education of the heir to the throne was regarded as a matter of no little importance, is shown by the letter of Rotrou of Rouen already mentioned. He expresses the unanimous wish of the Norman bishops that young Henry should be most carefully educated in letters, reminding the king that all the great rulers of the past, including Caesar, Alexander, David, Constantine, Theodosius, Justinian, and Leo, were men of learning. "A king without letters is like a ship without a pilot or a bird without wings."[91] Archbishop Rotrou's epistle seems to have been written as a protest against the too exclusively military training of the young prince, and no doubt the advice had some influence, although "it is curious ... that in none of the panegyrics of this unfortunate boy is any special stress laid on his knowledge of letters."[92] We should not credit him with great proficiency in letters,[93] but it is probable that he learned enough Latin to be able, for example, to read the lost *Liber facetiarum* which Gervase of Tilbury wrote for his amusement.[94] His chief interest, apparently, so far as letters were concerned, was in this lighter literature, especially that written in the vernacular which he patronized generously. As Miss Marian Whitney has written, "Perhaps no one historical personage had such a reputation for largesse among the men of his own age and that immediately succeeding it as did Henry."[95]

Richard I was far ahead of his brothers in learning. Stubbs has conjectured that the future hero of the Third Crusade "may have obtained the elements of that *scientia* which is markedly ascribed to him in contrast with his brothers" at the schools of Tours where his half-brother Geoffrey, later archbishop of York, was educated.[96]

We must certainly allow [him] some amount of literary knowledge and skill. We may not perhaps credit him with the quotations from the classical poets which the historians of the third crusade put in his mouth, but we cannot refuse to believe those writers when they tell us of the lampoons of the king's own composition which were sung in the camp in contempt of the Duke of Burgundy; and the stream of time . . . has brought down to us some few *sirventes* or satiric lays that entitle Richard to the name of a trouvère.[97]

His ability to use Latin is revealed in an anecdote told by Giraldus Cambrensis.

It came to pass, one day, that Richard, king of the English, in the presence of a large crowd of magnates used the Latin phrase "Volumus quod istud fiat coram nobis," and that Hubert Walter, the archbishop of Canterbury, wishing to correct the king, said: "My lord, *coram nos, coram nos!*" The king thereupon turned to Hugh, the bishop of Coventry, a learned and witty man, who replied, to the amusement of all present: "Stick to your own grammar, Sire! it is better."[98]

In another place Gerald describes Richard as a "man endowed by nature and training with everything that befits a prince, except letters,"[99] but he doubtless means by this that Richard is not himself an author of Latin letters, and especially that he is not so generous a patron as seemed desirable to Gerald.[100] Certainly the Welshman did not mean to imply that Richard lacked a knowledge of Latin. We have noted above[101] Gerald's use of a similar expression in describing both Henry II and Richard.

John, too, evidently had received some training in Latin, but his literary ability never equaled Richard's. Our chief source is again that admirably frank cleric, Giraldus Cambrensis. In a letter to John accompanying a revised edition of his *Expugnatio Hibernica,* Gerald suggests that the king may as well have the work translated into French, but by a competent scholar, since a reader translating at sight never does justice to the original.[102] John must have had some interest in literature, because we know he owned a library which included a Pliny, Valerian's *De moribus,* the *Sententiae* of Peter Lombard, the *Sacramenta* of Hugh of St. Victor, a *Librum Candidi Ariani ad Marium,* the Old Testament, and Origen's commentary thereon;[103] John is said once to have borrowed a book from the abbot of St. Albans.[104]

With Henry III (1216–1257) the English court seems definitely to have taken up the French vernacular as its literary language. The king is described as a man of "a refined mind and cultivated tastes, . . . liberal and magnificent," who "took interest in the work of Matthew Paris and enjoyed his society."[105] He is said, moreover, to have been the first English king to employ a *versificator regis* to whom he paid a regular stipend.[106] His wife, Eleanor of Provence, who had "had for her instructor that Romeo whom seventy years later Dante celebrated for his merit and his misfortunes," was herself a poetess.[107] There is no evidence that either of them understood Latin. The order of the day in literature by this time was French court poetry and romantic tales.[108]

Up to this point we have considered almost exclusively the extent of the knowledge of Latin among the rulers of Norman and Angevin England. What can be said of the state of culture among the noble class as a whole? Despite the fragmentary nature of our evidence, there is good reason to believe that the English nobility of the high Middle Ages were more familiar with Latin than is commonly supposed. Certainly it can be shown that there were lettered laymen in the twelfth century. The Beaumont brothers, Waleran and Robert, are examples. Moreover, William of Malmesbury does not seem to regard it as at all unusual for a layman to have a knowledge of letters. In telling Robert of Gloucester why he chooses him as a patron, William says that at first he considered *many* persons; and, making no distinction between laymen and clerics, he goes on to relate that he found some distinguished for nobility, some for prowess in arms, others for justice, and still others for their knowledge of letters (*litteratura*), finally choosing Robert as the embodiment of all these qualities.[109] He does not seem to regard Robert's learning as extraordinary *in a layman.*

Some interesting light is thrown on lay culture by the travels through England of the copy of Geoffrey of Monmouth's work which was given originally to Robert of Gloucester. It was borrowed from the earl by Lord Walter of Espec, the hero of the Battle of the Standard.[110] From him it passed to Ralph Fitzgerald and his wife Constance. This noble lady was a patroness of Geoffrey Gaimar, whom she was helping to collect material for his *Lestorie des Engles.*[111] These facts seem to imply that Walter of Espec and perhaps even Ralph had some interest in Geoffrey of Monmouth's Latin

Historia. Concerning Constance they probably show only her interest in vernacular literature. We also know that she was a patroness of David the Trouvère.[112]

Even Giraldus Cambrensis, who complained so bitterly of "illiterate" princes, did not at first despair of the progress of Latin letters
among the laity. In the introduction to his *Expugnatio Hibernica,* written about 1190, he apologizes in somewhat strong terms
for the simple style he has adopted in his book, saying that his ob-
ject has been to make himself clear and understandable to "laymen
and princes not too well grounded in letters."[113] Not until the early
thirteenth century, in the letter to King John referred to above,[114]
does Gerald, now past sixty and completely disillusioned about his
own success, unmistakably reveal the tendency of the times. His
friend Walter Map, who goes about preaching in the vernacular,
has won recognition and reward, while he, who has devoted himself
to the composition of long Latin works, has gained neither. If his
books are to be understood, they have to be translated into French.
His sole remaining hope, besides eternal bliss, is the future revival
of Latin letters, when he will come into his own.[115] Thus Gerald's
life witnessed perhaps the most flourishing period of Latin letters
and the beginning of the decline. When he set out on his literary
career he probably had good reason to hope for the favor of princes
and lords to whom Latin was something more than the language of
the Church and the law courts.

The decline set in about the last decade of the twelfth century.
Walter Map, writing about 1190, complains that "the nobles of our
land are either too scornful or too indifferent to apply their children to letters."[116] By the early thirteenth century, there were probably few laymen left in England who had a practical knowledge of
Latin. In a plea of 1198 before the king's court, the testimony shows
that, at a previous hearing in a manorial court, proceedings had to
be interrupted while the court sent for a clerk who could read the
writ.[117] Doubtless the chief cause of this decline of Latin letters was
the rapid rise of the vernacular as a literary medium. By this is
meant, of course, French, the native tongue of the Anglo-Norman
aristocracy. A striking fact about the new movement, however, is
that it received its great impetus and encouragement from those
who still had some knowledge of Latin, the generation of nobles
born about the middle of the twelfth century.

Finally, we should note that the distinction between literate clergy and illiterate laymen in medieval England has been unduly exaggerated. Ignorant clergy can be found in almost every period of the Middle Ages, both in England and on the Continent. Naturally, the lower clergy, mostly identified with the peasantry, could hardly have had much learning of any sort, but even the higher clergy were by no means all well trained. The bishop of Chichester, when speaking before the papal Curia late in the twelfth century, got so tangled in his Latin grammar that his blunders provoked laughter.[118] Richard the Lion-hearted, we have seen, spoke better Latin than Hubert Walter, archbishop of Canterbury. Louis of Beaumont, bishop of Durham (d. 1333), knew so little Latin that "before his consecration he had to take several days' lessons before he could read his part of the service," and had great difficulties even then.[119]

Notes to Chapter VII

[1] This chapter was in page proof before there became available to me Professor V. H. Galbraith's "The Literacy of the Medieval English Kings," *Proceedings of the British Academy*, XXI (1935).

[2] *Chronicon*, III, 27 (ed. Chavanon, 148): "Tunc Roso [Rollo] defuncto, filius ejus Willelmus loco ejus praefuit, a puericia baptizatus, omnisque eorum Normannorum, qui juxta Frantiam inhabitaverant, multitudo fidem Christi suscepit, et gentilem linguam obmittens, latino sermone assuefacta est." As Freeman has suggested (*The Norman Conquest of England*, ed. of 1870, I, 180 and 606), by the phrase "latino sermone" Adhemar probably meant the Romance vernacular, though we should expect *lingua romana* or *gallica*, since Adhemar was writing in the eleventh century. It is impossible to believe that the "entire multitude of those living nearest France" learned Latin.

[3] *De moribus et actis primorum Normaniae ducum*, III, *in* Migne, *PL*, 141, 657: "Quem [Willelmum] genitor . . . Bothoni cuidam ditissimo comiti sacro baptismate perfusum ad educandum commendavit, eumque ad erudiendum ut decebat tradidit." Though Botho was at this time decidedly pro-Christian and pro-French in his interests (cf. Freeman, *op. cit.*, I, 180), at the time of Richard's education he was stationed at Bayeux, the most Danish town in Normandy. Dudo makes William Longsword address Botho thus (Migne, *PL*, 141, 690–691): "Quoniam quidem Rothomagensis civitas Romana potius quam Dacica utitur eloquentia, et Bajocacensis fruitur frequentius Dacica lingua quam Romana; volo tua custodia [Richardus] et enutriatur et educetur cum magna diligentia, fervens loquacitate Dacica, tamque discens tenaci memoria, ut queat sermocinari profusius olim contra Dacigenas."

[4] See the panegyric verses addressed to Richard II and Count Raoul (Migne, *PL*, 141, 613, 615); and cf. Duchesne's preface, *ibid.*, 607, and Molinier, *Les sources* . . . , III, 214, no. 1962.

[5] *Historia ecclesiastica*, IV, 6 (ed. Le Prévost, II, 210). Cf. R. W. Church, *Life of St. Anselm* (New York, 1905), 25.

[6] Cf. A. J. MacDonald, *Lanfranc* (Oxford, 1926), 25.

[7] See the *Vita S. Herluini*, written by Gilbert Crispin, abbot of Westminster (d. 1114), in Migne, *PL*, 150, 700: "Prima litterarum elementa didicit, cum jam existeret annorum prope quadraginta. . . ." Cf. Armitage Robinson's edition of this *Vita* (Cambridge University Press, 1911).

[8] See the following passage in Gilbert Crispin's *Vita Herluini* (*ibid.*, 708): "Litteratus aliquis volens fieri monachus, quando ad illum [Herluinum] veniebat, qua exsultatione suscipiebatur, quae suscepto benignitatis, et veneratio exhibebatur. Laicos qua instantia ut ad discendum psalmos intenderent, agebat!" The sharp contrast between *litteratus* and *laicus* is worth noting.

[9] Ordericus Vitalis reports that Waltheof, earl of Northampton and Huntington, during his imprisonment at Winchester after his capture by William the Conqueror, daily recited the Psalms of David "which he had learned in his

childhood (quos in infantia didicerat)." See *Hist. eccles.*, IV, 14 (ed. Le Pré-vost, II, 266), and cf. Freeman, *op. cit.*, IV, 258, n. 2.

[10] See the well-known story of the prior of Bec who ordered Lanfranc to change his pronunciation of *docēre* to *docĕre*, in Milo Crispin's *Vita Lanfranci*, 2, *in* Migne, *PL*, 150, 32, and cf. Macdonald, *op. cit.*, 22.

[11] Witness the story of the interview of Herfast, the chaplain of William the Conqueror, with Lanfranc concerning the duke's marriage with Mathilda. According to William of Malmesbury, Lanfranc saw at once that the chaplain "knew nearly nothing," and facetiously placed an alphabet (*abecedarium*) in Herfast's hand and asked him to read it aloud; whereupon the latter returned to William in high dudgeon. Cf. Macdonald, *op. cit.*, 35–36.

[12] *Op. cit.*, V, 526.

[13] His biographer, William of Poitiers, reports (*Gesta Willelmi conquestoris, in* Migne, *PL*, 149, 1240): "Accipere solitus est avido auditu suavique gustu sacrae paginae sermones, iis ut animae epulum sumeret delectari desiderans, castigari atque edoceri." To this, Freeman (*op. cit.*, III, 271) remarked: "I do not know that the word *auditu* absolutely proves that William could not read, but it looks like it."

[14] In general, with regard to the men to whom Robert the Devil entrusted young William, see Freeman, *op. cit.*, II, 191–192, 195. As to the "Turoldus, teneri ducis paedagogus" of William of Jumièges (*Historia Normannorum*, VII, 2, *in* Migne, *PL*, 149, 847), he is undoubtedly the same person as the "Turchetillus . . . ducis paedagogus" of Ordericus Vitalis (*Hist. eccles.*, I, 24: ed. Le Prévost, I, 180), the *seigneur*, therefore, of Neuf-Marché-en-Lions (cf. Ordericus, V, 9, VI, 8, VII, 15, *in* Le Prévost, II, 369, III, 42, 229). Le Prévost has suggested (*ibid.*, II, 370, n. 1) that Turchetillus may be a diminutive of Turold, after the analogy of Anschetil from Hans. Be that as it may, that the two names refer to one and the same person seems certain; and we cannot regard the *seigneur* of Neuf-Marché as a pedagogue in the usual sense of the word. It may be added that he was killed in the uprising immediately following the death of Robert the Devil, in other words, before William had reached his tenth year. His name is found spelled in almost countless forms: Turold, Torold, Thorold, Therould, Turchetil, Thurcytel, Turquetil.

[15] VIII, 174.

[16] William of Jumièges (VII, 1, *in* Migne, *PL*, 149, 847) says only: "Is itaque dux in puerilibus annis patre orbatus, sagaci tutorum providentia liberalium morum instituebatur ad incrementa." The fact that both William of Poitiers and William of Jumièges dedicated their histories to the Conqueror (cf. Molinier, *Les sources* . . . , II, 215, nos. 1964 and 1965) shows only that literary patronage in the Middle Ages did not always indicate a knowledge of letters on the part of the patron.

[17] In a very interesting letter to a correspondent, Freeman wrote, *Life and Letters* (London and New York, 1895), II, 216: "All I can say about William's and Matilda's power of reading and writing comes to this. First, W. makes a bold broad cross . . . M. a spider-leggy kind of one. Does this suggest that the use of the pen was familiar to them? I need hardly say that their making their

crosses does not prove that it was not. But second: the chances are against princes of that day reading and writing unless we have some statement that they could, and W's early life was specially unfavorable for study." We may add that it is conceivable that a prince who could read should be unable to write, but hardly vice versa. The mere *signa* of documents prove nothing, one way or the other, since it was common practice in that day for all subscribers of a document to sign by making a cross, irrespective of whether they were literate or not; see, for example, the photographic reproduction, in the catalogue recently published by Maggs Bros. (London) announcing the sale of the original document (*ca.* 1067–1075), of a grant to St. Stephen's at Caen, containing the *signa* of William, Mathilda, and Lanfranc of Canterbury. The last was certainly *able* to sign his own name, even if he did not do so.

[18] *England and Normandy*, IV, 720.

[19] *Hist. eccles.*, IV, 5 (Le Prévost, II, 189): "Reginam hanc simul decoravere forma, genus, litterarum scientia, cuncta morum et virtutum pulchritudo." Cf. Ch. Jourdain, *Mém. de l'Inst. Nat. de France: Acad. des inscr. et belles-lettres*, XVIII, 90 and n. 5. She could probably read and understand the poem of Marbode, bishop of Rennes, addressed *Ad reginam Anglorum* (Migne, *PL*, 171, 1660), if, as it seems, it was actually intended for her.

[20] See Ch. W. David, *Robert Curthose* (Cambridge, Mass., 1910), 6 and, for further references, his notes thereto.

[21] *Ibid.*

[22] *Hist. eccles.*, V, 10 (Le Prévost, II, 379): "Huc, domine mi rex, non accessi pro sermonibus audiendis, quorum copia frequenter usque ad nauseam imbutus sum a grammaticis."

[23] David, *op. cit.*, 6. The poem was attributed to Robert in a MS (now lost) written about the year 1500; for fuller particulars as well as for the poem itself, see *ibid.*, 187–188.

[24] *Life and Letters*, II, 216.

[25] Her tutor in grammar and dialectic was the Flemish schoolmaster, Arnulf of Choques, afterward patriarch of Jerusalem; see David, *op. cit.*, 219, and cf. the poem of Baudri or Baldric of Dol addressed to Cecilia, in Migne, *PL*, 166, 1203.

[26] See *Epist.*, I, 4 (Migne, *PL*, 171, 146): "Si nescis quis iste cursus sit, Augustinum lege..." *Epist.*, I, 6 (*ibid.*, 151): "Scio, charissima mea, quia Salomonem legisti dicentem..." Cf. also I, 10 (*ibid.*, 162).

[27] See his poem addressed to her, in Migne, *PL*, 166, 1202.

[28] See his epilogue, *MGH. SS.*, IX, 353: "Sed tam compendiosum et honestum volumen non illiteratis principibus, quibus ars litteratoria spretui est; sed vobis merito dedicavi, ne nominis vestri monimentum ulla valeat umquam vetustate corrumpi, quae posterorum memoriae solet inimicari. . . . Multis igitur estis preponenda proceribus, sicut in huius libri primo prologo dixi; tum generositate praeclara, tum probitate precipua, tum quoniam estis litteris erudita, quod est gentilitium sive civilitas magna." The prologue referred to, that is, the dedicatory letter, *ibid.*, 349, is to the same effect. Cf. Molinier, *Les sources...*, II, 308, no. 2191.

[29] See the letters, *in* Migne, *PL*, 162, *passim*. Cf. *Hist. litt. de la France*, X, 125 ff., and d'Arbois de Jubainville, *Histoire des ducs et des comtes de Champagne*, II, 251–252.

[30] "The Claim of King Henry I to be Called Learned," in *Anniversary Essays in Medieval History presented to Charles Homer Haskins*, 56.

[31] *Ibid.*, 51; cf. 48 ff.

[32] *Ibid.*, 51–53. Freeman's "proof" of this assertion was questioned much earlier, by J. H. Round, "Henry I as an English Scholar," *The Academy*, XXVI (1884), 168.

[33] "It was apparently the anonymous author of the *Brut* or *Chronicles of England*, writing in the second half of the fourteenth century, who first called him Henry Beauclerc" (David, *op. cit.*, 48); but Thomas Wykes, who died *ca.* 1293, in his *Chronicon* (in *Annales Monastici*, ed. H. R. Luard; London, 1846–1849, IV, 11) describes Henry as the king "quem vulgus Clericum nuncupabat." Cf. David, *op. cit.*, 46–48, and esp. n. 16.

[34] *Gesta regum Anglorum*, V, 390 (ed. Wm. Stubbs, II, 467): "infans jam tum omnium votis conspirantibus educatus egregie, quod solus omnium filiorum Willelmi natus esset regie, et ei regnum videretur competere. Itaque tirocinium rudimentorum in scholis egit litteralibus, et librorum mella adeo avidis medullis indidit, ut nulli postea bellorum tumultus, nulli curarum motus, eas excutere illustri animo possent. Quamvis ipse nec multum palam legeret, nec nisi summisse cantitaret; fuerunt tamen, ut vere confirmo, litterae, quamvis tumultuarie libatae, magna supellex ad regnandum scientiae, juxta illam Platonis sententiam, qua dicit 'Beatam esse rempublicam si vel philosophi regnarent, vel reges philosopharentur.' Philosophia ergo non adeo exiliter informatus, sensim discebat ut successu temporis provinciales mitius contineret, milites nonnisi diligentissime explorata necessitate committere sineret. Itaque pueritiam ad spem regni litteris muniebat; subinde, patre quoque audiente, jactitare proverbium solitus, 'Rex illiteratus, asinus coronatus.'" Although my English adaptation of this passage is abridged, it adheres faithfully to the sense of William of Malmesbury's Latin. As to the text itself, it seems to me that the sense of the passage suggests that the punctuation needs correction: that there should be a comma or semicolon after "possent," and a period after "cantitaret."

[35] *Op. cit.*, 54. The story may well be apocryphal. The same anecdote is told of Fulk of Anjou and Louis IV. See above, Chap. VI, 125–126. Freeman, who was not sure whether William was illiterate or not, observed in reference to this passage that the proverb must at least have been "approved" by the Conqueror (*Norman Conquest*, II, 271).

[36] *Op. cit.*, 54. It should be added, however, that Professor David also calls attention to the contrary view, expressed by Freeman (*Norman Conquest*, II, 228–229), that the royal birth of Henry I was actually a matter of special importance, even in his youth.

[37] It is impossible to give a literal translation of Malmesbury's words— "fuerunt tamen, ut vere confirmo, litterae, quamvis tumultuarie libatae, magna supellex ad regnandum scientiae"—in idiomatic English. It is true, of course,

that Malmesbury is not quite as definite as we could wish him to be. He does not say specifically that Henry I read this literature himself. It is possible, therefore, that he employed a sort of *lector,* a clerk whose business it was to read aloud to him. But none of the evidence demands such an assumption, and I think it more probable that Henry I ordinarily read to himself, as suggested above.

[38] Apropos of Ordericus Vitalis' account of Henry's reading a letter from the French court (see below), Le Prévost remarked (in his edition of *Orderi-cus,* IV, 195, n. 3) : "Cette lecture ne dut pas être une petite besoigne pour le monarque anglaise ; car nous savons par Guillaume de Malmesbury que, malgré son surnom de Beauclerc, il ne pouvait lire haut, c'est-à-dire couramment, pendant longtemps."

[39] *Hist. eccles.,* IV, 4 (ed. Le Prévost, II, 182) : "Hic, dum dociles annos attigisset, litterarum scientiam didicit, . . ."

[40] *Ibid.,* VIII, 1 (Le Prévost, III, 267) : Hic in infantia studiis litterarum a parentibus traditus est, et tam naturali quam doctrinali scientia nobiliter imbutus est."

[41] *Hist. eccles.,* XI, 9 (Le Prévost, IV, 195) : "Litteratus vero rex epistolam legit." Professor David questions the historicity of this letter. He says (*op. cit.,* 55) : "The letter in question is said to have been from Bertrada de Montfort, the notorious wife of Philip I of France, though purporting to be from King Philip himself and bearing the royal seal ; and it called upon Henry, who was then entertaining Louis the king-designate of France at his court, to arrest him and place him in life-long confinement. The tale, which is mentioned by no other writer, is one of the most fantastic to be met with in all the thirteen books of *Ordericus Vitalis,* and to the present writer it seems evidently legendary. Henry I may have read other letters, but that he ever read one purporting to come from King Philip and urging him to imprison Philip's own son, the king-designate of France, while on a visit to the English court, seems hardly to be believed." In fairness, however, David directs attention to the fact that A. Fliche, the modern biographer of Philip I, takes the tale seriously.—*Le règne de Philippe Ier, roi de France* (Paris, 1912), 83–84.

[42] Robert of Torigni, *Historia Henrici Primi* (i.e., the eighth book of the *Historia Normannorum* of William of Jumièges), chap. 10 (Migne, *PL,* 149, 886) : "Quantae autem sanctitatis et scientiae tam saecularis quam spiritualis utraque regina, Margareta scilicet et Mathildis, fuerint ; liber qui de Vita ipsarum scriptus est, plano sermone describit." Robert (d. 1186) is evidently not referring to the contemporary *Vita* of Saint Margaret, which says very little concerning Mathilda, but to the later *Vita* of the abbot Ailred (d. 1166), which is no longer extant in its original form. All that we now have of it is an abridgment from the hand of some unknown author, first published by Surius, and reprinted from this edition in Pinkerton's *Vitae SS. Scotiae* (London, 1789), 371–383 ; in this abridgment there is a short chapter on Mathilda's sanctity. But neither of the *Vitae,* as we now have them, makes any special mention of the *scientia saecularis* of either queen. Concerning the contemporary *Vita,* see the following note.

⁴³ See Papebroch's critical commentary to the *Vita* published in *AA. SS.*, June, II, 320; and cf. Sheriff Mackay's article on Margaret in the *Dictionary of National Biography*.

⁴⁴ *Vita S. Margaritae*, 2: *AA. SS.*, June, II, 326: "Nam, quod ego in illa multum admirari solebam, inter causarum tumultus, inter multiplices regni curas, miro studio divinae lectioni operam debat, de qua cum doctissimis assidentibus viris etiam subtiles saepius quaestiones conserebat. Sed sicut inter eos nemo illa ingenio profundior, ita nemo aderat eloquio clarior. Evenit itaque saepius, ut ab ea ipsi rectores, multo quam advenerant abscederent doctiores. Plane sacrorum voluminum religosa, nec parva illi aviditas inerat, in quibus sibi acquirendis familiaris ejus caritas et caritativa familiaritas me ipsum me fatigare plerumque cogebat. Nec in his solummodo suam, sed etiam aliorum quaesivit salutem: primoque omnium ipsum Regem, ad . . . opera virtutum, ipsa, cooperante sibi Deo, facerat obtemperantissimum. . . . Quae ipsa respuerat, eadem et ipse respuere; et quae amaverat, amore amoris illius amare. Unde et libros, in quibus ipsa vel orare consueverat, vel legere; ille, ignarus licet litterarum, saepe manuversare solebat et inspicere; et dum ab ea quis illorum esset ei carior audisset, hunc et ipse cariorem habere, deosculari, saepius contrectare. Aliquando etiam advocato aurifice ipsum codicem auro gemmisque perornari praecepit, atque perornatum ipse Rex ad Reginam, quasi suae devotionis indicium, referre consuevit."

⁴⁵ *Ibid.*

⁴⁶ *Ibid.*, 324: ". . . quae [i.e., Matilda] a Rege Angelorum constituta Regina Anglorum, vitam matris Reginae . . . non solum audire, sed etiam litteris impressam desideratis jugiter inspicere; ut quae faciem matris parum noveratis, virtutem ejus notitiam plenius habeatis."

⁴⁷ William of Malmesbury, *Gesta regum Anglorum* (ed. Stubbs), II, 493: "Matildis . . . A teneris annis inter sanctimoniales apud Wiltoniam et Rumesium educata, litteris quoque foemineum pectus exercuit." Cf. Miss Norgate on Mathilda in the *Dictionary of National Biography*.

⁴⁸ See, for example, in the collection of Anselm's letters, *Epist.*, III, 119 (Migne, *PL*, 159, 156): "Quoties epistolari beneficio vestrae mihi sanctitatis municipium impertitis, toties innovatae laetitiae luce nebulosam animae meae caliginem serenatis. Est etenim vestri quaedam et absentis qualiscumque revisio, et chartulae contrectatus, et litterae perjucunda saepiusque recitata relictio. Quid namque vestris, domine, scriptis aut stylo ornatius aut sensu refertius? Non his desunt Frontonica gravitas Ciceronis, Fabii, aut Quintiliani acumina. In his sane doctrina quidem redundat Pauli, diligentia Hieronymi, explanatio Augustini, et quod his majus est, hinc dulcor evangelici stillat eloquii." Or again, *Epist.*, III, 96 (*ibid.*, 134): "Chartulam quidem a vobis missam loco Patris amplector, sinu foveo, cordi quoad possum, propius admoveo, verba de dulci bonitatis vestrae fonte manantia ore relego, mente retracto, corde recogito, recogitata in ipso cordis arcana repono." There are four other letters to Anselm, *Epist.*, III, 55 (in which Cicero is again mentioned), 93; IV, 74, 76.

⁴⁹ The one extant letter from Mathilda to Paschal is in Migne, *PL*, 163, 466–467. From Hildebert we have two panegyric poems addressed to the queen

(Migne, *PL*, 171, 1408, 1443–1445) and several letters (*ibid.*, 153, 160–162, 289–290), but no reply of Mathilda's.

[50] See J. H. Round's article in the *Dictionary of National Biography*, and cf. the *Hist. litt. de la France*, XIII, 61, 66.

[51] Migne, *PL*, 171, 179–180.

[52] *England under the Angevin Kings*, I, 94.

[53] See the prologue to the *Historia Novella* (ed. Stubbs), II, 525: "Pleraque gestorum praecellentis memoriae patris vestri stilo apponere non neglexi, et in quinto libro regalium actuum, et in tribus libellis quibus Chronica dedi vocabulum. Nunc ea quae moderno tempore magno miraculo Dei acciderunt in Anglia, ut mandentur posteris, desiderat animus vestrae serenitatis: pulcherrimum plane desiderium, et vestrorum omnium simile." See also the dedicatory letter of the *Gesta regum Anglorum* (ed. Stubbs), II, 355–356: "Vestrum est igitur, O duces, si quid boni facimus; vestrum profecto si quid dignum memoria scribimus; vestra industria nobis est incitamento ut, quia pericula vestra paci nostrae impenditis, vos vicissim per labores nostros omni aevo inclarescatis. . . . Nullum enim magis decet bonarum artium fautorem esse quam te, cui adhaesit magnanimitas avi, munificentia patrui, prudentia patris; quos cum aemulus industriae lineamentis repraesentes, illud peculiare gloriae tuae facis quod litteris insistis. . . . Quia enim natura indulget sibi, quod quis probat in se ipso non improbat in altero consentaneos igitur sibi mores experiuntur in te litterati, . . . Continentiam autem operis prologus primi libri exponit; quem si placuerit legere, materiam totam poteris de compendio colligere."

[54] *Gesta regum Anglorum*, V, 446 (ed. Stubbs), II, 519 ff.: "Cum enim alios considero, in uno nobilitatem, in altero militiam, in isto litteraturam, in illo justitiam, in paucis munificentiam invenio; itaque in aliis aliqua, in singulis singula, in vobis admiror universa. . . . Litteras ita fovetis, ut cum sitis tantarum occupationum mole districti, horas tamen aliquas vobis surripiatis, quibus aut ipsi legere aut legentes possitis audire. Digno itaque moderamine fortunae vestrae celsitudinem componitis, dum nec militiam propter litteras postponitis, nec litteras propter militiam, ut quidam, conspuitis: in quo etiam scientiae vestrae patescit miraculum, quia, dum libros diligitis, datis indicium quam avidis medullis fontem eorum combiberitis; multae siquidem res, etiam cum non habentur, desiderantur, philosophiam nullus amabit qui eam extrema satietate non hauserit. . . . multa enim sublimitati ejus [i.e., Henry I] mea humilitas debet, et adhuc plura debebit, ut, si nihil aliud esset, quod se talem filium habere gaudet, nam et olim felici sorte susceptum, non perfunctorie, ut hodie claret, litteris erudiri praecepit. . . ." Cf. Freeman, *The Norman Conquest of England*, V, 250.

[55] In Migne, *PL*, 179, 1771.

[56] Norgate, *op. cit.*, I, 94 and n. 2.

[57] *De nugiis curialium*, V, 4: (ed. M. R. James; 1914), 235.

[58] The translation is that of Acton Griscom in the introduction to his edition of the *Historia* (London and New York, 1929), 87; the text, *ibid.*, 219.

[59] *Ibid.*, 87 and 220.

[60] Ordericus Vitalis, *Hist. eccles.*, XII, 33 (ed. Le Prévost, IV, 438): "Ipse rex filios Rodberti, comitis Mellenti, quem multum dilexerat et a quo ipse in primordio regni sui admodum adjutus et consolatus fuerat, post mortem patris ut propriam sobolem dulciter educavit, geminisque pubescentibus: Gualeranno et Rodberto arma militaria dedit."

[61] William of Malmesbury, *Gesta regum Anglorum* (ed. Stubbs), II, 482: "Et ut nihil cumulatae pompae deesset, adolescentulos clarissimi generis, filios comitis de Mellento, ut contra cardinales de dialectica disputarent, subornavit: quorum tortilibus sophismatibus cum vivacitate rationum obsisti nequiret, non puduit cardinales confiteri, majori occiduas plagas florere litterarum peritia quam ipsi audissent vel putassent in patria." Cf. Griscom, *op. cit.*, 54 and n. 2, where this story is told on the authority of Le Prévost (Ord. Vit., *Hist. eccles.*, IV, 405 n.), who first drew attention to the incident but failed to give his reference.

[62] See J. H. Round, *Calendar of Documents*, 124, no. 370; cf. Griscom, *op. cit.*, 81 and n. 2. It is, of course, to be understood that the "subscripsi" may refer to a *signum* made *manu propria*, and does not necessarily mean that Waleran wrote out his name. Griscom (*ibid.*, 55 ff.), it should be noted, writes entirely too freely of documents "signed" by Waleran of Mellent, Robert of Gloucester, and others, giving the impression that it was customary for witnesses and other subscribers to charters actually to sign their names with their own hands. That this was not ordinarily done, has already been shown and hardly needs elaboration here.

[63] Published by Howlett in his edition of the *Chronicles of the Reign of Stephen, II*, 767:

> "Hic Paris in facie, statura Nestor, Ulixes
> Consilio, belli viribus Hector erat:
> Croesus divitiis, in causis Quintilianus,
> Eloquio Cicero, versibus ipse Maro."

[64] VI, 462 n. (1830). As far as I know, these verses have never been published; nor can I give any information concerning their author, Siger Lucanus. For biographical details on Robert and Waleran, see the articles of J. H. Round in the *Dictionary of National Biography*, under "Beaumont."

[65] *Dialogus de scaccario*, I, xi (ed. of Hughes, Crump, and Johnson, 103).

[66] William of Newburgh, *Historia rerum Anglicarum*, I, 4 (ed. Howlett, I, 31): "Stephanum adhuc impuberem regi avunculo nutriendum promovendumque direxit [sc. Adela]." Cf. Norgate, *op. cit.*, I, 273.

[67] The text in Griscom, *op. cit.*, 86; cf. *ibid.*, 88 ff.

[68] III, 2, in Howlett, *op. cit.*, II, 714.

[69] See the *Gesta ducum Normannorum: Continuatio Roberti*, VIII, 10, *MGH. SS.*, XXVI, 9: "Deinde consecratam reginam usque ad tempestivum tempus nuptiarum studiose nutriri precepit, [sc. Bruno of Trier] in quo nutrimento et linguam addisceret et se secundum Teutonicos mores componeret." Cf. Meyer von Knonau, *Jahrbücher unter Heinrich IV und V*, VI, 121 and n. 17, and Norgate, *op. cit.*, I, 275.

[70] *Anon. Chronicon*, in Bouquet, *HF*, XII, 120: "Hic [sc. Gaufridus] filium suum Enricum natu majorem ad erudiendum tradidit cuidam [Petro] scilicet

Xantonensi, qui in metris instructus est super omnes coaetaneos suos." I am unable to supply any further information concerning the identity of this Master of Saintes. Miss Norgate (*op. cit.*, I, 375 and n. 1) accepts the name, but since the editors of the *Recueil* fail to offer any explanation for what is evidently an emendation or addition of their own, it can hardly be regarded as proved.

[71] Gervase of Canterbury (ed. Stubbs), I, 125: "Puer autem Henricus sub tutela comitis Roberti apud Bristorian degens, per quattor annos traditus est magisterio cujusdam Mathaei, litteris imbuendus et moribus honestis ut talem decebat puerum instituendus." Cf. J. H. Round, *Geoffrey de Mandeville*, 405–408, and Norgate, *op. cit.*, I, 334, 375. Though he is reliable in other essentials, Gervase needs correction in his chronology. In a recent article on "Henry Plantagenet's Early Visits to England," *English Historical Review*, XLVII (1932), 449–450, R. L. Poole has proved conclusively that Henry could not possibly have been in Bristol for four years.

[72] See C. H. Haskins, "Adelard of Bath and Henry Plantagenet," *English Historical Review*, XXVIII (1913), 515–516. The dedication of the treatise shows that Henry must already (before 1149) have made good progress in his studies. I quote the most remarkable passage (*ibid.*): "Inde fit ut non solum ea que Latinorum scriptis continentur intelligendo perlegas, sed et Arabum sententias super spera et circulis stellarumque motibus intelligere velle presumas."

[73] C. H. Haskins, "Normandy under Geoffrey Plantagenet," *English Historical Review*, XXVII (1912), 423 and n. 28. For a refutation of the statement advanced by Oudin in the eighteenth century (*Commentarius de scriptoribus ecclesiasticis*, II, 1231) that Henry studied under William at Paris, see R. L. Poole, *Illustrations of the History of Medieval Thought*, 299.

[74] *De nugiis curialium*, V, 6 (ed. James, 237): "Vir . . . litteratus ad omnem decenciam et utilitatem, linguarum omnium que sunt a mari Gallico usque ad Iordanem habens scienciam, Latina tantum utens et Gallica." Cf. W. Rhys Roberts, "Gerald of Wales on the Survival of Welsh," *Transactions of the Society of Cymmrodorion*, 1923–1924, 54, and Haskins, "Henry II as a Patron of Literature," in *Essays in Medieval History Presented to Thomas Frederick Tout* (Manchester, 1925), 72; the former, incidentally, takes the "French Sea" to mean the Bay of Biscay, the latter as the English Channel.

[75] Disappointed in the patronage of Henry II and Richard I, Gerald addressed his *Itinerarium Kambriae* to Stephen Langton, *Opera*, VI, 7: "Sed quia principibus parum literatis et multum occupatis, *Hibernicam* Anglorum regi Henrico secundo *Topographiam*, ejusdemque filio, et utinam vitiorum non succedaneo, Pictavensium comiti Ricardo *Vaticinalem Historiam*, vacuo quondam quoad accessorium illud et infructuoso labore peregi; tibi, vir inclite, Stephane Cantuariensis archiepiscope . . . laborem nostrum per horridos Kambriae fines non illaudabilem, in duabus particulis scholastico stilo tam digerere quam destinare curavi." The dedications are, respectively, in the *Opera*, V, 20–21 and V, 224. Cf. Holzknecht, *Literary Patronage in the Middle Ages*, 140.

[76] *Expugnatio Hibernica*, I, 46 (*Opera*, V, 303): "quod his temporibus

conspicuum est, literis eruditus." In the same place, Gerald credits Henry II with having an unusual memory and with being especially well informed on historical matters: "Quicquid aliquando memoria dignum audierat, nunquam a mente decidere poterat. Unde et historiarum omnium fere promptam notitiam, et cunctarum propemodum experientiam rerum, ad manum habebat." See also Gerald's letter to John, *Opera*, V, 405, where Henry is described as a "principi, quod nostris rarum est diebus, literarum eruditione conspicuo." Cf. Stubbs's preface to the *Chronicle of the Reigns of Henry II and Richard I* (Benedict of Peterborough) *in the Historical Introductions to the Rolls Series* (ed. A. Hassall; 1902), 105.

[77] In his *Defloratio Plinii,* dedicated to the king, Robert of Cricklade writes: ". . . notum est quia cum sis in bellicis negotiis invictissimus, parto otio non minus es in liberali scientia studiosus."—From the excerpt pub. by K. Ruch, *Akad. der Wissenschaften, München,* Sitzungsb., phil.-hist. Kl., 1902, 265.

[78] *Epist.,* 66 (Migne, *PL,* 207, 198): "Semper in manibus ejus sunt, arcus, enses, venabula et sagittae; nisi sit in consiliis aut in libris. Quoties enim potest a curis et sollicitudinibus respirare, secreta se occupat lectione, aut in cuneo clericorum aliquem nodum quaestionis laborat evolvere. Nam cum rex vester bene litteras noverit, rex noster longe litteratior est. Ego enim in litterali scientia facultates utriusque cognovi. . . . Verumtamen apud dominum regem Anglorum quotidiana ejus schola est litteratissimorum conversatio jugis et discussio quaestionum." Cf. Stubbs, *Lectures on Medieval and Modern History,* 137.

[79] *Historical Introductions,* 105.

[80] See Ralph Niger, *Chronica* (ed. R. Anstruther; 1851), 169, and Giraldus Cambrensis, *loc. cit.*

[81] Haskins, in *Essays . . . to Thomas F. Tout,* 77.

[82] Found among the letters of Peter of Blois, 67 (Migne, *PL,* 207, 210 ff.).

[83] In Stubbs's edition, I, 145–146: "Tunc quia comites et barones Angliae minime intellexerant sermonem illorum; praecepit eis rex ut scriberent hinc inde petitiones. . . ."

[84] *Court Life under the Plantagenets* (London, 1899), 83–85.

[85] *Seventeen Lectures,* 139 (3d ed.; Oxford, 1900).

[86] See V. LeClerc, *in the Hist. litt. de la France,* XXI, 784–787.

[87] Stubbs, *Seventeen Lectures,* 141.

[88] *Ibid.,* 141–142; Norgate, under "Joan," in the *Dictionary of National Biography.*

[89] See William Fitz-Stephen, *Vita S. Thomae,* in *Materials for the History of Thomas Becket,* ed. J. C. Robertson, III, 22: "Rex ipse, dominus suus, filium suum, haeredem regni, ei [i.e., Becket] nutriendum commendavit; quem ipse cum coaetaneis sibi multis filiis nobilium, et debita eorum omnium sequela, et magistris, et servitibus propriis, quo dignum erat honore, secum habuit." Cf. the *Vita* of Herbert of Bosham, *ibid.,* III, 176–177; and Stubbs, *Lectures,* 140.

[90] See Haskins, in *Essays . . .,* 73 and nn.

[91] Migne, *PL,* 207, 210 ff.: "Licet prudentia vestra sibi sufficiat et eruditionis alienae suffragia non mendicet, quod tamen vobis ad utilitatem cedere credimus

et honorem, dissimulare non possumus, nec debemus. Experimento siquidem didicimus, quantum commoditatis accesserit terrae vestrae in eo, quod liberalibus disciplinis vestrae primitias adolescentiae imbuistis. Cum enim aliis regibus fit rude et informe ingenium, vestrum, quod exercitatum est in litteris, in magnarum rerum administratione est providum, subtile in judiciis, cautum in praeceptis, in consilio circumspectum. Ideoque omnium episcoporum vestrorum unanimiter in hoc vota concurrunt, ut Henricus filius vester et haeres litteris applicetur, ut quem vestrum exspectamus haeredem, habeamus tam regni quam prudentiae successorem. Scitis, quod totius prudentiae compendium in litteris continentur, si respublica regenda est, si (etc.). . . . libri haec omnia erudiunt ad perfectum.

"Rex equidem sine litteris, navis est sine remige, et volucris sine pennis. . . . Date igitur operam, amantissime princeps, ut filius vester pueritiae cursum litteralibus disciplinis impendat, quatenus sic et malitiam dediscat innatam beneficio litterarum, et laudabilium exemplis operum assuescat."

[92] Stubbs, *Seventeen Lectures*, 140.

[93] As Miss Norgate seems unintentionally to have done in her statement (*op. cit.*, II, 228) that, on his deathbed, young Henry "dictated" a letter to his father. The contemporary accounts (Geoffrey de Vigeois, *Chronicon*, II, 24 [Bouquet, *HF*, XVIII, 220], and the *Gesta regis Henrici*, ed. Stubbs, I, 300–301) tell us only that a Latin letter was sent signed with the seal and the ring of the young prince, and do not warrant the assumption that young Henry took any personal part in the letter's composition.

[94] See the dedicatory letter of the *Otia imperialia,* written for Otto IV, *MGH. SS.*, XXVII, 366.

[95] "Of Medieval Virtues: Largesse," *Vassar Medieval Studies* (ed. C. F. Fiske; Yale University Press, 1923), 203.

[96] *Seventeen Lectures*, 141.

[97] *Ibid.*, 140–141. On Richard's interest in the vernacular literature see also T. A. Archer, in the *Dictionary of National Biography*.

[98] *De invectionibus*, I, 5 (*Opera*, III, 30).

[99] See the letter to Richard, accompanying the gift of a copy of the author's *Topographia Hibernica:* ". . . vir, inquam, in quem fere, praeter litteras, quicquid principem decet, tam industria quam natura congessit."—*Opera*, I, 242.

[100] That this is Gerald's meaning is clear from his subsequent remarks, *ibid.:* "O utinam, sicut universis fere naturae dotibus, sic quoque nec hoc industriae dono caruisses, novus musarum factus incentor, et carminum incitator, diuque sepulta, defectu principum, tam litteratura quam largitate carentium, suscitans poemata, et antiqua tam studia renovans, quam tempora. Non enim desunt litterae, sed principes litterati. Non desunt artes, sed artium honores, nec hodie destitissent scriptores optimi, si non destitissent imperatores electi. . . . Hunc itaque defectum quem tibi non propria sed parentum contulit incuria tali redimas et releves virtutum incitamento, ut litteratis viris latera semper ambias, et bonum quod fortunae non naturae injuria in te non repperis, in aliis amplectendo diligas et venereris."

[101] Above, note 75.

[102] *Opera*, V, 410. Quoted in full below. Cf. Ruth Wallenstein, *King John in Fact and Fiction* (University of Pennsylvania diss., 1917), 14.

[103] See the entries in the *Rotuli literarum clausarum*, under these writers, acknowledging to the abbot of Reading the receipt of these books, which apparently had been in store at the abbey, and which evidently belonged to King John, since the formula used is the same as that employed for other royal goods returned.

[104] According to Stubbs, *Seventeen Lectures*, 41, and Holzknecht, *op. cit.*, 221, who, however, give no reference.

[105] Wm. Hunt, in the *Dictionary of National Biography*.

[106] Holzknecht, *op. cit.*, 222.

[107] T. A. Archer, in the *Dictionary of National Biography*.

[108] Holzknecht, *op. cit.*, 221.

[109] *Gesta regum Anglorum*, V, 446 (ed. Stubbs, II, 519).

[110] See Freeman, *The Norman Conquest of England*, V, 266, 581, 832; also F. M. Powicke, "Ailred of Rievaulx," *Bulletin of John Rylands Library*, VI (1921), 476.

[111] See vv. 6435–6458 of Gaimar's poem, edition of T. D. Hardy and C. T. Martin, I, 275; II, pp. ix ff.

[112] *Hist. litt. de la France*, XIII, 63, 66.

[113] *Opera*, V, 207–208: "Videor tamen jam mihi videre, quoniam cuncta evidentia, cuncta facilia, cuncta patentia cunetis lector inveniet, qualiter naucipendendo nunc in nauseam nares contrahit, nunc labellum porrigit, nunc libellum projiciendo contemnit. Sciat autem in primis, quod laicis haec, et parum literatis edita principibus, plano facilique stilo, solam desiderant ad intelligentiam explanari. Popularibus quippe verbis uti licebit, ubi tam populi quam majorum in populo res gestae literarum beneficio declarantur." For the date of composition see Dimock's introduction, *ibid.*, lvi.

[114] Above, note 102.

[115] *Opera*, V, 410–411: "Verumtamen, quoniam res gesta per interpretem non adeo sapit, aut animo sedet, sicut proprio et idiomate noto prolata, alicui, si placet, lingua simul et literis erudito, ad transferendum in Gallicum ocius non otiosus liber hic noster committatur: qui forte fructum laboris sui, quoniam intelligi poterit, assequetur, quem nos quidem, minus intellecti, quia principes minus literati, hactenus obtinere non valuimus. Unde et vir ille, eloquio clarus, W. Mapus, Oxoniensis archidiaconus, cujus animae propitietur Deus, solita verborum facetia et urbanitate praecipua dicere pluries, et nos in hunc modum convenire solebat: 'Multa, magister Giralde, scripsisti, et multum adhuc scribitis: et nos multa diximus. Vos scripta dedistis, et nos verba. Et quanquam scripta vestra longe laudabiliora sint, et longaeviora, quam dicta nostra, quia tamen haec aperta, communi quippe idiomate prolata, illa vero, quia Latina, paucioribus evidentia, nos de dictis nostris fructum aliquem reportavimus, vos autem de scriptis egregiis, principibus literatis nimirum et largis obsoletis olim, et ab orbe sublatis, dignam minime retributionem consequi potuistis.'

"Sane, quoniam dulciores anni nostri, et tempora robustiora, quoad literatos labores nostros, jam transierunt irremunerata, nunc senescentibus nobis, cum tanquam in januis assistens mors immineat, de cetero nos temporaliter remunerari nec expetimus a quoquam, nec expectamus. Solum hoc etenim amodo desideramus, et desiderare debemus, ut divinum in primis et praecipuis favorem nobis ... comparemus; et humanam per opuscula nostra gratiam, si literarum decus quoandoque resurgat et in statum redeat, saltem in posterum,

" 'Cum suus ex merito quemque tuebitur honor,' assequamur."

For the date, cf. *ibid.*, p. lviii.

[116] *De nugis curialium*, I, 10 (ed. M. R. James, 7): ". . . generosi partium nostrarum aut dedignantur aut pigri sunt applicare litteris liberos suos."

[117] *Rotuli curiae regis* (Rec. Com., ed. F. Palgrave, 1835), I, 46.

[118] Robertson, *Materials for the History of Thomas Becket*, II, 338.

[119] T. A. Archer, in the *Dictionary of National Biography*, under "Beaumont."

CONCLUSION

THE ART OF WRITING lagged behind the art of reading. Hartmann von Aue, the German poet, was unable to write. But the ability to read and to understand Latin and French, especially the latter, if not general, was at least not unusual among the noblesse in the twelfth century.[1] In the thirteenth century a rounded education required a knowledge of French,[2] and a knowledge of Latin was desirable, if not indispensable. In the *Speculum regale,* about 1200, we read: "If you wish to be perfect in knowledge, read all the languages, but first of all Latin and Velsco (i.e., French), since these idioms are the widest known."[3]

Consideration of the foregoing evidence forces us to the conclusion that we must modify the old belief in the almost total illiteracy of the laity in the Middle Ages. It is not justifiable to state categorically that only clerics had a knowledge of Latin. Many an ecclesiastic was ignorant, and numerous laymen were trained to read, if not to write, Latin. Nor can the usual contrast between the general condition of illiteracy and ignorance in the Middle Ages and the enlightenment of modern times be accepted without reservation. Illiteracy has continued to be the state of the masses from the early Middle Ages down to the nineteenth, and into the twentieth century. Even among the upper classes we meet with startling examples of illiteracy in the periods following the Middle Ages. When Nicholas of Cusa in 1433 proposed to introduce a secret written ballot in the Electoral College, he had to make provision for the attendance of secretaries, because some of the imperial electors were unable to read or write.[4] The pronunciation of Latin by the Germans in the fifteenth century was considered particularly barbarous. In 1482, ambassadors from the pope were sent to Germany, to whom the chancellor of the University of Tübingen was deputed to reply. But his pronunciation was so barbarous as to be nearly unintelligible, and the duty was therefore transferred to Reuchlin on the ground that he could at least make himself understood, and had a "sonum pronuntiationis minus horrendum." In the *Ancient Customs of the City of Hereford,*[5] the oath required of the town officials in the fifteenth century throws light on the state of culture among the burgher class. The provision reads: "If so be that he shall be a *laie* or unlettered man he shall do all things belong-

---

[1] Superior figures refer to notes on p. 198.

ing to his office by the counsel of his faithful citizens." And in the Steward's Oath we read: "He shall both counsel and assist the bailiff as often as shall be needful, and especially if the bailiff be a *laie* or unlettered man." It would seem that not a few town fathers of the fifteenth century were unable to read and write even their own tongue. Some of the French noblemen of the *ancien régime* were illiterate. The great Constable Montmorency (1493–1567) could write only "d'une façon suffisante pour l'époque."[6] In 1614, at the last meeting of the States General before the Revolution, it was justly said that it was not poverty which kept the nobles from holding judicial offices, but their own ignorance, the fact that they had been trained to believe that study and learning were inconsistent with their position.[7] In England we hear of an illiterate noble as late as the eighteenth century.[8]

Notes to the Conclusion

[1] Alwin Schultz, *Höfisches Leben zur Zeit des Minnesanges* (1st ed.), I, 120.

[2] Que tout li grant seignor, li conte et li marchis
 Avoient entour aus gent francoise tous-dis
 Pour apprendre francois leurs filles et leurs fils.
  —*Romans de Berte* (ed. Paulin; Paris, 1838), p. 10.

[3] Sundby, *Della vita di Brunetto Latini* (Florence, 1884), p. 70.

[4] *De concord. cathol.*, III, 37, in the Basel edition of 1565 of the *Opera* of Cusanus, 817.

[5] Edited by Richard Johnson (2d ed.; London, 1882), 15.

[6] F. de Crue, *Anne de Montmorency* (Paris, 1885), 5–6.

[7] J. B. Perkins, *France under Mazarin* (New York and London, 1894), II, 422.

[8] See the case of Lord Grantham in *Some Materials towards Memoirs of the Reign of George II*, by John Hervey, ed. by Romney Sedgwick (London, 1931), III, 823.